JANET PYWELL

Someone Else's Home

A story of determination, ambition and honesty.

First published by Kingsdown Publishing 2024

First edition

ISBN: 978-1-7395374-1-8

This book was professionally typeset on Reedsy.
Find out more at reedsy.com

Good Luck Denise
with your own
writing.

Love
Janet x

Foreword

"The ache for home lives in all of us."
Maya Angelou, American memoirist, poet and civil rights activist.

Acknowledgments

Many readers ask me about my inspiration for writing a novel.

In this case it came from a conversation one evening - in a pub. I was swapping funny, and incredible, stories about business adventures with Jayne and Linda when I began to develop the inkling of an idea. The seed was sown.

This book is the result of that fun evening.

Many thanks to Jayne Jackson and Linda Hill.

Also, Tracey Falcon, Jenni Perry and Colin Bachelor, Pete Bennett and Marc Brown for their feedback and constant support with early drafts, my countless friends and readers who give me encouragement and support.

And most importantly, my wife, reader and critic - Amanda - who encourages my enthusiasm and determination, and who makes our *home* a very special place filled with love.

Chapter 1

Carmen Bailey's long stride is matched by her son's easy gait as they hurry through Westbay's harbour. They are a striking couple, both over six feet tall with smoky green eyes and long dark, flowing hair hanging effortlessly past their shoulder blades.

Carmen, once a model, carries herself gracefully. Her yellow and red floral dress hovering just below her knees reveals long, tanned, slender legs. She ignores the curious glances and the turn of heads from people in the street. She knows their gaze is not really on her - it's on Luis.

Walking under the clock tower into Harbour Street, they pass Jane's Jewellers and the male grooming salon on the opposite side of the road, then up the pedestrianised street with its colourful array of unique and independent shops. Today the pretty stores have their awnings down, protecting shoppers from the midday sun.

Carmen has memorised Google maps. She has a vague recollection of the street from her last visit to Westbay some years ago, but just to make sure, she checks the numbers of the shops against the map grid on her iPhone.

'Past the florist, the art gallery and Harbour Bistro,' she mutters, her Andalusian accent still noticeable after almost thirty years in England. 'It's across the road from the café and beauty salon – beside the pet shop.'

'I wonder if it's always like this. It's very busy for a small town,' Luis says, quickly stepping aside and pressing his back against the window of the art gallery, to avoid a family pushing a baby's buggy over his shiny, silver boots. Distracted, Luis glances into the shop admiring the paintings in the window – an assortment of seascapes, rocky beaches and rugged skies. Carmen nudges him ahead of her trying to cajole a smile.

'You're too serious,' she says lightly. 'It's July. It's almost the school holidays, remember?'

'Holidays? No! I don't remember when we last had one.' Luis replies.

'Your life is one long holiday,' she teases.

'I've been studying.' His voice holds a note of caution while he points a finger with satisfaction. 'Here. This is it.'

Carmen stops suddenly in front of the shop doorway. There's a curved bay window with small square panes and a mustard yellow door. The paint on the old wood is peeling giving it an air of abandonment and the glass windows are dulled with dust and grime. It's set slightly back from the main street, in a small alcove, as if it's harbouring a secret.

'Ah, yes. Here it is.' Her soft voice holds a tone of cautious wonder. 'It has an air of opulence and mystery,' she whispers as if she's discovered something magical. She presses her nose against the dirty pane and shades her eyes from the sunlight with her long slim fingers. 'It's big considering it was a mobile phone shop. What do you think?'

Luis shakes his head, doubt creasing his forehead. 'Mama, I still don't—'

'I think it's perfect.' Carmen's smile lights up her whole

face. Her angular cheeks seem softer, her eyes radiate happiness and she looks nearer thirty than her forty-seven years. Although Luis is used to his mother's good looks and is proud that strangers sometimes stop and stare at her, he much prefers it when people look at him, like the woman now who is going into the Beauty Salon across the road. She has a head of curly red hair, and she pauses without concealing her interest in them. She does a double take and inside his heart, Luis smiles.

Thirty years ago, Carmen had begun her modelling career striding out on catwalks across Europe, but today the people in the street aren't looking at her, they're staring at Luis. Their eyes rest on his perfectly painted scarlet nails and the navy and lime cotton sarong hanging from his waist. Luis' shirt is open, revealing an unflawed, olive-tanned chest. Luis, who will soon turn twenty, has inherited his mother's regal demeanour and he lifts his chin in defiance and turns his attention away from the red head. Following his mother's gaze, he leans his forehead on the cold glass. It's cool against his throbbing temple, and he breathes deeply wishing this nightmare was over instead of just beginning.

'It was a mobile phone shop, but the owner went back home - up north, presumably,' Carmen explains, rubbing her palm against the grubby pane. 'It looks a mess inside, and it might take some work to do it up.' She knows that she will enjoy this type of work. It will be a change, and it will give her a sense of purpose. She notices the rotting wood around the door frame and sighs with determination and positive spirit. 'I think this will do, perfectly.'

'Are you *really* so desperate?'

Carmen glances into the street. 'Look how pretty it is, and

how busy...'

'It's not as busy as London.'

'You know I don't want to stay in London. We need a change, Luis. We...'

'But where will we live?'

'There's a two-bedroom apartment above the shop.' Carmen steps back to look up at the three storey building. 'There's a gate at the side. Look! That must be the entrance to the flat.'

'It looks tiny,' says Luis doubtfully, looking up at the building. 'And it's very old. Is it made of wood?'

'It's cladding.' Carmen grins.

'It needs painting.'

'Think of it as an adventure.'

'We're downgrading.'

'Nonsense.'

'Carmen Bailey?' A man's voice makes them turn simultaneously. 'David Chesent, estate agent.'

They all shake hands, and David is unsure who is more beguiling. The tall and elegant Spanish lady or the equally, unusual and attractive young man at her side who is wearing makeup that makes him look more beautiful than David's own young wife. To cover his confusion and to stop staring at them both, he smiles. 'Let me show you inside.'

* * *

It takes under two minutes for Carmen to decide. 'This space is enough for me.' She runs her hands along the side of the wall, ignoring the cobwebs and spiders.

'It was a mobile phone shop, and they divided it in two so that there is a larger workspace at the back.' He taps the wall with a knuckle and smiles. 'This can easily be taken down. What type of shop do you plan to open?' He pushes thick-rimmed glasses back up onto his nose. He's thinking, probably fashion boutique, high-end handbags, expensive shoes or perhaps even a classy makeup shop that his wife says the town is crying out for. 'There's quite a variety of shops in Harbour Street and there's already a boutique and a beauty salon, perhaps...'

'Interior design - soft furnishings.'

'Ah.' David smiles brightly. 'There's only one other shop like that, up in the new part of town, beside the supermarket.'

Carmen ignores him. She's too engrossed in her own thoughts, imagining the shop she'd always dreamed of owning with a deep blue chaise longue in the window, large shining crystal candelabras hanging from the ceiling and heavy framed mirrors. Expensive artwork on the walls with an assortment of pretty ornaments, vases, hand-blown glass, suede cushions and candles. This shop - her shop - would be a statement. Her clientele will have money and taste, and they will travel to find her.

'And,' David says, 'the town is busy all year round. This weekend is particularly busy as the schools have just broken up, but everyone flocks here - especially at the weekend. I know it's hard to imagine in this heat, but you should see it at Christmas. Everywhere is so pretty. There's even a Harbour Street Christmas committee.' He smiles.

Luis yawns. He hovers in the window, gazing out into the street. It's all so different to London. He watches an elderly woman, holding a small terrier on a pink lead, enter the pet shop next door. They both look hot and irritable - that's exactly how Luis feels too.

He sighs. It's all too hot. He pulls at the shirt that's sticking to his back. 'The shop is airless,' he complains. 'It smells musty. I'm going to be sick.'

Carmen ignores this declaration and she holds out her hand. 'Come, cariño, look at this my darling. There's even a kitchen in the back.'

'Oh goody.' Luis' brow creases but his mother hooks her arm through his. 'Don't be sarcastic, my darling. It doesn't suit you. Besides, it will give you an ugly resting face.' She smiles. 'And you are so beautiful.'

David shifts uncomfortably, pushing his hands further into his trouser pockets, wondering if he's met Carmen before. She has a beautiful face. Perhaps she's been in a film or on TV. Maybe an advert?

Carmen catches him staring at her. He blinks suddenly and turns quickly away wishing his glasses didn't keep slipping down his perspiring nose.

'And the apartment upstairs?' Carmen asks.

'It's through the back. There are stairs and a door that you can access from the kitchen and lock down here.'

'Lock?'

'Yes, for example if you have someone working here and you don't want them to have access to your private space upstairs.'

'Ah.' Carmen smiles. 'This has everything we need, isn't that true, Luis?'

Luis shakes his head and unwraps his arm from his mother's grip. 'It smells of damp.'

'That's the sea.' David beams. 'It's only a short walk through the alleyway and you're on the beach. The sunsets here are breathtaking.'

Luis regards the salesman with disdain. He hadn't expected

his mother to be so enthusiastic quite so quickly. It was the only reason that he had agreed to come with her. He'd hoped it might be a whim and that he would be able to persuade her that this was all a silly idea and that they should just go home - back to London.

'Come, let's see upstairs.'

Carmen follows David, ignoring the darkness of the rickety, narrow staircase and instead, much to Luis' distress, takes great delight in the minutest details, gushing over the originality of sash windows, the additional shower room that's so cramped he'd bang his head if he used it, and the old-fashioned kitchen unit that has rusty hinges and doesn't fit properly.

'The kitchen is smaller than our utility room at home in London,' Luis declares scornfully but Carmen ignores him and continues to smile brightly, causing him to trail sulkily behind her into the long lounge that runs the length of the shop below, and a smaller room tucked behind the stairs.

'Another bedroom?' Carmen suggests happily.

'A dormouse wouldn't sleep in there.'

Carmen grins and heads upstairs to admire the two larger bedrooms and the main bathroom.

'It's tiny,' Luis whispers. 'How can you even consider moving here?'

Carmen taps his chest just above his heart with her palm. 'Have faith, cariño.'

After the tour which takes much longer than David expected because Carmen opens every cupboard inspecting every detail, from hinges to running water to the flushing of the toilet - Carmen holds out her hand. 'Take off ten thousand and I'll buy it today.'

'I'll check with the owner.'

'There's no counteroffer. No messing around. If he wants to do the deal tomorrow, I'll want twelve thousand off.'

'I'll tell him.'

'Phone him now.'

David needs to escape from this alluring but captivating woman. 'I'll call him from my office.'

When they are downstairs, and standing in Harbour Street, Carmen says, 'We'll wait in the café across the road.'

'I hope he takes my call.' David pushes his glasses up his nose.

'He'd be stupid not to.' Carmen smiles.

They watch David walk away. His mind is racing. He's trying to work out the identity of this alluring woman and child. If he'd been into sport, or if he was interested in social media like his young wife, then maybe he might have known sooner. It wasn't as if the name Bailey would mean anything to him, but he strides it out, dashing quickly up the road unsure if he should google Carmen Bailey first or call the seller of the building about her offer. The name rang a bell. He has a vague recollection of his wife telling him about Bailey, a footballer, and his glamorous wife. Is it her? If so, why is Carmen Bailey moving here? With all the money they must have, why does she want to open a shop? And, even more importantly, where is her husband?

David's wife loved gossip - or as she calls it, social media. Perhaps she might be the one who can find out all the details. Whoever she is, famous or not, he'd have lots to talk about when he got home tonight.

In Harbour Street, outside the empty premises that holds so much hope for her, Carmen links her arm through Luis'. 'Is it warm enough for ice cream?'

'It's probably twenty-six degrees and as warm as it will get for July.'

Carmen pauses in the street to look at the shops around her, feeling brighter and more hopeful than she has done in years. 'Have you ever seen such a beautiful street with so many original shops? It's all so pretty and unique.'

'I have. Yes. Remember, London? Camden?'

'Don't be a grump Luis, or you'll end up like your father.'

Luis grins. They both know that out of the two children, Luis is like their mother in both looks and temperament, whereas his elder sister, Elena, is more like their father - smaller, broader and more serious.

They sit at an outside table under the awning, sheltering from the sun. A good-looking Rastafarian comes out dressed in a long, French-styled apron.

'Hello, would you like a menu?' Karl, the waiter, grins at them both, impressed by their unusual look and originality. He'd noticed them earlier stepping into the empty shop opposite with David the estate agent.

Carmen reads his name tag.

'Hello, Karl. Thank you.' She smiles and before he turns away, she asks, 'Has this café been here long?'

Karl pauses and scratches his head. 'I guess almost four years.'

'Is Westbay a good place to live?'

Karl's face shines with pride. 'I love it. Just about everyone here in Harbour Street is top-notch. You know, friendly - there's a great sense of community.'

'And all ages?' Carmen glances across at Luis who is busy studying the menu.

'Of course, young and old. We're all here - and some in-betweens.' He laughs. 'Are you on holiday?'

'We'd like to move here.'

'Good choice.' Karl looks at Luis' bent head noticing that the beautiful black hair has an almost purple sheen.

Luis looks up suddenly. 'We're from London.'

'I moved here, and I have no regrets. In fact,' Karl frowns, 'a few people have moved here from London, including my boss. Amber owns the café and Harbour Bistro across the road.' He nods at the restaurant. 'She was a successful lawyer, but she gave it all up and she loves it here now. Ben runs the art gallery. He still travels up to London with his charity. Then there's Eva from the flower shop, she's Polish, and Sanjay owns the Indian, and well, I'm not from here originally. But it's an inclusive community.' He grins at Luis who deliberately won't return his smile.

But Carmen does smile back at him. This is more than she could have hoped for. Then she notices how Karl and Luis have locked eyes - perhaps this could be the start of a new friendship. It will do Luis good to have a new start, a break before he goes to university in a few months' time. He'll have time to make friends and return here during the holidays. He will be able to find work and friendship in the local community.

'I'll have a coke.' Luis thrusts the menu back at Karl without smiling and turns rudely away to gaze up the street.

'Karl, my name is Carmen. And, if I'm not mistaken, there's a man hurrying down the street from the estate agents to tell me that I'm the new owner of the shop across the road. The empty one, beside the Pet Shop.'

* * *

Jack phones her when Luis happens to go to the bathroom. She tells him her news.

'What will we tell Elena?' her husband asks.

'We'll have to tell her the truth.'

'Everything?'

'Yes. Certainly about the house.'

She can hear his sharp intake of breath.

'She has to know,' Carmen insists. 'She might want to take her things. Do you want me to speak to her?'

'No. I'll do it.'

'We can speak to her together if you think that will be easier?'

'I know how much she loves this house,' Jack replies slowly. Carmen imagines him standing at the kitchen island with the bi-fold doors that open onto the manicured lawn. She isn't about to become emotional now.

'It can't be helped.'

'I know, but maybe we should wait until it's definite. You know, until there's no turning back?'

'There's no going back now Jack and we both know it.'

'I just think if we waited a few more weeks...'

'It will be more of a shock to her. It's best to tell her now. Be truthful. Tell her how it is and then she'll know what to expect.'

Jack's voice rises a notch. 'Even I don't know what to expect.'

'You need to start thinking about the future, Jack. Everything is changing.'

'This is our *home*,' says Jack, tersely.

'It's a house,' Carmen replies.

Chapter 2

It takes six weeks for the paperwork to go through and the contracts to be exchanged. Then Carmen has to find plumbers and painters to renovate the shop and flat and by the beginning of September she's stressed but excited.

During these past few months, Jack has been trying to get her to change her mind. He's pleaded with her, cajoled her, begged her and the night before the move nothing between them has changed. Carmen is resolute.

'How can you go to Westbay? What about me?' Jack's normally twinkling blue eyes are full of pain and confusion. He runs his hand through his dirty-blonde hair, a habit that once had football fans enthralled.

'I've asked you to come with me, Jack. You still can.'

'What about our home here?' He casts his hands around their palatial kitchen. The bi-fold patio doors are open revealing their rose garden, where plants and shrubs had been planted with professionalism, and the sweet smell of the blooms wafts into the room. To the left, the water in the swimming pool glistens in the dusky evening light, and Carmen has already admitted that it's the one thing she'll miss.

'Jack, I've told you a hundred times. If we don't earn money, then we won't have this home.'

'It's not my fault.' Jack thumps his fist in frustration on the marble island. 'I didn't know what would happen.'

'I know, cariño.' Carmen deliberately lowers her voice. 'But we must do something - for the long term. Something with purpose.'

'Anything but this, Carmen. What will people say?'

Carmen raises herself, extending her torso and lifting her shoulders back. 'I don't care.'

'But I do,' he argues. He points his thumb at his chest. 'It's my reputation.'

'Jack, tell me truthfully. What is your reputation?' She pauses. 'What is your reputation today?'

He stares back at her. His twinkling blue eyes that once danced with love and teasing are now burning angrily. 'Don't do this!' He warns.

Carmen's accent becomes stronger when she argues. It was something that Jack had always seen as both charming and exotic but tonight it holds no allure for him at all. 'We must be honest, Jack. That is what has kept our twenty-six-year-old marriage alive. Honesty. And I will not lie to you. Not now. Not ever! You must be truthful with me. And the truth is – we're bankrupt. It's gone! All the money gone. Phssst.' She flicks her wrist toward the patio doors. 'And what little we have left, we must use to invest in business.'

'Your shop in Westbay?'

'My business,' she says firmly.

'I'll earn money again.'

Carmen can see the desperation in her husband's eyes. 'I know, cariño. But until then, I must do what I can.'

'A shop!' Jack shouts scornfully. 'And it's not even in

London.'

'I know London is important to you. But we loved Westbay when we went there for a break.

'That was before Covid!'

'I know.' She places her hand on his and adds softly, 'But we loved it. We were happy there and we felt better after being by the sea. It's a very special place.'

Jack shakes his head. 'I'm sorry.'

'You don't have to be sorry. Just come with me, please?'

He turns away. 'I can't. This is my home. I love this place.'

'You have to be realistic. We will probably lose this house by Christmas. The mortgage rates are ridiculously high, and we can't afford—'

'You're blaming me again.'

'I'm not.'

'It's not my fault that Covid came along. It's not my fault that we didn't pay off the mortgages on all our properties and it's not my fault that they're going to foreclose on our—'

Carmen holds up a slim finger. 'Jack! Stop! Please. We've been going over this for weeks. The past is in the past and we must move forward.'

'Forward? To a bedsit over a shop? I didn't even live like that *before* I was playing football in the Premiership.'

She moves her finger from side to side as if conducting her words like a musical composer. She had been determined to stay calm but now her temperature and anger are rising as one. 'It's not a bedsit. It has two bedrooms and the lounge is large. It's *not* a bedsit.'

'That's not the point!'

'Then what do you want me to do, Jack? Sit around here moping all day?'

He slumps onto a white leather covered barstool and covers his head in his hands. 'I wish my career wasn't over.'

'Madre de Dios, Jack! That was twenty years ago. You're not a young boy anymore'

'I know.'

'It's like me wishing I was still a top model.'

Jack looks up. 'There are lots of older models.'

'Do not go there! My modelling days are over, as you well kn—'

'Loads of models are still famous. You could have done celebrity Bake Off - that would have paid—'

'No! No! No!' Carmen shouts. 'You did all the celebrity stuff; the Jungle, the celebrity SAS and all of that. But not me. I will not do *that.* I have been your wife for over twenty-five years, and you should know me better. Shame on you.' Carmen turns her back.

'Look,' Jack's voice is softer. 'All I'm saying is that if you did Strictly, or celebrity, then all our money troubles would be over - for a while at least. Just until I think of something.'

'You've had twenty years to think of something.'

'That's unfair.'

They lock eyes across the kitchen island. There's a noise on the patio and they both turn in unison. Luis appears wearing purple and pink eyeliner and false eyelashes. He's wearing a one-piece lilac bathing suit with a short beige dress unbuttoned at the front, revealing his hairless chest.

'Arguing about me, again?' he asks.

Jack turns away.

'No,' Carmen replies.

'That makes a change.' Luis wanders past them, pulling his towel over his narrow shoulders. Carmen is impressed with his posture, the turn of his head and the muscled tone of his olive skin.

'I'll be upstairs,' Luis adds, 'in case you're looking for me.'

'Make sure you pack everything tonight,' Carmen says. 'We'll be leaving early.'

Jack shakes his head and stares into the garden. His life is falling apart, and he seems unable to stop it. After Luis leaves, he turns to her. 'Why?'

'Come with me? Try it for a month - you may even like Westbay.'

'I mean, why does *he* have to dress like that?'

'Because *they* want to.'

'They. *They*. THEY!' he shouts. 'That's grammatically incorrect. *They* is plural - *he* is my son.'

'They, them and their is used for someone who might not identify strictly as male or female. Luis is non-binary.'

'I don't care who he sleeps with—'

'It's not about sexuality, it's about identity. They don't want to conform to traditional ideas of male and female so they choose to be non-binary, rather than one of the only two options available to describe their identity.'

'But what's the point?' Jack shouts.

'Pronouns are like a personal name - they connect to a person's identity. Like you're a man and I'm a woman - Luis prefers *they*.'

Jack rubs his hand through his hair. 'It doesn't make sense.'

'You may not always get it right. Sometimes I don't, but we have to try.'

'Why does he want to do this to us?' Jack grumbles.

Carmen leans toward her husband and hisses. 'It's not about you - it's about them. It would take so little to make your child happy, Jack. One word. One tiny, small, insignificant word. That's all it would take. Is it really so difficult?'

* * *

Although Luis had refused to accompany her since the first visit, she knows that there is no way he would stay at home with Jack. Carmen is pleased Luis is coming to Westbay with her.

Luis admires the shop front. 'It looks better. You got it all painted and the sign too, *Carmen's Soft Interiors* - I like the name. But I thought we had no money?'

'We have no money on Papa's scale but on mine - we still have enough to live on.'

'What does that mean?' Luis lifts a heavy suitcase up the narrow stairs.

'It means, that we can afford necessities.'

Luis laughs. 'Like a cleaner?'

'Perhaps a few luxuries, but it's important to remember where you come from. Our heritage. You know where your grandparents are from. Your abuelos are simple people. Your grandparents are simple people.'

'The country.' Luis stands up rubbing his back. 'They're from the Spanish countryside miles and miles away from any major city.'

'Don't turn your nose up, cariño. This is our history too. This is where we came from and makes us who we are.'

'Not me.' Luis lifts his shoulders in a shrug, in a similar manner to Carmen's. But now she places a hand on his arm.

'Don't! Not today. We all think we can leave our roots behind, but they make us who we are. You can never run from yourself and who you are, no matter where you live.'

Luis shrugs off her hand and ventures downstairs for the next box while Carmen glances out of the window.

Harbour Street is busy. Schools go back next week, and against everyone's advice, she is setting up a new business in a fishing town in September, where she probably won't get established before Christmas. And, according to Jack, she will never be able to pay the mortgage off on their London home.

She sighs. This morning before they left, Jack had brought up the same argument. Why couldn't they be on Instagram or TikTok filming every detail of their move? Why couldn't they look good to the public? Why can't they capitalise on their past?

Carmen had ignored him and continued to pack the final pieces of her London life. It had all seemed like a fantastic dream until today. This morning had been surreal. Leaving had been traumatic and heartbreaking, but she knew it was for the best. She'd spent her life adapting and today was no different. There were no difficulties ahead only the next decision to make or the next hurdle to jump on this crazy adventure.

How her life has changed. She'd become a model by accident and her career had taken her away from her family and the pretty village in the Andalusian countryside. Although she tried to visit once a year, she knew she would never go back to live there just as she knows she can't continue to live in the shadow of her handsome husband.

She had spent Jack's glory years as a world-class footballer living under a microscope. God! She remembered him when they met at a charity function. Jack had been handsome and charming. He was also on the cusp of world fame. They had fallen deeply in love and married quickly. A top footballer and a top model. It was perfect.

She was recognised as the face of perfumes and beauty products and with his career about to explode they faced fame together. But she'd fallen pregnant with Elena - and within a few years of her birth, Jack tore his first ligament. Luis was born and Jack did everything he could to keep physically fit.

But life had been a challenge. Twenty-six years of continual challenges. But since the day they met, Jack had understood her. He knew the sacrifices she made for his future and football.

But Carmen had never wanted any of his fame or fortune. She only wanted Jack, the father to her children and her husband. The investment properties, cars and their homes had diminished over the years. There had been bad decisions and disastrous investments, but she was getting older. Now she needed her own security. Her own life.

'Mama?'

Carmen turns from the window.

'Are you alright?'

'Si, cariño. I'm fine, my darling.'

Luis moves to stand beside her. 'Is this my fault?'

'What?'

'Are you doing this for me?'

Carmen places her arm around his waist and pulls him closer. 'Nooo.' It's a low Spanish growl.

'I'll still go to uni next month. I was leaving home anyway.'

'I know.'

'So, you will be here on your own.'

'Not unless Papa misses me.' She smiles.

Luis shakes his head. 'I can't imagine him in this place.'

Carmen shrugs. 'You never know what anyone will do for love.'

Luis grins. 'I know Papa. He likes the good things in life.'

'We are all guilty of that, Luis. We must also remember that while we have so much, there are many people in the world who still have so little.'

'Some still have lots more than us.'

Carmen folds her arms and gazes at her beautiful child noting the small creases forming on his forehead. Has she spoilt her children to the point that Luis no longer understands that a fortuitous life is a gift and not a given? Or that Elena felt so ignored and hates the fame and money so much that she became a long-haul cabin crew member to escape them?

'I think,' Carmen says slowly, 'that when you understand the intricacies of life and know how precarious everything actually is, that is true maturity.'

'Some of Papi's friends still play football. They still have lots of money and still have big houses.'

'That's not what life is about Luis and well you know it.' She shakes a finger at him. 'We raised you better than that.'

'I know Papi hates me.'

'Nooo. He loves you very much, cariño. He just can't express his feelings at the moment.'

'He hates me dressing like this.' Luis pulls on his turquoise summer dress. 'Did you see his face this morning? He barely said goodbye. He hates me.'

'He doesn't h—'

'He's embarrassed.'

Carmen doesn't deny this. She turns to open one of the boxes. 'Pass me the scissors cariño, por favor.'

'I don't care,' Luis continues, 'I don't care about him. I don't care that he doesn't accept me or that he wants to disown me. His behaviour hasn't always been brilliant, has it?'

Carmen doesn't answer.

'He was an arse in celebrity.'

'But he was one of the last left in the competition - one of the finalists.' Carmen pulls saucepans from the box. 'Come on, help me with this and then I'll take you for dinner somewhere nice.'

'He'll never accept me, will he?'

Carmen smiles brightly and with enthusiasm. She says, 'You have enough to worry about, cariño. Give him time. Your Papi needs to learn to love himself again before he can love either of us like he used to.'

* * *

Later that evening they manage to get a table in Harbour Bistro. There's a pretty courtyard at the back decorated with small shrubs and trees with warm golden lights and white aromatic candles on each table.

'There was a cancellation,' explains the waitress, showing them to the table.

'How wonderful. It smells of jasmine.' Carmen sniffs the air with appreciation.

'It's a warm evening but if you get cold later, we can light the patio heaters.' She nods to the heaters under the overhead umbrellas.

Carmen gives her a warm smile. 'We'll be fine. We have jackets. Thank you for squeezing us in.'

'Amber will be over later to say hello. She recognised you when you came in.'

Carmen smiles and focuses on the menu.

'I'm not sure if that's a good thing,' Luis whispers. 'Did she recognise you because of Papi or because you're a shop owner now?'

'It doesn't matter,' Carmen answers calmly although her heart is thumping wildly against her rib cage.

They both order lamb chops on a bed of mash with roasted vegetables, and chat easily as they enjoy their meal.

'This is as good as any London restaurant,' Carmen says, relishing the hint of garlic and rosemary on her tongue.

'Not quite.' Luis winks at her.

She raises her wine glass. 'A small toast to say thank you for coming with me and for helping me with my dream.'

Luis sips his wine. 'Is this really a dream?'

'I have told you a hundred times, cien veces, Luis. I was going to study interior design before I became a model.'

'Do you ever wish you'd stayed modelling?'

'No.'

'You could have made more money than Papi.'

She shakes her head. 'It's all about creativity.'

'You're talented and creative. I suppose I must have got my artistic talents from someone. It certainly wasn't from him.'

They both laugh and a sense of calmness overcomes Carmen. Although Jack isn't with her, she's suddenly aware that she has definitely made the right decision. There's something that's so comforting about sitting in this small courtyard with soft lighting and low music that is making her relax. Her shoulders begin to ease, the tension in her stomach disappears and her heart is lighter.

They are busy studying the dessert menu, discussing the pros and cons of each mouth-watering option seriously when

Amber comes over to their table.

'Welcome to Westbay.' Amber shakes hands with them both and the introductions are over in seconds. 'I saw you move in earlier. I'm sorry, I didn't have time to pop in to welcome you.'

'Please don't worry.' Carmen takes in Amber's steady gaze and warm smile.

'I hope you're settling in okay?'

'Now we've eaten this delicious meal, I'm much better.' Carmen grins. 'The Bistro is so pretty and the food is amazing. It's better than so many restaurants in London.' Carmen's eyes are twinkling in the light and Luis realises again how beautiful his mother is when she's relaxed and happy. How lucky she was, to have been born in the right body. How wonderful that must be, he muses.

'Have you much to do before you open?' asks Amber.

Carmen returns her smile. She's attracted to Amber's warmth and friendliness. 'It will take time, but I hope to open the shop next week.'

'*Carmen's Soft Interiors*? I like the name.'

'Thank you. I'll be selling cushions, lamps, small items of furniture, that sort of thing. Quite particular.'

Amber frowns concentrating. 'That's great. There's only one other interior designer in town but they're over by the supermarket at the top end of town. It's always good to have different businesses here in Harbour Street.'

'I hope so.'

'Well, you never know with a new business,' Amber pauses. 'Do you do the interior design as well or just sell soft furnishings?'

'I'll offer some bespoke interior design. I've done up

numerous properties in London and abroad,' Carmen says truthfully. In the early years of their marriage, they owned at least eight properties in London and three in Spain. 'Why?'

'It's only that Paul was talking about getting the pub refurbished.'

'Which pub?' asks Luis.

'The Ship. At the top of Harbour Street. You could ask him?' suggests Amber. 'Or I could mention it to him?'

'That would be great,' Carmen replies. 'I'd really appreciate you speaking to him.'

Amber nods. 'Consider it done.'

'Do you own the café, too?' asks Luis.

'Yes. And, my partner, Ben, owns the art gallery next door. I came here four years ago and...' She spreads her arms wide. 'I'm still here. I love it.'

'Karl said you were a lawyer in London?' Luis says.

Amber frowns. 'That seems a long time ago now, but yes, I was.'

'You don't want to go back to London?' Luis insists. 'You don't miss it?'

Amber shakes her head. 'Not at all. Sometimes Ben and I go up to London working with his charity or to a show and dinner but to be honest, I think Westbay has something magical about it. Those that come here just don't want to be anywhere else.'

Carmen smiles.

Luis glances at his mother. 'Papi might come and join us.'

Carmen nods vaguely.

Luis continues looking at Amber. 'He's sorting out paperwork and things...'

'Well, he'll also be very welcome. If there's anything I can do or if you need anything then please let me know.'

Luis leans earnestly across the table. 'Papi was a footballer, Jack Bailey. Have you heard of him?'

Amber shakes her head. 'Sorry. I'm not a great football fan.'

'He's also a celebrity—'

'Luis!' Carmen says quickly.

Luis shrugs. Although he doesn't think his father likes him, he's secretly proud that his father was famous and is recognised most of the time.

Amber grins. 'Sorry, I'm not one for celebrities either.'

'Me neither,' agrees Carmen warming to her new friend. This, she decides, is just the sort of woman she wants in her new life.

Luis laughs. 'That's not true Mama. What about all your WAG friends.'

Carmen smiles patiently but her cheeks flush. 'That was a long time ago.'

'Mama was a top model,' Luis says to Amber. 'Very well known.'

'Luis. Please.' There is an edge to her voice. 'That was also many years ago.'

Amber grins. 'Well, I'm not surprised. You're still very beautiful and—' She turns to Luis. 'I see that you take after her.' Amber is distracted by the waitress waving her over. 'I have to go but now you know where I am, come by any time.'

After she's gone, Carmen and Luis order dessert and sit in silence.

'Are you angry with me?' Luis asks.

'No.'

'You've gone quiet.'

'Not everyone has to know our business.'

'So, you are angry with me. Because of the WAG...?'

'No! But the past is called the past because that's exactly where it is. No one needs to know who we were or what we did.'

'But...'

Carmen holds up her hand as the waitress places two crème caramels on the table. After she leaves, Carmen says, 'You would not like me to speak about you to strangers, would you?'

Luis pulls his hair behind his ears and watches his mother closely wondering if his nose flared like Mama's nose when she's angry.

She continues speaking quickly, her Spanish accent growing rapidly. 'You wouldn't like me to talk about you, your achievements or lack of them. And besides, not everyone likes celebrities. I want to get away from all that. I want to know people for who they are, not for *what* they are or the job they do and for that reason, I think this lovely little town is going to suit us perfectly.' Carmen takes a delicate bite of her dessert and the flavours melt on her tongue. 'What more could you possibly ask for? Great food, good neighbours and a new business.' She doesn't add that refurbishing a pub would be perfect.

Chapter 3

Carmen's Soft Interiors opens a fortnight later. She keeps it low-key and invites a few of her new neighbours from Harbour Street for a glass of fizz and tapas; albondigas, queso manchego and jamon serrano. There is no grand statement, no big announcement and it's a small crowd: Luke and Mario - her neighbours from the pet shop, Amber and Ben, Eva from the flower shop and her partner Sanjay who owns the Indian takeaway. There's also Jane from the jewellers and Tommy who volunteers for the RNLI, Frances, the vicar, and finally Tracey, the red head from across the road in the Beauty Salon.

Carmen smiles brightly as they exclaim over the shop and the contents for sale.

'So pretty.'

'Very original.'

'My mother would love this...'

'This might go well in our lounge?'

'This would make a fabulous present...'

'Love this colour.'

Carmen mingles between her guests joining random conversations, a part of each group yet floating freely. It's a trick she's mastered from so many public engagements, as a model and also from when she was married to Jack. She's lost count of the dinners, receptions, award ceremonies and events they've attended together, but almost always, she's had Jack at her side. Now, even after asking him again today, he has refused to come to her opening. But there's a small part of her that's hoping he will arrive and surprise her - and surprise everyone - with a grand entrance but as the evening wears on, she realises her romantic and foolish notion will remain a wishful dream. She does, however, take heart from having Luis at her side. Luis looks beautiful in an off-the-shoulder white blouse and a long, flowing navy skirt and eye makeup in shades of blue and yellow.

Carmen fills glasses, floating on the soft chatter and bursts of laughter while enjoying the relaxed and friendly atmosphere when a tall man, carrying a luxurious bouquet of flowers, opens the door.

'I hope you don't mind me gate-crashing? I'm Paul from The Ship.' He holds Carmen's hand for a fraction of a second too long, which causes a flutter of excitement in the pit of her stomach.

'You're more than welcome. It was an open invitation to all the shop owners in Harbour Street.' She smiles.

'Beautiful,' he says.

'Beautiful?' Carmen laughs at his obvious flirting, takes the flowers and tosses her hair over her shoulder.

'The shop I mean,' Paul says hastily, unable to take his eyes from her.

Carmen is used to this reaction. She grins.

Paul is younger than her by a few years. He has dark eyes, grey hair receding at the temples and laughter lines at the corner of his wide mouth. He maintains eye contact with her as if she holds the answers to the universe and although she's a little uncomfortable, she's also flattered. Perhaps getting the refurbishing job in the local pub might be easier than she thought.

Tracey, the red head, from the Beauty Salon, pushes between them. 'I know I've seen you before,' Tracey says. Her curly mop of red hair is escaping from a clip and she pushes it irritably from her eyes. 'Have you been on TV?'

Carmen shakes her head and moves away to avoid the conversation, but then Luis is suddenly blocking her path.

'You'll have seen Papi on TV. He's the footballer, Jack Bailey.'

'No way!' Tracey covers her mouth with a hand full of ringed fingers. 'Oh my gosh. I had such a crush on him when he was in the Jungle. Is he really your husband?'

Carmen smiles. All eyes are on her and the conversation stops. The guests are all listening. It's as if the shop is one united being, holding its breath, waiting for an answer. Carmen exhales deeply. 'Yes.'

'Gosh. Are you still married? Is he—'

'Tracey that's none of your business—' Amber interrupts.

'Sorry,' Tracey continues, 'But he's always been my hero. My Dad supported West Ham back in the day.'

Carmen moves away to pour more fizz, but Tracey lays a hand on her arm.

'Is he coming here? Is Jack *really* going to come to Westbay?'

'He will do, yes.'

'When?'

Carmen swallows. 'He's tying up a few business details then he's going to join us.'

'And live upstairs?' Tracey's mouth is oval and drops open in shock.

'That's the plan.'

'Don't you have a big house in the country with a pool? I saw it in *Hello* magazine.'

'We do.' Luis steps forward. 'That's our main home. This is just a place by the sea - Mum's hobby—'

'So, you're not serious about this business?' Paul interrupts frowning at Carmen.

'Yes, I'm very serious.' Carmen raises her torso and straightens her shoulders. 'As selfish as it sounds, Jack's career has always come first, but now the children are older, and Luis is the last to fly the nest, it's time for me to pursue my own career.'

Tracey is scrolling on her iPhone and reads aloud. 'You were a top model - Coco Channel, Dior and oh my god, Versace...'

'Oh, the trials of social media. Everything's at everyone's fingertips.' Carmen can't keep the bitterness out of her voice.

'Tracey, put the phone away- now!' Frances, the vicar attempts to take the phone. 'Let's give our new neighbour all our support. Carmen doesn't want people gawping at her or gossiping behind her back. Carmen and Luis need to know they are safe here and amongst friends.'

Tracey pulls away.

'This is a new adventure,' adds Eva. 'Well done, Carmen.'

'We shall swear allegiance to you.' Sanjay holds up his palm and places it sincerely on his heart. 'We will never speak to anyone in the press or betray your confidence.'

'Hear, hear.' Ben raises his glass. 'We've all had secrets and a past that we don't want to share. Privacy is very important.' He turns to the small group and his eyes fix firmly on Tracey. 'Let's not ask Carmen anything else, Tracey. Let's leave her in peace and wish her all the best in her new venture.' He raises his glass. 'To Carmen's new adventure. Here's to *Carmen's Soft Interiors.*'

They all toast her success and although Carmen smiles, at the first opportunity to escape she hurries to the kitchen in search of a new bottle of bubbly and wipes a tear from the corner of her eye.

Earlier today Jack had been adamant he wasn't coming to this poxy town and now Carmen realises that the friendships she's craved for all her life, might finally be found in this charming street.

She pushes a tissue into her pocket and takes a deep breath. As she turns around, Paul is standing in the doorway watching her. He's muscular and his white shirt is taught across his chest. His skin is still tanned from the summer and with his grey hair and cheeky grin he looks more like a handsome surfer than a pub owner.

'I must go now. It's going to be a busy night in the pub, but if you want to come and look around, we could talk about the refurbishment tomorrow. If you're up for it?'

'I'd like that.'

Paul holds her gaze. 'Around eleven?'

'I'll come over.'

'Great.'

He doesn't move and Carmen can't get past him. Their bodies are close together and their faces inches apart. She laughs and holds up the bottle. 'You'll have to let me through Paul, or my new friends might die of thirst.'

* * *

After the guests are gone and they've tidied the shop and gone upstairs Luis goes straight to his bedroom. Carmen would like to think that Luis is in touch with friends but his two closest friends have spent the summer travelling and are currently in Australia. Luis had wanted to go with them, but as Jack had so bluntly explained, 'If you don't get off your arse and get a job to earn money, you'll have to sit and play computer games all summer.'

But Luis doesn't play computer games. Carmen knows that Luis spends most of his time on social media following makeup artists, fashion influencers and hanging out with LGBT+ groups.

Carmen kicks off her shoes and picks up her laptop. It was going to be a long night. She hadn't expected Paul to turn up this evening and she had assumed it might take time for Amber to mention her to him, but news travels fast in Westbay. Now she has a business meeting tomorrow morning and the opportunity to refurbish the local pub - but has absolutely nothing prepared.

She scrolls the Internet and buys two domain names. Then she creates two simple logos; one for Carmen's Soft Interiors and the other for Carmen's Bespoke Designs.

She finds a suitable hosting website and template and spends a few hours uploading photographs from the properties they previously owned in England and Spain.

Over the years she has managed all the Airbnb reservations. She has added and deleted their properties as they bought and sold, on the rental booking sites, and has had to be creative with the interior decor. It was fortunate that she'd kept a folder on her laptop with all the photographs.

After Jack's football career was finished through health reasons, he had succumbed to depression and found solace in alcohol. It had taken a disastrous car accident, when Jack had rolled his car over with no one else involved, to change their lives again.

It was the sobering moment he needed. For a few years afterwards, Jack had felt reborn and invigorated, thinking he'd been saved for a purpose and a greater destiny. He'd had a few business alliances and invested in several start up online companies. In contrast, Carmen invested in property. She learned about, and understood, growing and developing markets and got to know the up and coming areas in London.

The Spanish Costas were also booming and new apartments were springing up, so Carmen created her own property portfolio.

She hunts for images of the various properties that, one-by-one, had been sold. When Covid hit, no one travelled. No one rented their homes and then interest rates hit the roof. That's when Jack's construction businesses collapsed with massive debts. They sold the properties, and used the money to finance Jack's disastrous online business investments.

Carmen's anger is directed at herself. How could she have been so naive as to believe that they could have so many mortgages and not pay off their own home? They'd always lived on borrowed money and in the past eighteen months they'd been forced to pay off the interest. But they were seriously short of money, and although the bank agreed to an extension, it will take possession of their London property on the 24th December.

Carmen makes a second black coffee and listens to Luis' soft snoring, as she stands outside his bedroom door for a while. She wonders how he will get on at university next month. She's sad that she will no longer be a major part of his life, but for now she can keep an eye on him. She can look out for him and read every flicker of emotion and hurt that crosses his face. Here, at home, she can protect him.

How will Luis fare alone?

She returns quickly to the sofa. Pushing away emotions and an overwhelming wave of sadness, she picks up her computer.

One thing at a time. One problem at a time.

After the photos have uploaded Carmen begins to write the script for her website. Although her spoken English is good, her written English is not, so she opens ChatGPT as Luis once showed her. She types in what she would like to write about her business, descriptions of the properties and a brief bio about herself and within minutes a polished text about her and her business is written. She reads it slowly, checking, editing and then changing an unfamiliar word. When she's happy she uploads the text to her website. She then finds a similar site to the one she's creating and copies their Privacy Policy. It's not as if anyone reads it but it's imperative.

By the time she's finished working, her neck and shoulders are sore from leaning over her laptop and her head is beginning to throb. Dawn is breaking and she glances down into Harbour Street. Any other morning she'd go for a walk by the sea, but she needs to sleep. In five hours, she'll be meeting Paul but at least she now has some credentials to support her bid for his business.

Carmen climbs onto her bed and falls asleep immediately. She dreams of Jack arriving in Harbour Street. He's striding down the road waving something in the air, and she runs toward him. Gradually she slows her pace. He's waving a pint glass. He's been drinking. Beer is flowing down his arm and over his shoulder - and then he laughs. He pulls her close to him and his strong arms are reassuring around her. She's happy and safe. But it's not his face or his bright blue eyes she's gazing into. The eyes belong to Paul.

* * *

Carmen arrives in The Ship at eleven fifteen. Paul is behind the bar and when he sees her, his face lights up and his mouth breaks into a warm smile. He finishes pouring a pint from the pump for a customer and then motions her to follow him to a table in the corner.

'It's quiet,' he explains. 'We can sit here in the window. Can I get you anything?'

'I'm fine, thank you.' Carmen shakes her head and removes her jacket aware that Paul's eyes have rested on her cleavage. She takes her laptop from her bag and opens it.

'Thanks for your time, today.' She smiles.

He shifts in his seat and seems unable to speak.

'So, this is your pub and it needs refurbishing?' She prompts him.

'What do you think?' he replies, following her gaze and looking around the room.

She takes in the tired and worn chairs, scruffy and marked tables, shelves of discarded books and board games. 'It does look a bit tired. What would you like? What are you thinking?'

Paul shrugs. His eyes don't leave hers. 'Surprise me?'

Carmen nods. 'Do you have any ideas? Any pub you've been to that you like?'

'Not really.'

'Any colour schemes, types of furniture, wall decorations?'

Paul lays his hands on the table and smiles. 'I'm open to

suggestions.'

Carmen closes her laptop and places it deliberately and slowly in her bag. Then she picks up her jacket and pushes her chair away from the table.

Paul stands up quickly beside her. 'What are you doing? Where are you going?'

'I'm here for a business meeting. But you're looking at me like I'm a piece of meat at the market and, to be very honest, I'm not used to businessmen who think with their dicks.'

'What?'

Carmen pushes past him.

'Wait, Carmen. Stop! I'm sorry. Please.'

Carmen faces him. Her dark, smoky eyes are challenging him.

He holds out his hand. 'Look, I'm really sorry if I've given you the wrong impression.' He looks at her imploringly. 'I'm really interested in your ideas.'

'That's not how you're coming across to me.'

'I'm sorry. But, in my defence, you are a very attractive woman.'

Carmen hitches her bag onto her shoulder. 'There are lots of attractive women here in Westbay. Some came to my opening last night. You didn't letch after Eva or Amber.'

'Letch?'

'Yes.'

'Do I letch? I'm sorry.' Paul stares down at the floor then raises his eyes to her. 'Can we please start again?'

'Only if you apologise.'

Paul holds out his hand. 'You're right. I'm sorry. Please forgive me and let's move forward.' He indicates her vacant chair. 'Please?'

Grudgingly Carmen sits down. 'Where were we?' she

asks, pleased that she's regained the boundaries of their relationship. After all business is business.

* * *

When she gets back, Luis is in the shop alone.

'So, how's the macho man?' Luis asks.

'He turned out to be quite decent. He even likes my website.'

Luis grins. 'What website?'

'I did it last night.' She takes out her laptop. 'Take a look.' She makes coffee in the kitchen at the back of the shop while Luis studies the photos and layout of her online business.

'I'm impressed. Your English has improved. How did you do this?' He laughs.

'You showed me, ChatGPT.'

'You're joking?' He laughs.

'Never.' She takes the laptop from him and sips her coffee.

'So, what happens now?' Luis asks.

'He's given me an idea of what he wants, so I have to come up with some designs and ideas.'

'Sounds simple.'

'The deadline is Friday.'

'Two days away? You're joking?'

'I have to do a presentation.'

'Just for him?'

'He said there was someone else who would want to see it too.'

'He's not hanging around then?'

Carmen shakes her head. 'He wants it done quickly and the work completed in October.'

'Well, I'm sure you'll do it. Look, can you take over here? I need to go out for a while.'

'Have you done any drawing today?'

Luis ignores her and pulls on a purple and lime green jacket. Today his hair is in a tight bun, but tendrils have escaped to frame his face. He doesn't wait for an answer and Carmen is too tired to go to the window to see which direction he goes in. Perhaps he might make some new friends, she thinks hopefully, before settling down to concentrate on her new project. Perhaps he might even begin to love living here in Westbay.

* * *

Luis appears in the late afternoon. He's in high spirits and his nails are now lime green.

'You've had your nails done,' says Carmen. 'Very pretty. I like the colour.'

'Ummm.' Luis holds them to the light and regards them carefully. 'I had a pedicure too.'

'Wonderful.' Carmen is unpacking a delivery. 'What do you think of this?'

Luis stares at the lampshade in her hands. 'It's like a pink flamingo has been skinned and you've stolen all the feathers.'

'I'll hang it here. What do you think?' Carmen holds it in front of a wall-sized mirror with a heavy gilt-edged frame.

'Have you sold anything today?' Luis asks.

Carmen looks up. 'Not yet.'

Luis leans against the wall. 'What's the point?'

'The point of opening a shop? Living here? Life? God? What do you mean?'

'Are you divorcing Papi?'

Carmen places the lampshade on the counter. 'Why are you asking me that?'

Luis shrugs.

She continues, 'I love Papi. You know that. But all relationships go through ups and downs.'

'What's this? Up or down?'

'Very funny.' Carmen turns her back and moves a black and gold-leaf vase to a different table.

'Mama, we've been here for three weeks and Papi isn't happy. He wants us back in London - at home.'

'Do you want to go home?' Carmen turns and faces him. 'Then go.'

'Not without you.'

'Luis, you're going to uni in a few weeks, you won't even be here.'

'What if I don't go?'

Carmen takes a deep breath. 'Why wouldn't you? It's the perfect art course for you.' She also knows that if he doesn't go, Jack will be furious, and he will blame her. 'If you don't go to university then you'll have to get a job. What will you do?'

'I can work in here.'

'I can't afford to pay you a salary, Luis. You'll have to find a proper job with proper hours.'

'Doing what?'

'Well, I believe there's a supermarket in the new part of town. Maybe you can stack shelves.'

Luis contemplates his nails. 'You'd make me work in a supermarket? How humiliating. As if I haven't been bullied enough. You'd really make me...'

'Make you?' Carmen wags a finger defiantly toward her child. 'Make you? No, no, no. I have let you be who you want to be. I love you. I support you and I defend you. Even though my heart breaks sometimes. BUT.' She holds up her finger. 'I have never made you *do* anything. I have protected you, changed schools and helped you find the art course that you like but now it's your turn to make decisions. I will never *make* you be anyone or *do* anything you don't want to do, but you must take responsibility for who you are – and more importantly – for who you want to be.'

Luis gazes at her and she sees her younger self reflected in his eyes. At nineteen she'd been invited to stay with her cousin in Madrid and one night they'd gone to a popular nightclub. Carmen wasn't confident. She was from the country and she had no experience. She also didn't know how beautiful she was until a stranger had slipped her his business card and whispered, 'Call me.'

It was a top modelling agency.

Carmen had to make her own decision.

* * *

Later that evening while Luis is in his bedroom studying the latest fashionable makeup influencer Carmen studies Paul's spec for the pub. It includes new wood on the bar and a feature fireplace.

She sketches a few ideas and thinks about soft furnishings. Which ones could she get hold of in time for her presentation to Paul on Friday afternoon? She'd measured the pub and taken the dimensions of the space, and although her drawings look good, she needs something special. Something that will really impress him. She needs to be very creative and persuasive.

* * *

As well as running the shop and ordering stock, Carmen has sourced all the soft furnishings for the presentation. She's nervous. At three o'clock she asks Luis to help her carry them over to The Ship. She hopes that Luis' presence will soothe her, but today he's gone overboard with his makeup and her heart drops. His eyebrows are too thick and heavy, his foundation too patchy and his cheeks too rouged. He wears Barbie pink lipstick, which matches his blouse, and a short lilac and navy skirt. The black ankle boots make Luis' feet look very large against his naturally slim frame.

'What's wrong?' Luis stares at her. 'Am I late? It's not yet three.'

'Can you carry this, please, por favor?' She hands him her portfolio and takes the heavier items; a lamp, a small fold up table and two cushions.

Luis walks across Harbour Street in front of her, very provocatively, sashaying his hips dramatically. As he reaches the pub door he turns to smile at her.

'Suerte, Mama. Good luck. I hope it goes well. I know what this means to you.'

'Graçias,' she whispers. 'Thank you, my darling.' Her heart beats a little faster as they step inside.

The bar isn't busy, but a few heads turn in their direction. It wasn't the entrance that Carmen wanted to make but under the circumstances, she's defiant. Luis is her child. She ignores the stares and hushed whispers, and casts her eyes around the room looking for Paul. He's sitting with a group of people in the corner, and he waves her over. As they approach his table he stands up, smiling in anticipation.

'What's going on?' whispers Luis. 'Who are the other people?'

'No idea, cariño. Thank you for helping me and for going back now to look after the shop.'

Luis looks around defiantly as if to say he's going nowhere but then he places Carmen's portfolio on a nearby table and turns away with an elaborate flourish.

Paul shakes her hand formally. His tone is reserved, distant and polite. 'Carmen, hello again. Come and meet everyone.'

Carmen smiles at the assembled group.

'These are my partners,' Paul explains.

'Partners?'

'Yes. They all have a stake in the pub. I just manage it for them.'

Carmen hadn't been aware that there are other people to please; two men and a woman who, at this present moment, can't take their eyes off Luis' retreating back, sashaying dramatically as if leaving the West End stage.

'Let me introduce you,' Paul says galantly. 'This is Pete, Brian and his wife, Ann.'

The next hour is excruciating for Carmen because Paul's ideas for the pub are very different to his partners. While Paul wants a modern, functioning and generic pub the partners are looking for something cosier and more traditional.

Carmen is thrown. The props and samples she's brought over are a waste of time and although they admire her drawings and creative skill, she knows they're not impressed by her ideas. She reads their reactions, gains a better understanding of what they're looking for and changes tack, coming up with alternative suggestions.

'Perhaps some thatched roofing over the bar? And, by using

smaller tables that can be pushed together for bigger groups... we can create snug areas... and perhaps hang old beer signs above the fireplace....?' After forty minutes they thaw to her new ideas and she relaxes.

At the end of her presentation, when she's packing up, one of the investors, Pete, regards her through narrow eyes. 'Am I right in saying that you're married to Jack Bailey?'

'I am.'

'How's he doing now? Don't hear much about him these days. He was on that celebrity programme - the SAS thing, wasn't he?'

'Yes.' Carmen forces a smile on her lips.

Pete addresses Brian. 'That could be a feather in our cap if he comes to drink in here.'

Carmen hastily gathers the cushions that are deemed too loud and the wrong colours.

Brian leans towards her. 'What pub experience do you really have?'

Carmen smiles. 'It's true that most of the time I refurbish apartments but it's the concept and creativity of any place - whether it's a home, rented accommodation, pub or restaurant. I can design anything. It's just that I was given a different brief for the pub initially.' She looks hard at Paul.

The only female partner, Brian's wife, Ann, says, 'You've done well in a short space of time. The other people have had weeks to prepare.'

'Other people?' asks Carmen. Her tone much lighter than her raging, darkening mood.

'The Spencers at the top of the High Street. They're very popular and they're *local*,' Ann emphasises.

'Well, I'm local. I'm across the road.'

Ann's laugh is high pitched. 'Nice try.'

'It's true. I couldn't be more local.'

'With your accent?' Ann smiles.

Brian places a hand on his wife's knee.

'I am Spanish, and I have designed lots of properties. Please check out my website.'

Brian says, 'Ann, it's not where someone is from. It's about the design of the pub.'

Ann stares icily at her husband. 'I don't want a hard sell.'

'Hard sell?' Carmen repeats, shaking her head angrily. 'Hard sell? No, no, no! It was his suggestion...' She gathers her portfolio and laptop. 'Paul asked for my help. He asked me. Nothing more. I do not hard sell.' She gathers her belongings. 'Luis will come and collect the rest of my things later.'

Paul stands up. 'I'll help you.'

'No! Leave them!' Carmen refuses to look at him but she turns her attention to the group. 'Thank you for your time. I'm sorry if I was not briefed properly.'

She doesn't make eye contact with Paul, and she turns and walks away with their hot stares on her back. It's only now that she appreciates Luis' sassy walk. She wishes she now had the confidence to sashay her hips and walk without a care in the world because inside, she's extremely angry and humiliated.

Chapter 4

Luis is serving a customer, and looks relieved to see her. 'Ah, Mama, this lady needs something very original and er...' his voice trails off.

A tall, smart-looking woman in her seventies with grey hair looks expectantly at Carmen. 'It's for my living room and I want something different, something unique with a hint of excitement...'

Carmen smiles and takes over. She welcomes the distraction and pulls out a new range of wallpaper featuring tropical and colourful birds. The client takes almost an hour deciding on the right design before she finally says:

'I'll think about it. I'll come back later in the week.'

She leaves Carmen without a sale and feeling as though her whole day is jinxed. She's more frustrated and exhausted than she's felt for a long time.

When they are alone in the shop, Luis turns the closed sign on the door. 'That was a waste of time. She was here for ages,' he complains. 'I hope you had a better meeting with Paul?'

Carmen shakes her head. She's still too upset about her encounter with Paul and his associates to talk about it and as it's closing time she replies with fake optimism, 'How about a takeaway tonight?'

Luis' face lights up. 'The Indian has a good reputation?'

'You're right. Sanjay was here at the opening and everyone says how good it is. Want to give it a try?'

Luis moves closer and puts his arm around Carmen's waist and she leans into him. 'Can we go home tomorrow?' he asks.

'*This* is home.'

'No, I mean our real home.'

She pushes him gently away. 'If you want to go, my darling, then go. I'm decorating a feature wall in the lounge this weekend so you can stay and help or go back to London.'

Luis sighs and moves away.

It's at times like this that Carmen wishes Luis had some real friends. Normally he befriends young people who define themselves by so many pronouns that Carmen gets confused or even forgets. Sometimes these friends have eating disorders, anxiety or depression and although she likes to see Luis with what he calls his own tribe, she desperately wants to see him happy.

Happiness, now there's a word. She sighs heavily. But going back to London and back to Jack will not make Carmen happy. She's made her decision, and she will make it work - somehow.

* * *

Carmen is sitting at the small table in Sanjay's takeaway waiting for their order, trying to distract herself from her disheartening mood and feeling of failure. She's also wondering about the right colour feature wall for her new flat when Tracey from the Beauty Salon bustles through the door. Her red head bobbing in delight when she spies Carmen.

'Hello. Have you settled in?'

'Hello, Tracey.' Carmen isn't sure about Tracey yet partly because she's been too inquisitive about Jack, but also because she's seen Tracey watching her in her shop. She knows she must be patient. It's not the first time someone has been a fan of Jack's and taken an extraordinary interest in her life, and it certainly won't be the last.

'Have you ordered? I phoned mine through so I didn't have to wait in here. Where's Luis?' Tracey gushes.

Sanjay reappears having taken Carmen's order to the kitchen and he smiles at Tracey. 'Hello.'

'Do you know Jack Bailey, the footballer?' Tracey asks.

Sanjay nods. 'Of course.'

Tracey nods at Carmen as if she's not there or even listening. 'That's his wife.'

'I know, Tracey, and I'm sure Carmen won't mind if you don't mention it again - ever.' He laughs and Carmen smiles gratefully.

Sanjay disappears and reappears seconds later with Tracey's order in a carry out bag. 'There.'

Tracey looks at Carmen. 'I could eat mine with you, if you like?' she says.

'Thank you, Tracey, but I'm taking mine home.'

'I could come with you?'

'That's kind of you, but I have work to do tonight.'

'Work? What sort of work?' Tracey folds her arms, the takeaway dangling from one hand.

'I have some designs to do for a client in London,' she lies.

'Luis says this is all new to you.'

Carmen smiles wondering when Luis spoke to Tracey. 'This is all *new* to Luis. I have been doing this for *years*.'

Tracey's eyes narrow. 'Do you mind him wearing makeup?'

'No. I don't mind *them*, wearing makeup.'

Tracey pouts. 'I did *their* nails.'

'They look lovely.'

'I'll do yours if you like, mates rates.'

'Thank you, but I'm too busy at the moment.'

'Where do you normally get them done?'

'Different places.'

'Luis said you had a woman who used to come to your house.'

'Sometimes.'

'He said you've got a swimming pool— '

Sanjay interrupts. 'Tracey, your takeaway will get cold. Perhaps you should go now and leave Carmen in peace.'

Tracey's eyes narrow at him. 'Who are you? The peace police?'

Sanjay laughs. 'It's just that it's been a long day and probably like you, Carmen wants to relax - in peace.'

Tracey glares back at Carmen. 'I hope we can be friends. I know Luis likes me.'

Sanjay raises his voice. 'Enough!'

But Tracey is already at the door. She slams it behind her without a backward glance.

'Sorry, Carmen.'

'It's not your fault, Sanjay. But thank you.'

He nods. 'I understand why Darren left her, now.'

Carmen looks up.

'She's a, how do you say? Man-eater? But she's also very nosy and she never knows when to leave people alone.'

'She probably means well.'

'Not always. Eva doesn't have time for her now.'

'Really?'

'Eva has twins at university. Tracey tried to seduce her son last year and Eva wasn't happy. I know he's probably not interested in her but - be careful with Luis.'

'I'll warn them. Thank you.'

There's a voice from the kitchen and Sanjay disappears leaving Carmen alone and wondering if Luis would be interested in Tracey. Wondering if Luis is interested in sex at all. This new generation is still a mystery to her and by all accounts just about everything she reads says that this generation barely have sex. They don't drink alcohol and are often too anxious to try anything different. On paper, it should be a walk in the park for this generation, especially after the hedonistic swinging sixties, and the indulgent eighties, but somehow, she thinks social media has made it all so much harder and more confusing for them all.

* * *

On Sunday morning, Carmen is painting the smallest lounge wall sage green. She wears an old pair of jeans and she has tied her hair back from her face. She's thinking about taking a break when there's a knock on the front door. There's no bell so Carmen leans out of the sash window.

She recognises Paul's peppered grey hair.

'Paul?'

He looks up, surprised, then smiles and raises his hand. 'I owe you an apology.'

Carmen stares down at him and doesn't reply.

'Have you time for a coffee?' He points across the road. 'I could wait in the café for you?'

Inside the house Luis calls out, 'What does that plank want? Tell him to piss off.'

Carmen calls down. 'I'll be over in five minutes, Paul.' She slams the rickety window shut. Carmen guesses that Luis won't get out of bed until past midday and at the bottom of the stairs she calls up to his bedroom.

'I'm popping out. I'll be back in half an hour.'

Luis grunts loudly. 'He's a user.'

She closes the lid on the paint, checks her reflection in the mirror, adds lipstick and picks up the house key.

Paul is waiting for her. He's sitting in the corner of the café nursing a black coffee. He looks tired as if he's had a late night. Night work and late shifts are exhausting. He stands up and asks her what she would like and goes to the bar where Karl is making coffee.

Karl waves and calls out, 'Morning Carmen.'

A few minutes later Paul slides the cup onto the table.

'Thank you for the coffee.' Carmen stirs it unnecessarily. It's something for her to do.

'You probably like Karl more than you like me.'

'That wouldn't be difficult right now.'

'Are you angry with me?'

'Why would I be angry?'

Paul shrugs. 'I'm, I'm not sure.... are you?'

'Have I reason to be?'

Paul shakes his head. 'I never know with women. Sometimes I get things wrong.'

'I wonder why that could be?' Carmen muses.

He frowns then changes the subject. 'So, how do you think it went on Friday?'

'You tell me.' Carmen places her hand on her chin and stares at him. He's ruggedly handsome. He hasn't shaved but it suits him and his eyes, although tired, are still beguiling.

'I don't want to upset you, Carmen. I like you - *a lot*.'

She turns to look out of the window and the people passing by. It's the last weekend of September and it's a fine day but Carmen feels disconnected from those around her. She feels Paul's gaze on her cheeks.

'I'll be honest Carmen. I feel as though I've done something wrong,' he says, 'I just want us to be friends.'

She imagines him as a small boy in the playground offering sweets to another child, his eyes full of insecurity, trying to be popular.

'Look, Paul. Friends can only be friends if they're honest with each other.'

'Yes,' he says eagerly. 'Exactly.'

'But you weren't honest with me.'

'I was.'

'You said that the pub needed refurbishing. You told me you could do with a hand. You told me about your ideas without a mention of anyone else being involved. You never said I was pitching to a group of people who are your associates, *and* you never said someone else was also tendering for the work.'

'Didn't I?'

'You know you didn't.'

'What difference does it make?'

'A massive difference. Your associates' ideas were the opposite of yours. Your ideas and their vision for the pub are completely different. They're not even similar.'

'They're not?'

'You know they're not!'

Paul looks at his hands and Carmen follows his gaze. There's a mark on his finger where his wedding ring might once have been, but it's been recently removed. He scratches his chin with rasping strokes and looks dolefully at her with a small grin.

'Sorry,' he mutters.

Carmen sips her coffee.

'I've never met anyone like you, Carmen. Let me take you out for dinner?'

Carmen shakes her head. 'I don't think so.'

'Why?'

'Because I'm married.'

Paul shrugs. 'I don't see Jack anywhere. And, I'll tell you something, if I were married to you, I certainly wouldn't let you—'

'That's not healthy.'

'I don't mean in a controlling way. I mean I'd just do whatever it takes to be with you.'

Paul's phone rings in his pocket. He pulls it out and checks the number. 'Sorry, I have to take this.' He stands up, pushes open the café door and steps outside.

Carmen watches him distractedly, wondering how different her life might have been had she married him and not Jack. To have married a man who wants to please her rather than the other way around. Someone who didn't have significant differences of opinion. Might Luis and Elena have been different too? But that's silly, she thinks. They wouldn't exist at all. And for all Jack's faults, she still loves him.

'Hello, Carmen.'

'Hi, Amber.'

She slides into Paul's seat. 'On your own?'

Carmen shakes her head. 'Paul wanted to apologise so he bought me a coffee.'

Amber grins. 'What's he done wrong?'

Carmen explains quickly about Friday's presentation and Amber shakes her head in disbelief. 'What a mess. Sorry, Carmen. Not everyone is as insensitive as Paul, but his wife left him a few weeks ago. He's probably not thinking straight. I know he misses his children.'

'I didn't know.' Carmen looks out of the window rethinking her conversations with Paul.

'The problem is that Paul is very flirtatious.' Amber sees Paul coming toward them in the street. 'He just can't seem to work out what women want - especially his wives.'

'Wives?'

'Yup.' Amber stands up. 'This is wife number three.'

Amber has already disappeared when Paul slips back into his seat.

'Where were we?' His smile is strained.

Carmen smiles. 'Thanks for the coffee but I'm going home now to continue my painting.'

'Look, I know I've messed up, but I'll sort it. My investors will decide by tomorrow and I'm sure—'

Carmen lays a hand on his arm. 'It doesn't matter.'

'It doesn't?'

'Not anymore.' Carmen stands up.

'I'll walk with you.' Paul opens the door and they step into the street. 'Come with me a moment.' He takes her by the elbow and steers her toward Eva's flower shop. He picks up an expensive bouquet and gives them to her with a peck on the cheek.

'Friends?'

'You don't need to buy me flowers, but they very are pretty. Thank you.'

He slips his arm through hers. 'So, dinner one night?'

'No, but thank you.'

They pause outside her closed shop. 'Well, if you change your mind, you know where I am.'

'Thank you.'

He stares intently at her. 'You're probably the most beautiful woman I've ever met.'

'You're a married man,' she says.

'Not anymore.' Without warning he leans quickly forward to kiss her on the lips. She pushes against his chest and turns quickly away.

Paul grins. 'I know we're going to be friends, Carmen. I just *know* it. We're meant for each other.'

Carmen holds the flowers to her chest and watches his retreating back. She smells sunshine on their stems, sweet blossom, a multitude of colours and intoxicating scents. It's the smell of the dying summer on a warm day and, although she senses the season is coming to an end, her spirits are lifted. She's pleased she's here in Westbay. She has a shop, and for the first time in a long while, she feels independent. She turns to admire her shop window. Standing inside the shop, gazing right back out at her, are two familiar piercing blue eyes that look murderous.

Chapter 5

'What do you mean, he's only a friend?' Jack shouts once she opens the door. 'I saw him kiss you.'

'He didn't kiss me.'

'It was on the lips. Where have you been with him?'

'We went for a coffee.'

'And he bought you flowers?' Jack is incredulous.

'Yes. What are you doing here anyway?'

'That's a warm greeting. You've been begging me to come here and when I do, I find you snogging some bloke in the street.'

'That was not snogging, Jack Bailey.' Carmen wrinkles her nose at him. '*As you well know*. This is a lovely surprise.' She smiles.

Jack gives a wry smile. 'What's going on?'

He follows her upstairs and into the lounge, stepping over the paint tin and dust sheets then into the kitchen.

'Paul's the manager of The Ship and I did a presentation for a refurb on Friday. But he blind-sided me. I had no idea there were other investors involved who would make the decision or that there were other companies competing for the project.' She reaches for a vase.

'He didn't tell you?'

'No.

'What a snake.'

'Exactly. Did you speak to Luis?'

'He let me in and now he's gone back to bed.'

'*They*, let you in and *they* have gone back to bed.' She corrects him gently.

Jack watches her arrange the flowers. 'You've made it look lovely up here. It was a dump before. I couldn't believe the photos you sent but it looks much better in real life.'

'Are you going to move in?'

Jack's eyes are sparkling and Carmen is pleased and excited to see him. He hadn't wanted to see the shop or the flat. He hadn't shown any interest at all. He'd even refused to come with her to Westbay. In fact, he hadn't been here since they last visited together in happier times before Covid.

Full of optimism and love she moves closer to him. 'Come on,' she whispers. 'It's so wonderful to see you. Let's take a walk and look at the sea together.'

Jack smiles and she kisses him with more passion that either of them had expected.

'Umm,' he murmurs. 'You still taste gorgeous.'

'You too, Jack Bailey. Let's go, before we disturb Sleeping Beauty.' She nods up at Luis' bedroom. 'We need some special time together.'

* * *

'So, this is what's so appealing, is it?' Jack says. They're walking arm in arm through the harbour, past the fishing boats bobbing on a turning tide. The pretty summer kiosks are open and it's busy with holidaymakers browsing the stalls and enjoying the end of the September sunshine.

'It's magical, isn't it?' agrees Carmen. 'Look, that's the Airbnb where we stayed before.'

Jack screws up his eyes and grins. 'I remember. It's overlooking the sea. Didn't we get fish and chips and eat them on the beach?'

'That was a fun weekend.' Carmen pulls his arm closer to her, pleased that he's here beside her sharing memories. She's missed him. They'd spent so much time arguing and disagreeing recently that she just wanted to get out of London. Now that Jack's here, her heart is lighter and she finally believes that everything might be alright at last. Jack might even stay.

'I love this boardwalk and these beautiful houses along the front overlooking the yacht club but there are some lovely homes on the street behind...'

Jack grins. 'Don't even think about it.'

She laughs. 'I won't. I need to get the business up and running first.'

They walk along the sea front, arm in arm, watching the sailing regatta out at sea. The sun and wind on Carmen's cheeks remind her of days past, happier times, and she closes her eyes dreamily. She's enjoying the peace in her heart as they chat about friends and family before they turn back toward the harbour.

Years of marriage has made them both comfortable with silence and Carmen feels an inner peace she hasn't felt for a long time. Jack has always had this reassuring effect on her and it's what she loves most. When they're together she feels complete again. She smiles and his blue eyes twinkle back, full of promise and excitement. She notices that he's also calm.

He appears happier and his frown has disappeared. He takes in the scenes around him and is enthusiastic and positive about everything.

In the harbour someone screeches and then suddenly they are besieged by a small group of women, clearly on a hen-do and still worse for wear. One wears a golden crown and a sash across her breasts and a white T-shirt declaring she's *Sandra on Tour.* Her friend has lipstick smeared across her cheek and another has heels so high, she can barely stand up. She screams again, swaying, holding onto Sandra's arm. 'It's Jack Bailey!'

'Jack!'

'Is it really you?'

'I can't believe it.'

'God, he's gorgeous.'

'Can I have a kiss?'

'Photo! Photo! Photo!' The one tottering on high heels grabs Jack's arm as she almost falls to the ground, pulling her mobile from her bag.

'Selfie! Selfie!' chants the one with lipstick on her cheek as her friend staggers to stay upright.

Sandra, the bride-to-be, seems unfocused. Her friends grab her arms and push her against Jack.

He steadies her, laughing good-naturedly. 'Easy girls. Out celebrating?'

'She's getting hitched,' says Smudged-lips.

'You're beautiful,' slurs, High-heels.

'Me. me.' Smudged-lips pushes between Sandra and Jack. 'Me, me. Take a photo.' She orders.

'You! You!' High-heels pushes the phone at Carmen. 'You take the photo.'

The three girls gather around Jack. Their arms are around his waist and over his shoulder and Lipstick plants a kiss on his cheek. He grins at Carmen and shrugs in a 'what am I to do?' expression and poses between the women smiling happily.

Carmen takes a few photos and realises that this is what Jack enjoys. He loves that he's still recognised, and people want a photo with him. After his rebranding as a celebrity, he's insatiable. Carmen hands the camera back and stands at the railing looking out to sea as Jack waves goodbye to the girls.

'Sorry,' he whispers, still basking in their attention.

Carmen shakes her head. 'No problem.'

But it is a problem. Jack loves it and they both know it. He loves the attention, fame and recognition. He links his arm through hers. 'Lunch?'

They opt for the Italian in the square and order pizzas and salad. Carmen tells him about the opening of her shop and the local people in Harbour Street. She's hoping that he'll be interested enough to stay and meet them, but Jack has other plans.

He leans across the table 'The book's coming out earlier than expected. They've brought the date forward.'

He's referring to his autobiography. *Jack's Boots.* It was an idea that originated after he sold his football boots for charity. The boots he wore when he scored the winning goal in the FA Cup. A story about his early years and how he made it as a Premier League footballer.

Carmen hasn't read it.

'I think there'll be a sequel.' He grins.

'But this one isn't on the shelves yet,' replies Carmen laughing. She's always impressed with Jack's naive enthusiasm.

'It's coming out before Christmas now. They reckon it will

go down a storm - a Christmas blockbuster.'

She wipes the corner of her mouth with her napkin. Listening to Jack's excited voice she's caught up in his enthusiasm. 'I've worked so hard to meet deadlines. It was a cathartic process,' Jack continues. 'You know, talking about my anterior cruciate ligament injury - my ACL - you remember how painful that was, don't you? I mean, when you tear your ligaments, it's no joke. It's that strong band of tissue that connects your thigh bone...'

Carmen nods. She remembers those painful years vividly.

'You know the effect it had on my career. It wasn't just me. You remember how it happened to Gazza in the 1991 FA Cup Final? He missed out on a multi-million-pound deal with that Italian club.'

'It was a terrible time.' Carmen inhales deeply as if it will block out the memory.

'I heard my ACL snap!' Jack adds. 'It's one the of most serious football injuries although it happens a lot more to women athletes now.'

'Why?'

'They say that it could be because women have thinner ACLs or it could be because of how they land when they're tackled. It's all changed. Now, in female football, they have injury prevention programs to combat the risk of it.'

'You've made a pretty good recovery.'

Jack leans across the table. 'I have now but it put an end to my career, Carmen. By the time my knee was fixed I was too old—'

'You've had other interests,' she interrupts. She likes the positive Jack. The Jack who is full of ideas and fun.

Jack stares at her meaningfully. 'I was prone to injury after that, especially when I was suffering from fatigue - when we had fixtures too close together. They've made so many medical advances in the last twenty years. Now you can get away with wearing a knee brace and have lots of physio. But I had a complete rupture.'

Carmen sees the anguish and hurt in his eyes.

'Do you wish you'd ever gone back to modelling?' He changes the subject quickly taking Carmen by surprise. 'I never understood what happened. You didn't want to be a WAG either— '

'I was never going to be known as your wife or girlfriend in that way— '

'I know but - modelling. You were so popular and so good at it.'

Carmen shakes her head. 'We had a family.'

'But you were with all the supermodels of the 1990s,' Jack says proudly.

'It wasn't enough just to model though Jack, was it? They wanted us on talk shows. We had to party in trendy nightclubs so that we'd appear in the gossip columns of the magazines.'

'You might have landed a movie deal?'

'Which I would have hated.'

'Linda Evangelista, Cindy Crawford, Claudia Schiffer, Kate Moss - they've all done well.'

Carmen smiles at the memory proud to have worked with some of the top names. 'Do you remember how Chanel made us use cool-toned browns and lighter neutral tones to enhance the eye shape and the vampy lips - that you liked?'

'I remember the bucket hats, bike shorts and combat boots.' Jack laughs. 'God you were hot!'

'And the velvet suits?' Carmen giggles.

'Supermodels were like superstars. You were a superstar. You don't see that anymore.'

'Everything changes, Jack.'

'I know.' He smiles. 'And, I have to go with the times. The thing is, Simon, my agent, reckons that if it goes well and I do a lot of promotional work on TV and book signings then I might even get more TV work. Perhaps even my own programme.'

'Like Gary Lineker?'

'No, more of a chat show host. Simon seems to think I'd be great interviewing guests and celebrities and things. He says I've got a natural ability to put people at ease.'

Simon, Jack's agent, is always spinning some new career carrot in front of Jack for him to follow; another idea as a celebrity, a new idea to get on TV. Suddenly Carmen has a feeling that this doesn't bode well.

'Would you like that?' she asks, already knowing the answer.

Jack reaches for her hand. 'It's for us, baby. It's for you and me. It's all about keeping our home. Our London home. The advance on the book has paid for...'

'Some of our debts?' Carmen adds.

'I know it's not a lot, but if it comes out before Christmas I'll speak to the bank again. I think it might be alright.' Jack makes eye contact with her. 'I'm doing my best.'

'I know.'

'And if I can resurrect my career then that will be even better.'

'Your career?'

Jack smiles sheepishly. 'Not the football one. Even I know I'm too injured and too old for that - but I mean the celebrity one. I would have done the cooking one but standing all that time - my knee....' He places his hand under the table on his trousers.

'They haven't asked you for Masterchef!'

'I know, but if they did. I couldn't do it. That SAS one almost killed me. But listen, Carmen. Simons says the public love me. He reckons I have the banter and I'm a cheeky chappie. I make people laugh.'

Carmen looks at her husband. He is charismatic and sometimes he's funny. It's just such a shame that when he is on the TV both she and Luis cringe at the over enthusiastic way he wants to please everyone. By doing this, it appears that he has no real backbone and that he's a people-pleaser, but worse, the public laugh at him, not with him. All this had come out in one of their arguments during the summer. Carmen wasn't going to bring it all up again but the feeling of peace and inner calm she'd felt earlier along the promenade has now completely disappeared.

Jack pays the bill. The restaurant is still busy and as they leave, he's recognised. He takes time to chat, shake hands and pose for photos.

Carmen drifts away to stand outside in the street. Jack follows ten minutes later.

'Sorry, babe.' He slips his arm through hers.

'Will we go home?' she asks.

'London?' Jack smiles and his whole face lights up.

'I mean the flat. Luis should be awake by now.'

Jack's smile fades. 'Yeah, of course.'

* * *

In the flat, Luis is sitting on the sofa, on his phone, eating toast and drinking tea.

'Hi Luis, how's it going?' Jack asks.

'Fine.' Luis wraps a pink kimono around his waist and reties the belt. Luis isn't dressed and hasn't put any makeup on yet. 'If you like living in the back of beyond where there's nothing to do.'

Jack flops in the chair opposite. 'You didn't have to come here. You could have stayed at home with me.'

Carmen sits beside Luis and regards them both with interest. They couldn't be more different. Luis with long slim arms and fingers and subdued dark eyes and Jack - broad and strong with twinkling blue eyes. Probably the only thing they have in common is their stubborn nature.

'Are you still drawing?' asks Jack. 'Looking forward to uni?'

Luis ignores him, yawns distractedly and then stares at his phone.

Jack raises his eyebrows to Carmen and she smiles back.

Luis waves his iPhone. 'It looks like everyone's seen you in Westbay. It's all over social media.'

'There's no privacy,' Jack mutters.

'You love it.' Luis' eyes darken.

'So, it's not long until you go to uni,' Jack says. 'Is there anything you need?'

Luis doesn't look up. 'I probably won't go.'

Jack sits up straighter in the armchair. 'What?' He glances at Carmen trying to read her expression before his gaze fixes back on Luis.

'I might not go.'

Jack stares at Carmen. 'Did you know about this?'

Carmen shrugs. 'Luis is constantly changing their mind.'

'*Their*,' mutters Jack.

Luis looks up from his phone. 'Not constantly. I told you last week, but you were too busy with your presentation.'

'I did listen.' Carmen nudges Luis and grins. 'You know I did.'

'Then you knew?' Jack leans forward, gripping his hands. 'Why didn't you say? Why hasn't anyone told me?'

'It's not important,' Luis says.

Jack begins to grind his jaw and Carmen knows that he's choosing his words carefully. His chest is rising as he controls his emotions. 'It *is* important.'

'To you maybe but I don't want a student debt hanging over me for years.'

Jack laughs. 'You know we'll pay it for you.'

Luis shrugs. 'What with? Mum says we're broke. We're going to lose our home.'

Jack's eyes blaze and he says slowly and carefully in a measured tone. 'We will *not* lose our house.'

'Is that because of your book deal?' Luis finally looks at his father. 'And the fact that you're going on a book tour next month.'

'How did...?'

'What?' Carmen's smile fades. 'What book tour?'

Jack flicks his gaze from one to the other.

Luis smiles slowly. 'Ah, so you haven't told Mama, yet. That's a shame. It's all over social media.'

Jack shakes his head and looks pleadingly at Carmen. 'I'm sorry. I was going to tell you.'

'When?'

'It's only for a few weeks.'

'When?'

'At the end of October.'

'It's for six weeks.' Luis reads from his phone. 'And he's going all over Europe and... yes, it looks like you're off to the States too.' Luis looks up and smiles triumphantly. 'It might be more than six weeks.'

Carmen stares at her husband and stands up. She suddenly needs to be alone. Jack has had all morning and lunchtime to tell her this news, but he hadn't.

'Carmen, wait! Please!'

Carmen shuts herself in the bathroom. It's the only room with a lock. She sits on the edge of the bath. Her heart is pounding wildly and she wipes a tear from the corner of her eye. She waits, and when her heart has calmed, she stands up and stares at her reflection. Then with one simple swipe of her hand, she pulls her wig from her head.

The face staring back at her is no longer the once glamorous model. She only sees the sick woman who has tufts of greying hair now growing back in random patches after gruelling bouts of chemotherapy.

Chapter 6

Carmen hears them arguing from inside the bathroom.

'Why did you have to tell her?' Jack is shouting.

'Because you didn't.'

'I was going to—'

'Liar!'

'Don't speak to me like that!'

'You've said worse to me—'

'I've apologised.'

'If you meant it - it might have helped.'

'I did mean it!'

'The problem with you is...'

'You never listen, Luis...'

Carmen covers her ears and closes her eyes trying to block it all out. She's spent the past two years trying to block everything out, from her diagnosis to Luis identifying as a non-binary person that she's no longer allowed to call her son. Then finally, Elena broke the news that she's seriously in love with her boyfriend - a controlling and narcissistic pilot. But through all of this, there has been Jack.

Two years ago, he had fallen apart when he thought he might lose her. Then he'd been stalwart and supportive and it seemed as if her being sick had given him purpose. But she didn't want a marriage based on her illness and him being her carer. It had been tough, but now she was determined. She had to live life to her best possible potential.

After she'd been given the all clear, she had re-evaluated her life. The outcome was that she needed more. She wanted to live. She was greedy for life, thirsty for new experiences and hungry to make changes. All those years ago she'd given up modelling to support Jack's footballing career and to raise the children. The family had been her sole purpose but now, with Elena flying all over the world and Luis leaving for university, she wanted to plan ahead. She didn't want them to be bankrupt, but she didn't want a celebrity lifestyle either. She just wanted to be normal. She wanted to prepare for the future - her future. She needed to be creative and to do something for herself.

That hadn't suited Jack.

With them still bickering in the lounge, Carmen puts her wig on and rearranges her hair carefully so it falls over her shoulders. She pinches her cheeks, smiles and then opens the bathroom door. When she enters the lounge, they both stop arguing and look at her.

Jack is now standing at the window and he takes a deep breath. 'Are you alright?'

Carmen assesses the situation. 'Yes. Luis, please go and get dressed.'

Luis frowns then rises to his feet and disappears upstairs to his bedroom.

Jack moves toward her. 'You can see why this place is not ideal, Cammy. Look, we can't even have a conversation in private.'

'You should have told me at lunchtime.'

'I was distracted.'

'And when we walked along the beach were you also distracted? Were you so excited to be with me in Westbay that you forgot to mention that you'd be travelling abroad for weeks - possibly months?'

Jack shakes his head. 'I should have told you.'

'Is that why you came here?'

Jack nods. 'I wanted to tell you in person.'

'Then why didn't you? Why did Luis have to read about it on social media?'

Jack spreads his arms wide. 'Look, the thing is, there's also something else. Something that Luis doesn't know. It's not on social media.'

Carmen tilts her head. Her breathing is rapid and her mouth feels dry. She wouldn't blame him for meeting someone else, even for having an affair. Her illness had been tough on him too. But divorce? It was something she'd never contemplated. Not when he stopped playing football or when he was depressed or when he was drinking and spent most of their savings backing the wrong horses. They'd got through everything together.

'Cammy? Are you listening?' Jack steps forward. 'Simon has got me a gig. On a dancing show - in Australia.'

'A dancing show?' she repeats hollowly.

'Yeah.' He rubs his chin.

'What about your knee?'

'I'll take pain killers.'

Carmen sits down on the sofa. 'So, you're not leaving me for a book tour but for a dancing show on the other side of the world?'

'I'm not leaving you! Besides, you left me - you came here.

There's no point in me sitting at home by myself.' Jack moves to sit beside her and takes her hands in his. 'Look, the thing is, I'll combine it with the book tour - all before Christmas.'

Carmen looks at the earnest expression in his eyes. Eyes that she's looked into for over twenty-five years. Eyes that have adored her, undressed her, hated her and more recently felt sorry for her. Now these eyes are pleading. They're asking her not to make a fuss, to understand him and to support him.

'Before Christmas?'

'Yes,' he replies softly, still holding her hands. 'I think it's a good idea.'

She stares at him.

'Please don't look at me like that, Cammy. You'll break my heart. Look, I know this is difficult. We're having a tough time - both of us. But if I do this, I might be able to pay off our debts and save our home.'

Carmen stares down at their entwined hands.

He continues quickly, 'It will give us the space we need.'

'Space?' She looks up sharply. 'Have you met someone?'

'God, no! You know I haven't.'

Carmen shrugs.

'Look, Cammy. This makes sense for both of us. We can have a break and sort ourselves out.'

Carmen stands up and walks to the window. Down in Harbour Street people are walking aimlessly, browsing shops, drinking coffee, heading to the beach - leading normal lives while her life is crumbling apart.

'I understand you need a break,' she says. 'It's hard being a carer and you've been through a lot.'

Jack stands up. 'It was never about me. I just knew I didn't want to lose you. I'd have done anything.'

Carmen notices the past tense. She wishes that she still wasn't so attracted to him. She wishes that she could nestle in his arms and feel safe like a girlfriend or wife and not as a patient.

'When do you leave?' she asks.

'I fly to Sydney tomorrow night.'

Carmen nods. He's already decided. He knew before he left London.

'It hasn't been on social media?' She laughs ironically.

'Someone dropped out at the last minute. It's all going to be a big reveal on the opening night.'

'Is this what you want?'

'Yes.'

'Goodbye then, Jack.'

'Is that it?'

Carmen shrugs, 'I don't know. We've never been apart for so long.' During all the years they'd been together, they'd stayed together, travelling and working, supporting each other.

Jack walks toward her. 'I want to call you every night, is that okay?'

Carmen smiles lamely. 'With a dance show on at a completely different time to the UK, that's going to be hard.'

'Well, let's at least try and speak each day?'

Carmen nods.

'I mean it, Cammy. I want to... I want us to—'

'To what?'

'To be okay.' He steps forward and pulls her close. She wraps her arms around his waist and rests her head on his shoulder. Feeling his beating heart and his reassuring presence, she experiences an overwhelming surge of love. Just for a second, she allows herself to close her eyes. She wants to beg him to stay. She would even go back to London right now for him but he's already decided. He needs a break from *her*.

Carmen steps away, kisses him very gently on the lips and says very quietly, 'Go with God, my darling. Vaya con dias.'

* * *

Luis is fuming. After their father has gone Luis storms around the apartment ranting.

'He's so selfish. All he does is to think about himself. His life. His bloody career. We've all paid a price for it.'

'Luis, please! Don't be angry.'

'How can you forgive him?' he shouts. 'How can you - not care!'

'I do care.'

'How could he bloody leave you? After everything you've been through?'

'Luis, STOP!' Carmen waves her finger at him. 'I will not have this. No self-pity. Remember? I am luckier than many, many, women who have had breast cancer. I am here and I am alive. So stop! Now!'

Luis has dressed in a short lime green skirt and purple blouse. He tosses his hair aside, over one shoulder, and then toys with the end of the curls, wrapping them around his fingers. 'I hate him.'

'No, you don't.'

'I do.'

'He wants to save our home. And he wants to have enough money for you to go to university and not have to worry about paying off your student debt and...'

'I'm not going to university. And, anyway, he doesn't have

to do that for me.'

'He's always looked after you. He's looked after all of us so try not to be too ungrateful.'

'I didn't ask him to—'

'Luis! Stop! Enough of this. I will not let you speak badly about your father. He loves you very much. Now, let's be proactive. Let's do something positive.' Carmen checks her watch.

'Like what?' Luis' voice is sulky, but he's interested.

Carmen grins. 'Check out the competition.'

* * *

It's late afternoon, the shops have closed, and there's a sleepy Sunday vibe as they walk up Harbour Street toward the square. Carmen pauses at the church, but the doors are closed.

'It may open later but the pub's open,' Luis says.

'We're not going in The Ship.' Carmen's voice takes on an edge and she slips her arm through Luis' and pulls him toward the modern part of the town with the supermarket and newer shops.

She stops outside the one that interests her. 'Opulence Interiors.' The modern double-fronted shop window is vastly different to her shop. This one is sleek, sophisticated and modern.

'What's this?' asks Luis.

'My competition.'

Luis pushes his face against the glass and looks inside. 'It looks very...'

'Chic?'

'No. Extravagant and expensive.' Luis mutters deciding on

the right words. 'Very expensive. Why are we here?'

'They've pitched for the job in the pub.'

'The refurb?'

'Yes.'

'You'll win then. This is all...' He waggles his fingers in the air. 'Show!'

Carmen looks though the windows again, admiring the pink sofa in the window and a glass and white coffee table decorated with fake champagne glasses. It's a much larger shop than hers and at the back is an oak dining table and four elegantly backed chairs, a range of bright cushions and throws, and lots of silver lamps hanging from the ceiling. There's an assortment of animal statues, icons and fancy table decorations.

'Dust collectors.' Sniffs Luis. 'They're pretty ugly, don't you think?'

'I like the vase - that big one with the pampas grass.'

'Swingers.'

'What?'

'Swingers used to put pampas grass outside in their front garden so that other swingers would know.'

Carmen laughs and Luis grins back.

This is what she loved about her child. He always had the ability to come out with something unpredictable that would make her laugh, and in that way, she is heartened. Luis is very much like his father too.

* * *

Carmen waits patiently all day on Monday hoping Paul will give her positive news, but he doesn't come to the shop. By lunchtime she thinks he's gone to *Opulent Interiors* to give them the good news.

She makes a few sales, orders a flamboyant pink lamp and does everything to not think about Jack jetting off to the other side of the world. She has been hoping he might call and tell her he's changed his mind but that wouldn't be Jack. Once his mind is made up, he's stubborn. But she also knows that it's the stubbornness of his nature that has kept them together. Following his parents acrimonious divorce when he was thirteen, he vowed that if he ever got married, he would never leave his wife.

Carmen is emotionally exhausted and a little down. After dinner with Luis she heads upstairs with a design book for an early night. She is sitting at her dressing table, contemplating her reflection and wondering if moving to Westbay had been the right thing when Luis peers around her bedroom door.

'Are you okay?' he asks, sitting beside her while studying the vibrant palette of makeup sprawled out across the tabletop. He picks up a metallic shade of eye shadow. 'Gold, champagne and bronze are perfect for enhancing blue eyes,' he says. 'Yours maybe a little too smoky but let's add a touch of sparkle.'

Carmen observes Luis through the mirror as he becomes engrossed. Meticulously blending colours and experimenting with eye shadows, his face is a canvas for creativity. It's not the first time they've done this but each time Carmen remembers the first time. Luis had been four and was enamoured with the range of her professional makeup.

He puckers his lips and Carmen laughs at the intent expression on his face.

'Mama, stop! I'm trying to create a masterpiece here,' Luis

declares, wielding a makeup brush like a magician's wand.

'But cariño, don't you think this shade is a little too bold?' She leans closer, inspecting the electric blue eyeshadow around Luis' eyes.

'It's a *look*, Mama.' Luis grins, adding an extra stroke of glittery gold. 'I'm going for avant-garde.'

Carmen sighs, her maternal instincts tingling. 'I know, but don't you want something more... subtle?'

'Subtle is overrated,' Luis replies, unfazed. 'Let's make a statement. Makeup is about self-expression, remember?'

'Of course, my darling. But a little guidance wouldn't hurt you. I used to do the perfect cat-eye.' Carmen remembered, her voice holding a hint of mischief.

Luis chuckles. 'Mama, you're a decade behind in makeup trends - at least.'

'Ah, I see.' Carmen pretends to be affronted. 'So, I suppose electric blue is the new 'in' colour?'

'Absolutely.' Luis leans forward to admire his handiwork in the mirror.

Carmen sighs, unable to contain her concern. 'Okay, but don't you think it's a bit... much?'

'Mama, you're killing my vibe here,' Luis teases, swiping on a bold lipstick shade.

'Just trying to help, cariño.' Carmen attempts a compromise. 'Maybe a lighter touch on the blush?'

Luis shakes his head. His determination is unyielding. 'I've got this, Mama. Trust me.'

'Alright, alright.' Carmen raises her hands in surrender. 'But promise me you won't scare the neighbours away with that neon glow.'

'Deal.' Luis grins mischievously and twirls around to face

her. 'Now, what do you think of my new look?'

Carmen smiles, looking at her child with unwavering love. 'Cariño, you're positively radiant. A trendsetter without a doubt.'

'See, I knew you'd come around to my taste in the end.' Luis beams, feeling validated in his choice of makeup.

Carmen kisses him on the forehead and speaks as if he's still a small boy. 'Now, it's getting late. You'd better take it all off before bed.'

* * *

After Luis has gone Carmen isn't sleepy. Her mind is busy. She wonders when she will next see Jack and what will happen between now and Christmas.

'Three months. That's a lifetime, for some,' she whispers.

She pulls off her long wig and puts it on the bust in the cupboard. She hates wearing someone else's hair and, worse still, she wonders about the person who grew it and shaved it off for money. She leans toward the mirror ruffling the untidy patches of feathered hair now with clusters of grey strands. This short, ragged hair makes her eyes seem bigger but without makeup she looks sad and old. She once had lovely soft, dark locks - she had been young.

She unbuttons her blouse, removes her bra and stands staring at her misshapen body in the mirror. The surgeon had offered to do reconstructive surgery at the time but to Jack's surprise she'd refused. Now she looks lopsided with a ragged scar across her chest where her left breast had been.

Jack hadn't understood until she'd explained about Kintsugi. Jack had never heard of the Japanese word. She told him how it's the Japanese art of putting broken pottery back together with gold. He'd immediately assumed that he needed to buy her an expensive piece of jewellery but she had smiled and elaborated quickly. She explained that it's built upon the idea that one embraces flaws and imperfections and by doing this create an even more beautiful piece of artwork.

Jack had frowned and turned away. He clearly didn't get it. She had planned on getting a meaningful tattoo where her left breast had been but if truth be told she hadn't been brave enough to face more pain.

Tonight, in her apartment in Westbay, Carmen accepts why Jack didn't understand her decision. She had once been a top model and now she was ugly.

She pulls on her nightgown, climbs into bed and reaches for her book.

Her iPhone rings.

She answers it quickly.

'Cammy?'

'Hello, Jack.' Her heart begins beating faster.

'The flight's boarding.'

Carmen looks at her clock. It's ten thirty. 'Have a safe flight.'

'Thanks.'

There's a pause then Jack asks, 'Are you alright?'

'Fine.'

'Sure?'

'Yes.'

'We'll be okay.'

'I know.'

'These weeks will pass quickly,' he says.

'Yes.'

'It will give you time to get your business off the ground.'

'Yes.' He doesn't ask her about the pub, but then he's probably forgotten.

'Thank you, Cammy,' he says quietly.

'For what?'

'For letting me do this.'

'You're a grown up, Jack. You don't need my permission.'

'It's not that...'

'What is it?'

'I'm sorry.'

Carmen waits wondering if he's apologising for something he's already done or for something he will do in the future. But when he doesn't say anything else she's overcome with a wave of deep sadness and regret that lodges in the base of her throat. She swallows hard. Her voice is barely a whisper. 'Go carefully, cariño.'

'I will. They're boarding the plane now. I love you.'

Carmen holds her breath. She can't tell him how she really feels, how much she already misses him or how frightened she really feels or she will crumble into a pathetic, quivering mess.

'You too,' she whispers. 'Te quiero.'

Chapter 7

It's a busy week and it's not helped by the fact that Luis isn't around to help. Since Tracey from the Beauty Salon across the road painted his nails, he's made friends with her. They either hang around over there or he's on an errand for her, collecting something or dropping something off. In the evenings, they often go to a bar together and Carmen is left alone. They communicate with text messages.

Carmen knows that if Luis goes to university the term will start in three weeks' time and she will have to manage the shop alone anyway. She has to get used to it, so she keeps busy; filling the shop with a variety of timeless pieces, some classical, all tasteful and some genuine antiques. She enjoys browsing websites as much as she enjoys speaking to customers and she's pleasantly surprised when she makes a couple of decent sales.

She has never been a person for routine and today is no different. After work Carmen huddles up against a cold northern wind. She needs fresh air, so she strides out along the boardwalk to the promenade and then past the pretty coloured beach huts until her frustrated energy subsides. When it does, she turns around and walks back towards the town, only this time more slowly. She tucks her chin into the collar of her jacket while watching the oyster catchers feeding along the high tide. Seagulls swarm excitedly overhead and in the distance a flock of gulls follow a fishing boat back to the harbour. She pauses to look up at the beach huts. They're already closed and boarded up ready for the winter. Only one man is in a pink beach hut and he's oblivious to her. He's re-organising, tidying up and whistling as he works.

Walking toward her is a beautiful black woman carrying fish and chips and she smiles.

'We have to make the most of it before the winter,' the lady says, laughing, holding up the bag in her hand.

'Absolutely.' Carmen's nostrils twitch at the salt and vinegar wafting from the paper.

The stranger holds out her free hand. 'You're Carmen? I'm Femi. Amber told me about your new shop but I haven't got down to see it yet. Life has got in the way.'

Carmen smiles. Femi's handshake is firm and her eyes are friendly. 'I can understand that.'

'How are you getting on?' Femi smiles.

'Very well. Thank you.'

'Good. Ah, Lawrence, this is Carmen from the new interiors shop.'

Carmen thinks Lawrence is like a bouncing puppy as he strides down the hill from the beach hut to join them. He's clearly in love with Femi. He slips his arm around her waist and his eyes shine happily.

'We have to make the most of it while the children are busy,' Femi explains.

'Children?' asks Carmen.

'Albert is on a trip with the school to see a play in London. Ricky is studying for his A-levels and Ahmed is in Turkey. Do you have children?'

'Luis is here with me but he's - they're going off to uni in London, in a few weeks time.'

'They? Ah, is this the new pronoun thing? I need to get used to it,' Lawrence says. 'I'm sorry, it's probably a generational thing. I don't mean any harm by not remembering it's just so unusual to use the plural form.'

Carmen smiles. 'I often forget myself.'

'I've seen Luis in town,' says Femi. 'They are striking. They were wearing a beautiful purple and lime dress. They looked very beautiful and I'd know you're his mother - sorry - their mother - by your beautiful long hair and those incredible cheek bones.'

Carmen touches her wig self-consciously.

'They seem very artistic,' Femi says.

'They're an artist, a very good one, and I'm just hoping that they will go to uni in a few weeks. You know what young people are like.' She crosses her fingers. 'Don't let your fish and chips get cold. I'll see you again.'

Lawrence calls out. 'Tell Luis to go and see Ben in the art gallery - Amber's partner. He's very supportive of local artists.'

'I will. Thank you.'

* * *

Walking under the clock tower between the harbour and Harbour Street, Carmen pauses to enjoy the view. The shops are quirky, unique - a real mixture of independent businesses. The male grooming salon is often busy and she's even seen queues outside. Sometimes Carmen's even seen a couple of young girls with short hair waiting. She crosses the road to look in the window of Jane's Jewellers. There's a young girl inside, maybe mid-twenties wearing butterfly dungarees. She knows Tommy's niece helps in the shop. Carmen looks at the jewellery designs in the window and thinks about Elena. She would love this modern jewellery. She loses herself for a few minutes picking out a pretty necklace for her daughter and then a ring for Luis. But it's October. Still too early to shop for Christmas.

She walks slowly past the butcher's shop and the greengrocers. The café is closed, as is the flower shop. At the art gallery she pauses to look in the window. There's a painting of red bullfinches that she thinks would be nice in her shop and she wonders if Ben would be open to a reciprocal arrangement where she hangs some of his paintings in exchange for a few small choice pieces of furniture to stop the gallery from looking so bare.

'Hello Carmen.'

She turns at the sound of a voice beside her.

'Hello Tracey.' Carmen keeps her voice light. She doesn't want to speak to Tracey and she's not sure why. 'How are you?'

'Just finished work. Going to get a burger then I'm meeting Luis.'

'Lovely,' says Carmen. She begins to walk away but Tracey matches her pace along the path.

'It's a shame, you know...' Tracey leaves the sentence hanging in the air like a bad smell.

Carmen smiles politely.

'Poor Luis,' adds Tracey.

'Why?'

'They're very upset.'

'Oh.'

'Are you worried?'

'Luis always knows they can talk to me.'

'Ah but that's it. No one ever wants to talk to their parents.'

Carmen walks toward her shop but Tracey stays at her side, her hot and excited breath on her cheek.

'Luis told me he was here.'

'Who?'

'Jack.'

'Ah.'

'I wanted a photo with him. A selfie.'

'That's a shame.'

Tracey smiles triumphantly. 'But I got one anyway.'

'Good.' Carmen fumbles at the gate for her house key.

Tracey shoves her iPhone under Carmen's nose. 'Look.'

Jack is smiling broadly with his arm around Tracey's shoulder. Looking at the background they must have been standing exactly where she's standing now. Right outside her gate. 'Lovely.' Carmen tries to move past, but Tracey blocks her path.

'How are you going to keep him?' she asks.

Carmen frowns.

'I mean, he's in the dancing programme in Australia with Shazzy B. Did you know that Shazzy B's a man-eater and she's always having affairs with her partners? That programme breaks up marriages. And then- as if that's not enough - he's doing a book tour.'

Carmen pushes to get past Tracey's shoulder. 'Please let me get into my flat.'

'I feel sorry for you, do you know that? I mean, it doesn't

matter how pretty you are, does it? It's an age thing. I had the same problem with my Dan a few years ago. He dumped me on Christmas Eve but I realised I was better off without him. I mean, who needs men anyway, right?'

Carmen steps around Tracey's shoulder.

'If you want to talk. I'm here for you.' Tracey places her hand on Carmen's shoulder and squeezes it. 'The world's your lobster. I'm sure you'll find someone else - one day.'

Carmen blinks and is about to close the gate on Tracey when she adds, 'Your problem is that you've never wanted any publicity. No one knows anything about you and Jack acts like he's a single man about town. He's all over social media. I couldn't put up with that.'

'You don't have to.' Carmen closes the gate on Tracey's surprised face, and unlocks her front door. Once inside, she leans against the wall and exhales slowly.

Why does Luis always choose such awful friends?

* * *

Inside her flat, it's quiet. Luis is out so she pours a glass of Pino Noir and checks her phone. There's only the message from Jack to say he arrived safely from two days ago. She guesses rehearsals, costumes and pre-publicity for the show are keeping him busy. It's the opening night tomorrow - Saturday.

There's a persistent banging on the door downstairs so Carmen walks to the window and looks down into the alleyway. It looks like there's a bald spot at the crown of Paul's head. She lifts the sash window and calls out, 'Hello?'

He looks up. 'Come down, quickly!'

'What do you want?'

'I'll tell you when you come down.'

Carmen closes the window and walks slowly downstairs. If he's guilty that they've given the contract to her competitors who have been in the business for fifteen years then so be it. She'll go on the charm offensive but keep him at a distance. She opens the door and Paul grabs her shoulders excitedly.

'You've got it!'

'What?'

'The pub contract. Congratulations.' Paul shouts. 'We're closing on Monday so I hope you can do everything in that time. You said you could. This is your opportunity.' He kisses her cheek.

'They've given it to me?' Carmen is beyond shocked. She had assumed that because the other business had been established for longer and were better prepared, that her rivals would have been given the contract.

'They want *you!* Aren't you happy?'

'Surprised, but I'm certainly not complaining.'

Paul laughs. 'It's meant to be. We'll celebrate. Dinner?'

'No.'

'No, of course. Okay, lunch?'

'Maybe. Do I get a contract?'

'Yes. I'll bring it over tomorrow - unless you want to come and have lunch in the pub and we'll talk it over?'

'Okay.'

'Late. After the rush. About 3:30?'

'I'll be there.'

After Paul has left, Carmen is floating on air. She got the contract. She wants to phone Jack, but she checks her watch. He'd be on set now, dress rehearsal, and there's no sign of

Luis. She opens his bedroom door, and the room is a mess. She sighs but then notices his open portfolio on the desk. She steps forward and glances at his latest drawings. Since he was a child there was art in Luis' blood. Everything he did was graceful, artistic and flowed. As he grew older, there has always been a sense of thoughtfulness. Luis is a thinker and always has been. As a child his face would crease up as he studied the rain falling outside. He'd spend hours watching it trickle down the window pane, his small finger tracing the route of each drop.

Luis was the only child who never wanted to blow out the candles on their cake. Instead, he was transfixed watching the beauty in the flickering flames, marvelling at the shimmering colours until they were finally extinguished.

Her beautiful child who sat in trees, mapping the rough bark with a small finger, absorbing the contours of each leaf, watching the light reflecting through the woods - he hadn't changed, at all. *They* hadn't changed.

The water colour drawing on the desk in front of her is simply beautiful. He hasn't painted the beach or the sand or the horizon, but he's painted a view looking down at the water's edge - an oyster catcher and its orange beak from above.

The simplicity of the colour reflects the opaque water as if it's cool to touch. There had been many times when she'd wondered where he'd gone in Westbay but now having seen these drawings her heart is at peace.

As long as Luis is painting, he's happy. *They* are at peace. It's when they stop painting or drawing that she has to worry.

Downstairs in the lounge her phone rings. Carmen closes the bedroom door and hurrying she answers the call without checking the ID.

'Jack?'

'Mamma? It's Elena.'

'Oh. Hola, my darling.'

'You sound disappointed.'

'Not at all. It's lovely to hear from you.'

Elena sighs loudly on the other end of the phone and Carmen tenses. They've barely begun talking and she knows she's already upset her daughter. 'How are you, my darling?'

'I'm fine. Have you heard from Papi?'

'He texted to say that he arrived okay. I guess he's busy.'

'I know he arrived okay. He was on my flight.'

'Wh—?'

'Didn't he tell you?'

'He, he - no,' Carmen says quickly.

'He left five days ago.'

'I know but he's busy.'

'We're all *busy*, Mama.'

Carmen sits on the sofa and crosses her legs. 'I know, my darling, so tell me about you. How are you? What have you been doing?'

'Flying, Mama. That's what I do, remember?'

'Guapa, don't speak to me like that! No me hablas así.' When Carmen gets angry she often reverts to her native language. She's proudly aware that after studying at European Schools both her children are bilingual and they understand her perfectly.

'Sorry, Mama. Let's start again. How are you?'

'I'm fine.'

'How's Westbay?'

'It's different and I think Luis likes it here.'

'It's not about Luis. He's going to uni. What about you?'

'Well, I opened the shop and - did you get the photos?'

'Sí, yes, thank you. It looks lovely. You've worked hard.'

'Thank you. And today I won a contract to refurbish the local pub.'

'Really? But you've never designed a pub before.'

'It's not designing. It's just a makeover with soft furnishing.'

'Can you do that?'

'Of course.'

'Did you tell Papi?'

'Not yet. When he has time and we have a longer conversation, then I will.'

'So, you have spoken to him?'

Carmen hesitates, hating the grilling that is customary with her daughter. 'Yes, why?'

'Luis said you weren't talking.'

'Luis worries too much.'

'So, did Papi tell you my news?'

Carmen hesitates. Whatever Elena told her father, Jack hasn't shared it with her. 'I think he wanted you to tell me....'

'Really?'

'Sí.'

'José has proposed. We're getting married.'

Carmen covers her mouth with her hand.

'Mama? Are you there?'

Carmen can't speak. They'd only met José once. He came to their house and strutted around as if he owned it. He lay by the swimming pool like a king and Elena had fetched and carried drinks and snacks for him all day. He had treated her like servant in a five-star hotel, even though it was Elena's home.

'Of course, I'm here, my darling. Congratulations. You must be so happy.' Carmen smiles. It's one thing that she learnt years ago. People can tell your reactions on the phone even though they can't see you. She knows the smile will echo in her voice.

'Well?'

'Well, what?' asks Carmen.

'Don't you want to know when?'

Carmen's smile grows wider until her cheeks hurt. 'I'm hoping that you'll fly over here to England and we can talk about your wedding plans together. We'll have great fun planning it all. You may even like to have it here in Westbay.'

Elena sighs impatiently. 'I have my own life, Mama. I'm busy and it's hard enough finding a time in our schedules, when José and I are both free, but we've blocked off the weekend before Christmas.'

'To come here?'

'No, Mama, to get married.'

'Before Christmas?' Carmen rubs her temple.

'Yes. I'll send you, Papi and Luis tickets. We're getting married in Florida.'

'Florida?'

Elena says impatiently, 'Stop repeating everything I say. You know how that makes me angry. I'm sure Papi told you all about it, so you don't have to pretend. If you stay for Christmas, then you can get to know José better and meet all his family.'

'They're all going to your wedding?'

'Mama, they live there. It's their home. That's why we're getting married at Christmas so that José can be with his family.

Carmen wants to shout, what about us? What about your family? But instead she says, 'That sounds amazing. It seems like you have it all arranged.'

'Sí, Mama. I know how busy you are so there's nothing for you to do. José's mother is helping me sort the dress and his sister is arranging the venue and flowers so that José and I can relax and enjoy it all.'

It has been a long time since Carmen has seen Elena relaxing and enjoying herself. 'I'm pleased for you, my darling.'

'You are?'

'Of course. If you're happy then I'm happy.'

'Good. Right, I have to go now. I'm flying to Cape Town tomorrow.'

'Okay, well then sleep tight and take care.'

'Mama, how are you? You know with the other thing?'

'I'm fine.' Carmen toys with the strands of her fake hair. 'All is good.'

'You're definitely cured?'

'Yes. Stop worrying and think about your lovely wedding.'

After they've said goodbye Carmen sits in silence. She's thinking about her daughter's wedding in Florida. What are José's family like? They seem to have everything arranged for her daughter's special day and there's nothing for her to do. Simply turn up as an invited guest. She had never imagined her beautiful daughter would get married in America. She had always imagined they would plan the day together as a family. Her mind races. How will she manage her shop the weekend before Christmas? Then there's Jack's book launch and Luis will be at uni. But worst of all it was Elena's future husband that Carmen worried about the most.

José had flirted openly with her. When they were briefly alone in the kitchen in her London home he had placed his hand on her bottom playfully before she smacked it away.

'Don't touch me!' she hissed. 'You're my daughter's boyfriend. Have some respect for us both.'

She stirs from her dark thoughts as Luis comes home. 'Hola, Mama.'

'Hello, Luis.'

'Are you alright? You look like you've seen a ghost.'

Carmen blinks quickly. 'Elena is getting married.'

'Yes, I know. To that prick of a narcissist. How does she not know he's a psychopath?'

Carmen shakes her head.

Luis continues, 'Don't think I'm going to Florida to their poxy wedding. He's a fake and I wouldn't give him the shit from my shoes.'

Chapter 8

It takes Carmen four calls and three messages left on Jack's answerphone before she finally gets through to him.

'It would be easier to speak to the Pope,' she jokes tersely.

'Sorry, Cammy. It's manic here. So many rehearsals. We're on stage in a couple of hours. It's bloody nerve-wracking!'

'Is it going well?'

'No! It's so hard. I never realised I was so unfit.'

'How's your knee?'

'Strapped.'

'What are you dancing?'

'The salsa. You should get it on YouTube later.'

'I'll ask Luis to find it.'

'Good. Look, I haven't got long. I have to—'

'I spoke to Elena.'

'Ah.'

'You didn't tell me she was working on your flight?'

'I didn't get chance—'

'You didn't tell me about her wedding plans either.'

'Don't tell me she's really going ahead with it?'

'So, she told you?'

'Yeah but I didn't believe her. I thought she was just pissed at me.'

Carmen breathes deeply. 'She's pissed at both of us.'

'I know. But to marry that misogynistic—'

'Steady, Jack.'

'I hoped that with all that flying she'd meet lots of pilots and fall for someone else - someone decent.'

'She's getting married in Florida the weekend before Christmas.'

There's a pause before Jack replies, 'She told me, but I can't be there, babe. I'm on my book tour and then I'll be in Vancouver.'

'Did you tell her that?'

'No of course not. She was mad enough with me.'

'Why?'

'Oh, you know, the normal. She doesn't want her Papi on TV making a fool of himself.'

'Ah.'

'Exactly. Look sorry, honey. I've gotta go. Barbs is waiting.'

'Barbs?'

'The producer.'

'Okay. Good luck.'

'You say, break a leg when you go on stage.'

Carmen sighs. 'Break a leg, Jack.' But before she can say goodbye, he's gone. But not before she heard a female voice purring in the background.

'Come on, Jack. You need to get dressed.'

* * *

'Morning, Carmen! Ready to work your magic?' Paul greets her as he's wiping down the wooden bar counter.

'Absolutely, Paul. We're going to give this place a facelift that'll make heads turn,' Carmen replies her eyes gleaming with excitement.

As Carmen unpacks her designs and sketches, Paul leans against the bar admiring her focus. 'Carmen, I've seen a lot of changes in this old pub but I think this transformation will be the talk of the town. I know it was supposed to be soft furnishings but those extra ideas you suggested went down really well.'

Carmen grins her eyes scanning the room. 'Well, Paul, we're aiming for a fusion of tradition and modernity. Think cozy nooks with a contemporary twist, a bit of vintage mixed with comfort.'

'Ah, just like your style, a perfect blend of classic and refreshing,' Paul says with a grin, earning a playful eye roll from Carmen.

'Flattery won't get you a discount on those vintage beer signs, Paul,' she teases, flipping through her design portfolio.

'Can't blame a man for trying, especially when faced with such talent.' Paul winks.

Their banter fills the pub as they refine the details of colour schemes, upholstery choices and lighting for ambiance. During the discussions Paul finds himself admiring more than just Carmen's designs. He admires her passion, her wit, and the way her eyes sparkle when she speaks about her work.

'Now, about that fireplace.' Carmen begins sketching out some ideas in her pad. 'Your associates liked the idea of a rustic touch with some reclaimed bricks and a mantelpiece that...'

Paul leans in closer, intrigued. 'A mantelpiece, you say?'

'What about adding a touch of mystery like a hidden compartment for some old pub treasures?' Carmen's eyes widen with excitement.

Paul grins. 'That's brilliant! A secret compartment for the pub's history - hidden right under everyone's noses.'

Their laughter echoes through the empty pub filling the space with shared energy and camaraderie. Paul finds himself captivated not only by Carmen's designs, but also by her infectious enthusiasm.

Carmen is in her element. This is the one time she can forget her problems. She can forget she's a cancer survivor and that she's a mother to a beautiful non-binary child who is riddled with anxiety and a daughter who resents her, and a husband who no longer values her. Now, absorbed in the refurbishment project, Carmen comes alive. She's inspirational and engaging and she has a vision that she can describe easily.

Paul is smitten. He finds it hard to take his eyes from her animated, smoky, dark eyes. He watches her fingers as they trace imaginary patterns in the air and the way her neck tilts gracefully over her sketchpad. He imagines the softness of her skin if he were to kiss her at the base of her neck.

'Are you listening, Paul?'

'Um, yes, of course.' He sits a little straighter in his chair and looks down at her drawings. 'I was wondering if there will be enough time. We close on Monday. The staff are coming in to help clear the place and the contractors are booked.'

'Great.'

He looks at her carefully. 'I'm also planning an opening night.'

'Perfect.'

'On the twenty-third.'

Carmen checks her iPhone. 'That's the date I'm taking Luis to university.'

'But you'll be home by the evening, won't you?'

'I suppose so.'

'Good.' Paul smiles. 'Let's make this the best celebration ever. One that we will both remember.'

They're interrupted by a tall, lanky boy who Carmen has seen working in the kitchen. 'Paul? Can you come to the kitchen a minute?' he says urgently.

'On my way, Ricky. Give me a minute to finish with Carmen here.'

After he's gone Paul says, 'That's Femi's son. He's a good boy and a hard worker.' He places a hand on Carmen's fingers. 'I'm so pleased you're here. You're already making a massive difference to this pub - and to me.'

* * *

That evening Carmen is roasting fresh salmon and vegetables when Luis wanders into the kitchen.

'You want to see it?' He holds out his iPhone. 'Or do you want a bigger screen on the laptop?'

'Is he okay?'

'Um.'

'Have you seen it?' she asks.

'Sí.' His voice is grave, and he won't look at her.

'How bad?'

Luis holds out the phone and Carmen sits at the kitchen table watching Jack's dance routine on the other side of the world. His partner, Shazzy B, is mid-twenties, slim, fit, blonde - and very energetic. The complete opposite to Carmen.

She flings Jack around on the dance floor and he wiggles his hips, frantically and out of synch, to keep pace with her.

His arms flail in the air as if he's trying to keep balance on an invisible tightrope. If he wasn't her husband, she'd laugh but then suddenly their dance is over and they're wrapped in each other's arms, panting heavily and gasping for breath. Shazzy B whispers in his ear and he nods, his blue eyes twinkling. Their gaze lingers on each other meaningfully before they stand with the TV host and wait for the judges scores.

Carmen hands the phone back to Luis then she stands up and opens the oven to check the vegetables.

'He got through to next week,' Luis says to her back. 'The judges like him.'

Carmen doesn't turn around but she nods. 'Good.'

* * *

The following week passes quickly. Luis has agreed to open the shop while Carmen is working in the pub. They settle into a routine with her toing and froing, changing ideas, experimenting with cushions and pictures. In the evenings Carmen does a stocktake of the things she's used from the shop and experiments with the next stage - wallpaper for the wall with the mirror. She orders a few more vintage beer signs and a secret box that can be cemented into the fireplace.

On Friday evening she's working in the flat above the shop when she suddenly looks up from her laptop. She would miss Luis' calm company. He's happy with peace and quiet as much as he's happy scrolling through his phone. Occasionally she hears the voice of a social media influencer persuading Luis to buy a new and innovative type of skin cream.

It's been a week since he mentioned his course.

'Do you need anything for university?' she asks.

He looks up from his phone. 'Aren't you working?'

She chooses her words carefully. 'I am, but I'm thinking about you leaving next week. Do we need to go shopping?'

Luis grins. 'You know I never turn down the offer of a shopping trip, but after the last time when I embarrassed you...'

'It was the sales assistant who was embarrassed. She thought the makeup was for me.' Carmen laughs.

Luis grins at her. 'I won't subject you to that again. I prefer to buy online anyway but there's a great art shop I'd like to visit.'

'Sunday?'

Luis smiles. 'Sunday.'

'Okay and then next week I'll drive you to London on Friday morning and you can spend the weekend settling in?'

'I'm going out with Tracey tomorrow night. We're going into town on the bus.'

'Okay.' Carmen looks back at her laptop, happy that she's scored a victory. He's going to university.

'You don't like her, do you?'

'She's very interested in Papi and it makes me a little wary.'

'She's my friend.'

'Good.' This is another reason Carmen is pleased that Luis is going to art school. It will get him way from Tracey.

'She's a good person,' Luis says.

* * *

It's early on Saturday morning and the town is still waking up when Amber appears in Carmen's shop.

'I've bought you a latte,' she says. 'Karl tells me it's what you normally order.'

Carmen's face lights up. 'Gosh, I haven't had a chance to think about coffee yet. That's kind of you.'

'Nonsense, I have a reason for bringing this over.' Amber laughs, placing the take-out cup on the counter. 'How's the refurb at the pub going?'

'It's all going well.'

'It was fortunate in the end, wasn't it? Fate was smiling on you.'

'What do you mean?'

'Well, Sabrine and George get most of the work around here.' Amber frowns.

'Sabrine and George - the owners of Opulent Designs?' Carmen says carefully.

Amber nods. 'A lot of people thought they'd get the contract but we - all of us in Harbour Street - were thrilled when you got it.'

Carmen smiles. 'Thank you.'

Amber shrugs. 'We're a small community but we try and look out for each other and we're very supportive - and - that's why I'm here. Because although it's still early and there's plenty of time, I want to plan ahead this year. Each December before Christmas we have a festive parade and lights are switched on, but last year it all got hijacked and it was a complete disaster.'

'Really?'

'Yes, Jane's Jewellery shop was burgled and she ended up in hospital.'

'That's awful.'

'It's not going to happen this year.'

'I saw a young girl working in there through the window,

last week.'

'That's Shelly, Tommy's niece. She works there now. Jane finally got together with Tommy.' Amber smiles.

'Gosh, it all goes on here in Harbour Street.' Carmen laughs.

Amber frowns. 'You could say that. Goodness. I'd never really thought about it.'

'There's you and Ben,' Carmen adds.

Amber laughs. 'I'd forgotten about us, too. Well, it's a good job that you're married, Carmen. You won't have to go through a romance in Harbour Street.'

Carmen smiles.

'So,' Amber continues, 'We usually meet at Frances' house - at the vicarage - and we talk about plans for Christmas. I'm hoping we can count on you to be involved.'

'If I can help...'

'You'll be very welcome. It will be great to have someone creative like you onboard.'

Carmen wonders about her December schedule. She can't tell Amber that her daughter is getting married in Florida the week before Christmas. She can't tell Amber much about her private life at all, for fear of it ending up in the press. For years she has confided in very few people, only her sister in Paris and parents in their small village in Spain. She learnt the hard way that information is money.

In the early years, when Jack was a well-known footballer, she had once blabbed innocently about where they were going for the weekend. When they got to the Cotswolds town it had been besieged with paparazzi taking photos for the tabloids. In more recent years, Jack had leaked a few stories of him meeting other well-known celebrities which had kept his name in the papers and made him relevant. Now, although

Jack isn't here, Carmen is still protective of her privacy. She knows not to give anything away or it might appear in the papers the next day or on social media. Although Jack might be working abroad and his absence is justified by TV or a book launch Carmen can't stand the scrutiny of their marriage or any detrimental gossip linked to their relationship.

'Amber, may I ask you about someone?'

'Paul?' Amber replies.

Carmen stares down into her frothy coffee.

'The thing is, Carmen.' Amber leans closer. 'This is like a village here and everyone knows everything. So, you have probably already learnt that if you want privacy, tell no one anything. Ben and I are also very private - but for different reasons. We didn't tell anyone when we were going through all the foster training - apart from Femi who helped us because she knows the process.'

'Femi? I met her and Lawrence.'

'She has three foster boys. Ricky, her eldest, works at the pub. Have you met him yet?'

Carmen recalls the tall boy who came to the table when she was talking to Paul.

'Paul has been very good for Ricky. At work he's a good role model but he's a disaster at home. All his energy goes into the pub and his relationships suffer.'

'It wasn't Paul I wanted to ask you about. It's Tracey.'

'Ah. Okay, well Tracey's complicated. I don't think she's a bad person but she's naive. Especially as far as men are concerned. Dan used to beat her and now I'm not sure what sort of relationship she has with this new boyfriend, Eric. Why do you ask?'

Carmen shakes her head. 'I'm not sure.'

'Is it because she's friends with Luis?'

'You know?'

Amber grins. 'The whole of Harbour Street knows that they're the best of friends - perhaps even the whole of Westbay,' Amber pauses before adding. 'She's lonely. Her last boyfriend Dan used to hit her and then he dumped her at Christmas.' Amber frowns. 'Would Luis be interested in her - you know, emotionally?'

Carmen shakes her head truthfully. 'I have no idea.'

'Does Luis have a... a partner, someone special?'

Carmen shrugs. 'I don't ask.'

Amber laughs. 'I guess that's Carmen speak for mind your own business.'

Carmen smiles. She likes Amber and perhaps one day she might even trust her but right now Carmen only has herself to rely on.

'Well, I guess things will all work out because Luis is leaving next week, isn't he? Sorry. I mean they. So *they* may naturally drift away from Tracey.'

Carmen looks up. 'You know they're leaving?'

Amber grins. 'You haven't been paying attention, Carmen. There are no secrets in Harbour Street.'

* * *

Carmen finds it hard to settle that evening. Against her principles she goes onto social media to find news of Jack who is caught up in the whirlwind of dancing and media notoriety in Australia. She watches his latest dance and tunes into an interview filmed twenty-four hours ago.

He's in front of the cameras, on the sofa, being interviewed on Australian daytime TV. Beside him, Shazzy B is snuggled up coyly. She's hugging his arm as if he's the most important man in her life.

Dios! God! How she misses him.

Her phone pings and she answers with amazement. 'Jack?'

'Hi baby.'

'This is a surprise. How are you?'

'Stiff and sore. I've never ached so much.'

Carmen laughs, pleased and relieved that he's remembered to phone her.

'Are you okay?' he asks.

'All good.'

'I got your text messages. How's the pub decorating going?'

'I'll finish on Friday.'

'You taking Luis to uni?'

'Yes.'

'Thanks, babe. I'm so pleased he changed his mind. I wish I was there to help.'

'Do you?' Carmen whispers.

'What's that? Is Luis okay?'

'Yes. Fine.'

'Did you get Elena's email?'

'I haven't opened it yet.'

'What are you doing?'

Carmen laughs. 'I've been looking at your rumba on YouTube.'

Jack laughs. 'Hot stuff, aren't I?'

'The best.'

'The judges' comments were positive.'

'What's your dance for this week?'

'The waltz.'

Carmen smiles. They had danced the walz together at a charity ball once in Vienna. It had been snowing outside and afterwards Jack had organised a carriage ride with white horses back to their hotel. It had been one of the most romantic moments of her life.

'Cammy?' he calls.

'Yes, Jack. I'm here.'

'Do you remember Vienna?'

'No. Not at all.' They both laugh. He had proposed that night. It was a night they still celebrate every year. Except last year. Last December Carmen's head was in a bucket. She was puking after her chemo.

'Is it hot there?' she asks suddenly, breaking the memory

'Yeah.' Jack's voice grows distant. 'I'm off to rehearsals. Read Elena's email.'

'How's Shazzy B?' Carmen didn't want to ask. She doesn't want to know. She wishes she hadn't asked and then he replies.

'She's lovely. She's a wonderful, funny, patient and kind person.'

* * *

Carmen is still mulling over the conversation with Jack when there's a loud commotion in the street; shouting, swearing, running, crashing and a loud bang.

She leaps up and runs to the window overlooking Harbour Street. She pulls up the sash window, but there's no sign of anyone. Then there's banging on the front door and the bell is ringing persistently. Someone is shouting her name. She runs down to the front door and Ricky, the boy from the pub, is holding a life size rag doll. It looks familiar and it groans.

Beside him Tracey's mouth is moving quickly but she can't understand a word.

'Dios mio, Luis.' Carmen takes her child's arm, but he doesn't respond. 'What's happened? Que ha pasado?' She backs away, helping Ricky carry her child inside. 'Come upstairs.'

Ricky is stronger than he looks and with Carmen's help they manage to drag Luis, stumbling upstairs and lay him on the sofa.

'What happened?' Carmen removes his long, trench coat.

'Arrgh,' he groans.

She takes Luis' bloody face in her hands. 'Cariño?'

Tracey has followed them upstairs and is busy appraising the lounge. 'Some boys beat him up,' she says vaguely.

Ricky appears with a bowl of water from the kitchen and a tea towel. 'Here.'

Carmen takes them gratefully and wipes Luis' face searching for damage.

Luis flinches. 'My ribs,' he mutters.

'He passed out,' Tracey explains. 'And Ricky was out the back of the pub kitchen having a fag and he came to help.'

Luis rubs his head and attempts to sit up. His other hand holds his ribs.

'I'll get Femi to come and take a look,' Ricky says. 'She's a paramedic.'

'I'll be fine.' Luis swings his legs off the sofa with a groan.

'Do you need a doctor?' Carmen asks.

'Stop fussing, Mama. I'm fine.'

Tracey and Ricky are standing watching him and Carmen is suddenly self-conscious. She's not dressed for the public. She's wearing navy track pants and a red jumper, and although she's wearing her wig, she hasn't checked her hair or makeup since she came home.

'Do you want tea? A hot drink will help with shock.' She goes into the kitchen. She needs to be alone.

'Are you alright?' Ricky stands behind her. His face is full of concern.

'I'm fine, thank you. Do you want tea?'

'I'd better not. I only popped outside for a fag break. Paul will be looking for me.'

Carmen places a hand on his arm. 'Thank you, Ricky. I really appreciate what you've done.'

Ricky lowers his voice. 'Has this happened before?'

'I don't think so, why?'

Ricky shrugs. 'I don't think everyone understands his way of dressing. You know? It doesn't bother me but maybe some blokes don't understand. They might not like it. Do you get what I'm saying?'

'I do.'

'I mean, I think he—'

'They.'

Ricky's frown deepens. 'I think *they* should dress how they like but not everyone gets it.'

She places a hand on his arm. 'I know. Thank you for understanding.'

Ricky nods, turns on his heels and leaves without saying goodbye.

Chapter 9

It's impossible to get rid of Tracey. Carmen makes tea for them and Tracey takes off her coat and makes herself at home, swinging her feet up under her bottom, settling into the chair where Jack sat only a few weeks ago.

She blows on her tea. 'I've often wondered how the stars live. I always thought it would be more luxury.'

'Luxurious,' corrects Luis sipping his tea.

'I still think we should call the police.' Carmen stares at her child. 'They shouldn't get away with this.'

Luis' right eye is bruised and swollen. It's turning pink and purple and his chin and hands are scratched. When he pulls up his shirt, there's swelling and the beginning of a bruise across his ribs.

Tracey insists on taking photos. 'For the police,' she says.

'We're not calling the police.' Luis is insistent. He tugs down his shirt and tucks it into the waistband of his trousers.

'Tell me what happened?' Carmen says, calmly.

It's Tracey who answers. 'We'd just got off the bus and we were walking down the street when they set on us.'

'Did you see who they were?'

Tracey shakes her head.

'No,' replies Luis. 'They came from behind.'

Carmen regards Tracey carefully. 'I'm pleased they didn't hurt you, Tracey.'

'No. They didn't.' Tracey looks away.

'So, they just attacked Luis.'

'Yes.' Tracey looks at the floor.

'You didn't speak to them? You haven't seen them before?'

They both shake their heads.

'Why do you think they attacked you?' asks Carmen.

Tracey chokes on her tea and looks at her with disbelief. 'Are you joking?'

Carmen stares back at her. 'No.'

'Look at Luis. They clearly hate the way they're dressed.'

'How did they know what Luis was wearing? They had on a long coat.'

'Yes but...' Tracey looks at the floor-length grey coat lying on the chair where Carmen had flung it.

'They must have known,' she says.

'Known what?' asks Carmen.

Tracey frowns. 'Known what Luis was wearing.'

'How?'

Tracey scratches her chin. 'They followed us.'

'Yes, you said that. You got off the bus. Were they on the bus?'

Tracey shrugs. 'Maybe.'

'No,' Luis' voice is gravelly like their throat hurts. 'We were the only ones who got off at our stop.'

'It sounds like they were waiting for you.' Carmen sips her tea and regards Tracey. 'I wonder why?'

Tracey shrugs. 'We didn't know them, did we, Luis?'

Luis shakes his head. 'It all happened so quickly.'

'How many of them were there?'

'Three, maybe more,' says Tracey.

'Two.' Luis frowns. 'Look, I'm sorry guys. I've got to go to bed.'

Carmen stands up. 'I'll see you out Tracey.'

'Do you want me to stay, Luis?' Tracey's voice holds a note of optimism.

'No. I'll see you tomorrow. Thanks for everything.'

Tracey grins. 'I didn't do much. I'm just pleased I could save you.'

Luis smiles. He stands up with a struggle and when Tracey moves closer for a hug, he holds up his hand. 'Not a good idea. Night Trace.' He blows air kisses and turns toward the stairs and the comfort of his bedroom.

On the way downstairs Tracey speaks quickly, 'I'm so glad I was there. I mean, it was awful. They were horrible and they kicked him on the floor. I tried to push them off. It was a good job I screamed. It was a good job Ricky was having that fag and he heard me. He soon chased them off.'

'Thank goodness for Ricky - and you.' Carmen opens the door and smiles. 'Night Tracey.'

'Night, Carmen. I'll call round in the morning.'

'Text first as Luis likes to sleep in.'

Tracey pouts. She doesn't look happy as Carmen closes the front door behind her.

Upstairs, Carmen taps on Luis' door. He's already in bed, sleeping naked as always. His hair is tied up in a yellow ribbon, his face drained of colour. His eyes are luminous and his purple cheek is growing darker. The scratches on his chin have dried leaving bright red weals.

'It's just as well that purple suits you.' Carmen grins, sitting on the bed.

Luis takes her hand. 'Ah, Mama...'

She looks down at this child who she loves so much. She takes in his sculptured features, soft skin and long black eyelashes. 'Why don't you tell me your version of what happened?'

* * *

'It's all a blur,' Luis says, attempting a nonchalant smile. 'It all happened very quickly. Just a little encounter with a stranger who didn't appreciate my eyeshadow choice.'

'What happened?' she insists.

'We got off the bus, walked across the square by the church and as we turned into Harbour Street they appeared from nowhere. They pulled my arm and pushed me against the wall. One hit me in the face and the other in my ribs.' Luis moves to make himself comfortable. 'I fell on the floor and curled up but they kept kicking me in the back and in the ribs—'

'Where was Tracey?'

'I guess she was pushing them off. I screamed or maybe it was her. Then Ricky arrived and he was kicking and punching and shouting at them. He was amazing. He bent down to help me up but I passed out as we were walking home. I guess he carried me here.'

'You were lucky,' Carmen says.

Luis stares at her. 'You mean after the last time?'

She squeezes his hand, remembering the time they'd gone to the hospital and he'd had ten stitches after a knife attack. There's still a faint scar across his right bicep.

Carmen's heart clenches. Her anger is bubbling and tears rise and sting her eyes. 'Oh, cariño.'

'It's just a bruise, Mama. I'm okay.' Luis' attempt to brush it off is evident.

Carmen struggles to contain her emotions. 'Shouldn't we call the police or something? This is unacceptable!'

Luis shakes his head. His expression is resolute. 'No, Mama. I don't want to make a big deal out of it.'

'But Luis, this is serious.' Carmen's concern spills over. 'What if it happens again?'

'I'll handle it.' Luis' tone is firm, a testament to his inner strength and resolve.

Carmen's heart aches. She's torn between her protective instincts and her respect for Luis' wishes.

'I understand but please let me help. We can't let this go unpunished.'

Luis hesitates then softens at Carmen's unwavering support. 'I appreciate it, Mama. But I'd rather not involve the police. I want to handle this my way.'

Carmen sighs, realising the depth of Luis' independence. 'Okay, but promise me you'll be careful out there, especially when you go to university.'

'I will, Mama. I promise.' Luis offers a reassuring smile.

Luis lies in bed, quietly reflecting. It's Carmen who breaks the silence, attempting to lighten the mood. 'You know, if those guys had seen your eyeliner skills, they might have asked you for a tutorial,' she quips, trying to bring a smile to her son's face.

Luis chuckles softly, a hint of gratitude in their eyes. 'Thanks, Mama. You always know how to make me feel better.'

'You're my child, Luis. Nothing will ever change that,' Carmen says, wrapping an arm around Luis' shoulder and in the serenity of that moment amidst the pain and the unspoken battles Carmen and Luis find solace in their unwavering bond of love.

'Why tonight?' whispers Carmen, 'How did they know where you would be?'

Luis yawns. 'I guess because Papi came here.'

'You can't blame your father.'

'I'm not. It's just that it was on social media that he was here so any nutter might know that I'm living here now, especially if they've spoken to any local people. You know how they all love to gossip and if there's a story for the tabloids - that's even better.'

Carmen sighs.

Luis looks at her intently and smiles. 'You can't run away from who you are.'

'I'm not running.'

'Neither am I,' he whispers.

Carmen smiles. 'We should still call the police.'

'No.'

Carmen kisses her child on their forehead and stands up. 'Get some rest.'

She's at the door when Luis speaks. 'Thanks Mama, for not asking me to change and to stop being the person I am inside.'

'Te quiero, cariño. I love you, my darling.'

'Te quiero, mami.'

* * *

On Sunday morning they were supposed to be going shopping for Luis' art supplies, but he says, 'I'd prefer to sleep, Mama, if that's okay.'

'Of course, cariño.' She kisses the top of his head. 'I'm popping out, but I won't be long.'

Carmen pulls on a jacket and heads over to the pub. Something about last night just doesn't make any sense. Why was Ricky having a fag break when the pub isn't even open to the public? It's closed for refurbishment.

She heads outside and she's surprised to see faces through the pub window. She knocks and suddenly Paul's face appears. He beams at her and opens the door.

'I was going to come over to you, how's Luis?

'Sleeping, but they'll be fine.' She looks over his shoulder. 'What's going on?'

Paul looks sheepish. 'I opened last night for a private party.'

Carmen's face changes in disbelief and her mouth opens wide. 'But we're not ready.'

He opens the door wider and she steps inside.

'Don't worry. It was only a small gathering. No one touched any of your designs and we only used the far end of the bar for a baby shower. It was a small group. Ann's cousin's sister.' One of the associates had clearly pulled rank and wanted her family celebration. 'We'd agreed to it before we contracted you.'

'You had?' Carmen replies.

'I told you, didn't I?' Paul rubs his hand over tired eyes.

'Was Ricky working last night?'

'Yes. He told me what happened. He disappeared and I thought he'd left me to clean up but... well, he came back in the end.'

'He was very good to help Luis.'

'I wish I'd been there too,' Paul says earnestly. 'I'd have sorted them out.'

Probably best you weren't. But I was wondering do you think anyone will have CCTV?'

Paul pulls on his lip thinking. Maybe we might have something. I'll have a look for you once we're cleared up.' He nods at a girl in the back of the bar sweeping the floor.

'Thanks. I'd appreciate that.' Carmen turns to go.

'Wait! Florence is leaving in a minute. Fancy a coffee and we can talk things through together?'

Carmen doesn't want coffee. She doesn't want to spend time with Paul either but she does want him to look at the CCTV.

'Why not?' She smiles.

* * *

It takes two cups of coffee and almost two hours before Paul is reluctantly ready to look at the CCTV. Behind the kitchen is a small storeroom that Paul uses as an office. There's a table, laptop and several screens revealing views from cameras placed outside.

He says, 'You shouldn't be in this office.'

'I won't tell anyone.' Carmen smiles. 'Promise.'

Paul returns her smile and looks closely into her eyes. 'It's all about trust,' he says.

They pour over the footage from last night together. Paul forwards the tape to the approximate time of night when Luis was attacked.

'The CCTV is on the side of the building so it should have a view of the street between the square and Harbour Street.'

Carmen holds her breath and concentrates on the screen. Two silent figures appear. They're grainy images but she recognises Luis' stride and long grey coat.

'That's them.'

Paul's finger hovers over the button to pause for a closer shot but the figures continue walking. They are moving out of the shot in the bottom right corner when two other figures appear in the top left. 'They're coming from the square,' Paul says.

Suddenly the figures are running and then they're out of range.

Carmen gasps. 'No!'

'Shit!' says Paul. He taps some keys on the pad and moves the mouse but there's no action to be seen. 'I can't believe it,' he says.

Then in the very corner there's an image. A very quick shot of a person taking pictures on their phone and suddenly they move out of sight again.

'Can you play it again, slowly?' asks Carmen.

Paul slows it right down. A figure in a light coat steps into the frame and Carmen gasps.

'That's Tracey, isn't it?' Paul freezes the frame.

'Yes.'

'The stupid cow is taking pictures.' Paul looks sideways at Carmen. 'Why would she do that?'

'Let's see if there's more.'

Paul lets the video unfold in slow motion. Ricky in the top left corner steps outside, lights a cigarette and looks up. He tosses the cigarette aside, runs to the bottom right of the screen and disappears off camera.

Paul rewinds the film and plays it again. 'What do you want to do?'

'I'll speak to Luis.'

'Do you want to call the police?'

'There's no point.'

'I'd call them if I were you.'

'They're too busy. Too understaffed and there's too much paperwork involved.'

'Do you mean too much judgement?' he asks.

Carmen frowns and thinks carefully before answering. 'It's not easy living in the public eye as we have done. It's been particularly difficult for Luis to be able to express themself. Sometimes, we have never been sure if it's because of how they are or if it's because of who their father is.'

Paul smiles uneasily. 'Everyone likes Jack Bailey.'

'Not everyone is popular all the time. One small mistake can haunt you for a lifetime.' Carmen doesn't add that Jack's made plenty of mistakes. Their life is plastered all over the Internet. 'All anyone has to do is piece all the information together.'

'I guess that's what turns a fan into a stalker.' Paul places his hand on Carmen's. 'I just want to say that you're safe with me. Trust me. I'll never tell another soul about anything you tell me. I'll never betray your trust.'

'Thank you, Paul.' Carmen doesn't pull her hand away. It's a shock that Luis has been attacked and one that she's busy processing. She needs to take care of her child.

'I'd best get back and check on Luis.'

'I'm here if you need me.' Paul stands up with her and in the small and cramped office their bodies are very close together. He makes no attempt to move. Their faces are close, and Carmen is aware of his breath on her cheek. She knows he wants to kiss her. She knows he's attracted to her, but she moves carefully away.

'Thank you for your friendship, Paul.'

He smiles back at her as if he's been rewarded with nectar from the Gods.

Chapter 10

Luis sleeps most of Sunday morning and Carmen brings him soup at lunchtime. 'The bruise is quite spectacular,' she says but Luis barely looks at her.

'Do you want company? I'll sit with you if you like?'

He shakes his head.

Later in the afternoon there's a knock on the front door.

'Hello, Femi. This is a surprise.'

Femi is dressed is a colourful dress of yellow and burnt ochre. 'Ricky told me what happened last night and I just wanted to check on Luis. Is he okay?'

'They'll be fine. They're resting. Do you want to come in?'

'I have a shift at the RNLI but I'm here if you need me.'

'Thank you.'

'I don't want to interfere but after something like this, there maybe a... reaction.'

'Do you mean depression or anxiety?'

Femi replies, 'You've been through it before, have you?'

'Unfortunately, yes.'

'Counselling helps.'

'They won't have any more counselling.'

Femi nods. 'Well, speak to Ben. It's an outside chance but he might be able to help. He has a gift for understanding young people. He does a lot of work with them for his charity in London.'

After Femi has gone, Carmen mulls over her advice. Harbour Street has lost its shine. Although it's a kind community, bad things happen here the same as they do everywhere else in the world.

Carmen had hoped they would be safe here. That Luis would have nothing to fear but now she isn't sure. Perhaps they're right. They can't keep running and they can't keep hiding.

'What's the answer?' she whispers, but there's no answer only the screaming emptiness in her heart.

* * *

On Monday Carmen wakes Luis. 'Can you please look after the shop because there's a delivery at ten and one of Paul's associates wants to see the progress we're making in the pub. I'll only be gone for half an hour.'

'Fine.'

'Luis please don't forget.'

'Mami, don't nag!'

Carmen grabs her coat and laptop and heads to the pub where Paul is waiting eagerly.

'Coffee is ready, and I've bought croissants from the bakery.' He's laid a table in one of the alcoves. 'Please take a seat, Carmen. The new mantelpiece will be here tomorrow which will get rid of that unsightly hole.' Paul slides into the seat opposite her and smiles. 'How's Luis?'

'Sleeping but they're working in the shop this morning.'

'Have you thought any more about the video?'

'No, but please keep it for me.'

'I will but it's not enough evidence to be absolutely certain, is it?'

Carmen shrugs.

Breaking his croissant, Paul asks, 'Will you ask Tracey about it?'

'After I've spoken to Luis.'

'He goes to uni on Friday. I guess you'll leave early and be back for our opening in the evening?'

Carmen smiles. 'That's the plan. Let's hope the new bar stools arrive by then. I'll call the suppliers later.'

They eat breakfast and discuss the progress of the refurb and afterwards Carmen makes a few phone calls and then checks her watch. 'Isn't your colleague, Pete, coming at ten? It's almost eleven.'

Paul looks surprised. 'He cancelled. I told you.'

Carmen is confused. Paul hadn't said anything about Pete cancelling and she has her own delivery this morning that she needs to sort out. She collects her handbag and computer.

'Can't you stay a little longer?' he asks.

Carmen shakes her head. 'I need to check a few things over at the shop.'

Paul is reluctant for her to leave. 'It's lovely having you working over here,' he says. 'Anytime when we're open come and use it as an office.'

Carmen barely says goodbye. She really doesn't have time for croissants with Paul in the pub. He's taking advantage of her.

* * *

Carmen crosses the road, and her shop is still in darkness. It's also locked so she goes around the back and pushing the front door open she calls out, 'Luis? Cariño? Are you home?'

Silence greets her amplifying the worry that gnaws at her insides. Her stomach churns, panic builds inside her chest and her mouth is dry. She might be sick. She drops her keys on the table. Her mind is conjuring up worst-case scenarios. Past experiences.

'Luis!' she calls with panic rising in her throat. 'Luis?'

She runs upstairs and pushes open his bedroom door. Her heart is thumping wildly but the room is empty. 'Luis?'

She fumbles in her pocket for her phone and there's a sound behind her.

'What?' He's standing in the doorway of the bathroom wrapped in a crimson towelling robe. 'Why are you shouting?'

Carmen swallows hard and taking great strides she crosses the gap between them. 'Are you okay?' She pulls him into a strong embrace. Her heart pumping erratically with relief and bewilderment.

'Mind my ribs.' Luis pulls her hands gently away. 'I'm fine. I've just had a bath. Enjoying quiet time away from the drama.'

Carmen regards him carefully, but he turns away. 'Quiet time? You had me thinking you were abducted by aliens or something!'

Luis chuckles. 'Nah, no aliens. Just your wonderful, responsible, totally-not-causing-any-problems - child.'

'Your eye is very swollen.' Carmen sits on the bed and asks gently, 'Are you okay, cariño? You know, after what happened...'

His smile falters for a moment before he shrugs it off. 'I'm tougher than I look.'

Carmen raises an eyebrow. 'You hungry?' she asks, breaking the silence.

Luis grins. 'Starving! Have we any pizza? I'm in the mood for some serious comfort food.'

'Absolutely,' Carmen replies, stroking Luis' hair. 'Pizza it is.'

'I'm sorry. I didn't open the shop. I overslept.'

'I was expecting a delivery.' Carmen scratches her forehead willing her heart to be calm. She's trying to change her point of focus and regain control of her fear.

'Call them, can't you?' Luis says easily, pulling his robe tighter as he glances through his wardrobe.

'Of course.'

After the relief that Luis is okay Carmen is overwhelmed. Her memories of the last attack are so ingrained. She grabs her bag and hurries out of the flat in need of some fresh air.

* * *

Carmen doesn't think about the shop or about the pub or about anyone. She's exhausted. There's too much going on and Jack's not here. She's putting on a brave face for Luis but all the time she's in turmoil.

She storms down Harbour Street, under the clock tower, toward the harbour and the fishing boats with the wind tugging against her face. She wants to pull off her long wig and throw it over the railing and into the water. She wants to shout and rant and curse. She wants her family. Suddenly she imagines her mother and the village where she was born, high up in the hills of the Andalusian countryside. Had she known her life was going to turn out to be so complicated, she might never have left her village. She might never have taken a modelling contract and moved away.

Perhaps she might have married a local man. Pepe, the neighbour's son, had talked to her about marriage, but she'd been sixteen and full of youthful ambition and plans to break away from her parents. Back then life wasn't complicated. Not like it is now. Then, everything was much simpler. There was no social media, no easy phone access and although it had been harder to stay in touch with people - it's worse now.

Everyone is at your fingertips. Unless you're ignored.

Jack's dancing with a young woman on TV in Australia, and although Carmen's only a button away on Elena's phone - she doesn't call. And now Luis, for all his bravery, is facing a life of difficulty, misunderstanding and constant battles.

We're all living separate lives.

Carmen can't bear the thought of losing her family.

After the last time Luis was beaten, he tried to take his own life. Carmen vowed then to do anything to keep her family safe - but then why is she here?

She gazes out to sea where the fishing boats are coming home, trailed by a flock of excited seagulls fighting over scraps thrown overboard by the fishermen. Carmen grips the cold rail and exhales slowly, closing her eyes, the wind washing over her face and tired eyes.

Four more days and Luis will go to university and she will be here alone. It's a scary thought and she's filled with fear.

Carmen has never lived on her own. But in the meantime, she'd better check on the parcel delivery.

* * *

It's not until Tuesday lunchtime that Carmen notices the

change in Luis. He hasn't been outside since the weekend and this morning he hasn't showered. He's also spent considerably more time in his bedroom. Carmen watches him visibly shrinking and when she knocks on his bedroom door with a sandwich, she knows something isn't right.

'I'm fine, Mama,' Luis replies, not meeting her worried eyes. 'Stop fussing.'

'We need to get you sorted for uni. We were going shopping. How about we go later?'

'There's nothing I need.'

'What about bedding or food and towels.'

'We have plenty of everything, don't we?'

'Yes, but perhaps you'd like something special?'

'No, Mama. Nothing.' He turns away from her and she returns downstairs to the shop. It's quiet, so she searches for bits and pieces online for Luis to take to university.

That evening, she's musing over the designs on the mood board for the bar when Luis wanders into the lounge. He hasn't dressed or shaved today. There are dark circles around his eyes and his long dirty hair is tied back making him look gaunt and lifeless. He sits on the chair opposite her.

'I'm not going on Friday,' he says.

Carmen regards her child with love. 'Why?'

Luis shrugs. 'It's not worth it.'

'But you've worked too hard to get accepted onto this course. Places are rare and you've got a natural talent for drawing.'

Luis stares at the floor. 'I can still draw if I'm here.'

'Of course, you can draw if you're here but you won't develop. You won't grow as an artist and you'll miss out on so many career opportunities.'

Luis shrugs. 'I don't care.'

Carmen waits patiently but he won't look at her. She knows that he really wants to go to university. It's fear that's stopping him.

'I would like you to go, Luis. Go and live life and embrace it with happiness and excitement. Not with fear for being the person that you truly want to be.'

If only Jack was here, they could be a team again. Parents together, supporting and loving their children and giving Luis advice.

He stands up. 'Buenas noches, Mama.'

'Good night, my darling.'

* * *

The following morning Paul has texted her three times, before nine o'clock.

What about the secret nook? Has she managed to get hold of the old beer signs? What about the new material for the bench seat in the window?

Carmen ignores the messages and crosses the road to the café. Karl greets her warmly and she waits patiently for her latte before heading back out into Harbour Street. Ben is opening the art gallery. Remembering Femi's words, she hurries over to him. She hasn't seen him since the opening of her shop but he smiles in greeting.

'How's the refurb project going?' He nods at the pub. 'Is Paul behaving himself?'

Carmen returns his smile. 'He needs a restraint but I'm managing.'

Ben laughs.

'I want to ask you a favour. It's about Luis.'

Ben's face turns serious. 'I heard what happened on Saturday night, is he okay?'

Carmen stares down Harbour Street oblivious of the people and businesses opening. 'I don't know what to do.' She's suddenly fighting back her tears. Ben takes her elbow and guides her into the gallery. 'It's quieter in here,' he says, closing the door.

The gallery has a calming effect on her; the light timber wood, soft lighting and there's a comforting aroma.

'Is that sage?' She sniffs the air and wipes her eye wishing her heart would calm its rapid and nervous beat.

Ben grins. 'Yes, it's a new candle. Amber's favourite.'

'It's lovely.'

'So, tell me about Luis,' Ben says. 'You know he's been in here a few times?'

Carmen's mouth drops open. 'They never said.'

Ben smiles. 'He said — *they* said, they like art and they're very perceptive. Luis came in a few weeks ago as I had an unusual painting in the window. It was created using tiny dots... so we talked about art and their work and what they liked. They're very knowledgeable. Luis' has a place at the Central Saint Martins, no?'

'Yes, it's a constituent college of the University of the Arts. I'm supposed to take them on Friday to London but they said last night that they're not going.'

'Ah.' Ben looks at her and scratches his chin. 'Is this because of what happened on Saturday night?'

'I think they're depressed - again.'

'Again?'

'The last time - it was bad... almost fatal. And I'm scared. If Jack was here...' Carmen's voice trails off and she wonders what Jack would do. He would be hurt and angry. After the last time it was Jack who had been in pieces in the hospital waiting for Luis' recovery, never leaving his side.

Carmen blinks away the memory.

Ben says, 'I'll talk to Luis if you like but I can't promise I can change their mind.'

A tear trickles down her cheek but she wipes it quickly away. 'I'd appreciate that.'

'I've a few calls to make but then I'll go and knock on the door. Is that okay?'

'More than okay, Ben. Thank you.'

He hands her his phone. 'Put your number in here and I'll let you know how it goes.'

Chapter 11

At lunchtime Carmen sends Luis another text message and says a silent prayer for a quick reply. She can't smother him, yet she needs to let him know she's here. It's Wednesday and she's still hopeful that he will go to university in two days' time.

There's cold chicken and salad for lunch. Let's get a takeaway for dinner? xx

Luis texts back.

Thanks.x

Happy that he texts straight back, she picks up the two packages with the vintage beer signs that were delivered that morning and closes the shop. She heads to the pub and she's about to step inside when she hears her name called across the street. Turning, she hides a sigh before smiling brightly.

Tracey is waving her arm and hurrying across the street toward her. 'How's Luis? They're not answering my calls.'

'They're alright. I think it's probably—'

'Is it 'cos of Saturday? It wasn't my fault.'

Carmen shrugs. 'I don't know what's going on,' she says truthfully.

'I've been round to the flat but Luis won't answer the door either.'

'I'm sorry.'

'I'll call round tonight. Will you let me in?'

'It's up to Luis if— '

'Why won't they speak to me?'

'I don't— '

'I'm upset. Tell him we're friends.' Tracey is mixing up her pronouns.

'I'll tell them.'

'Tell him to text me.' Tracey glances over to the apartment. 'Does he miss me?'

'They're not saying much.'

'Is he still going on Friday?'

'They haven't mentioned it.'

'It will be worse at university. He should stay here. No one will like him like I do. He won't have any friends.'

'I assume they are going,' Carmen lies.

'I want to talk to Luis. Tell him I've got to speak to them.'

'I'll ask them.'

* * *

Carmen steps into the pub and into Paul's wide smile.

'I thought you'd forgotten me.' He turns down the corners of his mouth.

'Hardly.'

'I felt abandoned.' He pouts.

'I doubt it.' Carmen places her packages on the counter.

'What's wrong?' Paul is standing too close. His breath is on her cheek.

'Nothing.'

He takes her hand and pulls her toward him. 'Is it about Luis?'

Carmen shakes her head but she doesn't move away. She's drawn to Paul's tenderness and care. He places a comforting hand on her shoulder.

'You know Luis is going away and, as hard as it is, it might just be what he needs. Kids are smart. They handle more than we give them credit for and I'm speaking from experience.' He grins.

'But they need their parents,' she replies tersely.

Paul pulls his lips together in a tight line. 'I know, that's why I'm working hard with Sandra to sort out our marriage. She's the one who looks after the kids mostly and I know it's not always easy. I do understand that.'

Carmen swirls a drink coaster on the bar with her index finger. 'It's hard knowing that your child is struggling.'

Paul leans closer. His voice is gentle. 'You're stronger than you think, Carmen. This is just a glitch.'

Carmen smiles. 'I have enough glitches in my life right now. Thanks, Paul.'

Suddenly, a lively group of builders burst into the pub. Their laughter is infectious and Paul winks at Carmen. 'Tell you what, I've got an idea. When they've gone, we'll go out for dinner and I'll take your mind off everything.'

'I don't think that's the solution, Paul. What about your wife and family?'

'I'm trying my best. At least Sandra and I are talking now.' He's twisting his wedding ring that's now back on his finger. 'I'm spending more time with Sandra and the kids but to be honest, Carmen, I have to work.' He casts his arms wide and nods at the workmen who are finishing the thatch-work above the bar. 'We need to get this place finished for Friday and that's my main concern. After that, I'll have more time.'

'Any chance of a pint, Paul?' calls one of the workmen, winking at Carmen.

'Dying of thirst over here, mate,' adds his partner.

'You're not getting a drop until this place is finished. What do you think I am, a charity?' Paul laughs.

The banter and camaraderie with Paul, eases her worries momentarily, and for the first time in days she's hopeful. She spends the next few hours managing to distract herself concentrating on the pub interior and the finer details that will make it the talk of the town and hopefully increase her business profile

It's just after four when her phone pings.

Talked with Luis. Fingers crossed. Ben x

* * *

Carmen works later than she had anticipated, partly because she wants to give Luis time to mull over and digest his conversation with Ben but also because the opening is on Friday and she wants the pub to be perfect.

Her mind is in overdrive although no one would guess. She works quietly and methodically until Paul wanders over and sits beside her. 'The kitchen's had a deep clean and we're pretty much sorted.'

'Good.' The kitchen is not part of her remit but it has kept Paul busy.

'Fancy a drink?' he asks. 'We can have a private celebration.'

Carmen checks her watch. 'It's just after six. I'm going

home, thanks.'

'Just one? A small one? It's not as if you have far to go?' Paul turns down his mouth.

'I'll have one on Friday because now, I want to get back to Luis.'

Paul smiles, stands up and looks at her meaningfully. 'It's probably for the best.'

'Yes.' Carmen gathers her things. 'This will give you more time at home with Sandra. How old are your children?'

'Max and Jemma are seven. They're twins.'

'How lovely.'

Paul frowns as if he'd like to disagree and he twists his wedding ring nervously.

'Have a lovely evening with them all. See you tomorrow.' Carmen slides quickly out of the pub suddenly in a hurry to see her child and hoping that above all hope, Luis is feeling better.

* * *

Carmen climbs the stairs to the flat but Luis isn't there. This isn't what she's expecting and her heart rapidly fires up, beating wildly. She reaches for her phone and there's a message from Luis. Sent ten minutes ago. If only she'd left the pub earlier. Her hands are shaking as she reads the message.

Gone to get a curry for us. Lxx

The front door downstairs bangs.

'Luis?' she calls, hardly daring to breathe.

She hears him come up the stairs and he walks in smiling and waving the takeaway bag. 'Ouch!' He clutches his ribs.

'That hurts.'

'You'll be sore for a few weeks still.'

'I wanted to invite you for dinner.' Luis leans over to kiss her on the cheek.

Carmen removes her jacket and follows Luis into the kitchen. He's showered and shaved and he's wearing purple flared trousers, high heeled boots and a sparkling yellow jumper. He's also wearing full makeup. Luis' hair is flowing free and clean down his back and her child looks radiant and beautiful.

Carmen's spirits rise.

'Wine?' Luis reaches for the glasses. 'I got a bottle of your favourite Rueda.'

'Graçias, cariño. Thank you. That's kind.' She rubs his shoulder as she reaches for forks and serviettes.

They sit opposite each other at the dining table. 'So? What's brought about this change?' She smiles.

'Ben came round this afternoon....' Luis spoons spicy basmati rice onto their plates. 'I ordered lamb biriyani, your favourite.'

'Thank you. Tell me about Ben?' Carmen pours the wine, caught up by Luis' infectious good humour.

'Well.' Luis leans across the table. 'He's such a nice guy. It turns out he works with a charity up in London and he goes up there a lot and we're going to meet up and visit a few galleries together. He and Amber want to go to the new Chanel exhibition at the Victoria and Albert, so we're going there next week and they're also coming with me to see *Boyfriend* at the Albert Hall.'

'So, you *are* going to university?' She grins.

Luis tilts his head and smiles.

'Wonderful.' Carmen raises her glass. 'Exciting times. I'm

so happy for you.'

'Ben said that it won't always be easy but that I should just be myself and understand there are people who won't always accept or even like me - regardless of how I look. He said it happens to us all. We can't be liked by everyone.'

'That's so true.' Carmen savours the spices on her tongue. 'Think of the negative comments Papi has received. It's all about how we deal with them.'

'It's about how we deal with challenges. Life is life but it's our attitude and how we deal with each difficulty that counts.'

'Our attitude is everything.' Carmen smiles.

Luis continues excitedly, 'It's about resilience.'

'And kindness,' adds Carmen, raising her glass. She's extraordinarily proud of her child with full makeup covering a battered and bruised eye. 'I think you should tell Papi what happened.'

'Why?'

'Because he would be proud of you and how you're dealing with it.'

Luis raises his eyes to the ceiling.

'I mean it.' she says.

'Okay.'

They spend the rest of the meal talking about Luis going to university in the morning and what they need to pack. It turns out that Luis has already done a lot in the past few hours. 'I still have tomorrow to sort things out. Can I take the TV from my room?'

'Of course.' As they clear up together Carmen says vaguely, 'I saw Tracey today.'

'Oh?'

'She's upset that she hasn't heard from you.'

Luis shrugs. 'I wasn't in a good place.'

'Do you want to message her? I think she blames herself.'

Luis places the plates carefully in the dishwasher. 'I don't want to see her but I will sort it out.'

'Why don't you want to see her?'

Luis turns to face her, and Carmen has a clearer view of his swollen eye covered with vibrant eyeshadow.

'I guess I'm embarrassed.'

'You don't need to be.'

Luis turns away. 'I'm going to see Ricky tomorrow to thank him.'

'That's a good idea.'

'Tracey wasn't much use. If it wasn't for him I might not be here.'

Carmen reaches out and pulls Luis closer feeling the tautness of his shoulders and the natural smell of his skin. This child was once a part of her, integral to her body and when they are this close it's like they're joined again. Inseparable.

'Mind my ribs, Mama. And my makeup!' Luis laughs and pulls away.

'Sorry.' She smiles but her heart is lifted. She's happy. Luis, her beautiful child is back to normal.

* * *

Jack's phone call takes her by surprise.

'Is everything okay?' Carmen asks, still groggy with sleep. She sits up in bed and checks the time.

'Why didn't you tell me?' Jack shouts down the phone.

'It's 5am here, Jack. What are you talking about?'

'Luis? Why didn't you tell me he was beaten up?'

Carmen rubs her scalp trying to get her thoughts together. 'Luis said he would tell you.'

'Well, Elena told me. She phoned me just now and I'm rehearsing for the live show tomorrow. You can imagine how I feel. What's going on?'

'Luis is alright. They're fine.'

'It didn't sound like it.'

'The bruise on their eye is fading and their ribs are sore. But they're going to uni—'

'I should bloody hope so. Did you call the police?'

'No, Luis didn't want t—'

'It's not bloody up to him. After the last time, Carmen. You should have called them. You should have—'

'I SHOULD HAVE WHAT, JACK?' Carmen shouts. Then conscious of Luis asleep in the flat. She lowers her voice and speaks quickly, her accent growing thicker with anger. 'It's all very well you telling me what to do when you have no idea what's going on—'

'I have no idea because you don't tell me—'

'You're always busy. Always rehearsing. Always—'

'I know you're angry I came over here.'

'I'm not. I'm honestly not. I don't care, Jack.'

Silence fills the air waves.

'Right,' he says quietly. 'I thought you did. I actually *thought* you cared.'

Carmen takes a breath and in a measured voice says, 'We've both decided to follow our own paths. There's nothing wrong in that. Both of our children are adults. You can contact your children any time you like.' Her voice softens. 'It's nice that Elena phoned—'

'She assumed I knew.'

'Part of me didn't want to worry you and also Luis didn't want any fuss—'

'Is he alright?'

'*They* are fine.' Carmen reminds Jack of the pronoun. '*They* had a wobble about going to university but Ben spoke to them and they're back on track.'

'Who's Ben?'

'Amber's husband. He works with disadvantaged children and he has a charity that—'

'I've got to go. Sorry, it's the middle of the afternoon and we're on stage next.'

'Well, good luck.'

'Thanks, Cammy.'

'I—' Carmen doesn't finish her sentence as Jack cuts the connection. She tosses the phone onto the bed beside her where Jack should be lying asleep. She wants to scream but she doesn't. She wants to shout and rant but she can't. Instead, she lies staring at the ceiling going over their conversation and imagining Jack dancing with a girl, young enough to be his daughter with a reputation for wrecking marriages and sleeping with her dance partners.

* * *

Carmen doesn't open the shop on Friday morning. They're too busy packing up the car. Luis owns a lot of clothes.

The conversation in the car is sporadic and formal as if they realise that their lives are about to change forever. Their words stop and start almost in unison with the traffic jams and changing lights as they get closer to London and their destination.

They're both dreading the separation and the fear of being alone for very different reasons.

Once they arrive at the university Luis doesn't want Carmen hanging around. They've barely carried the bags upstairs to Luis' room before he begins ushering her out of the door. Some students smile shyly and others turn quickly away but not before they've checked out Luis and his long beige skirt and bright purple shirt. His hair is tied up and his bright green eye shadow covers the bruising, and emphasises his cat-like eyes, making Luis look both interesting and alluring.

'Drive carefully, Mama. I'll phone you.'

'Will you be alright?'

'Of course. Now go!'

'What about food for tonight?'

'You've given me pizza and some curry meals. They're in the fridge.'

'I know but—'

'Mama! Go!' He laughs, pushing her out of the door and toward the staircase.

She grins and leans forward quickly to give Luis another quick hug. 'Te quiero,' she whispers.

'I love you too, Mama, now go!'

Carmen turns to wave from the top of the stairs. He grins. She turns the corner then she's suddenly alone. She walks down the stairs of the residential accommodation looking at the youthful expectation in the eyes of the students, wondering if any of them will make friends with Luis. Her heart is heavy as if it's been wrenched apart and the tears begin welling up in the back of her throat, choking her. She swallows quickly. She just wants Luis to be happy.

Carmen starts the car and leans forward over the steering

wheel to look up at the residential building. But there's no sign of Luis. He's not at the window. He has already moved on. He's already embracing the next stage of his life - without her.

'Dios mio,' she whispers, 'God, please look after my child.'

* * *

It's a lonely drive home to Westbay. She tells herself that she's ridiculous and that she's been on her own before but strangely this is all very different. When she gets home it's as if all the life has been sucked out of the flat. There's no soul to it any more. No atmosphere. She's overwhelmed with sadness and grief. Luis isn't going to appear tonight waving a takeaway. She's not going to hear him running a bath or his footsteps on the stairs. It's all eerily quiet.

She wanders from room to room and then strips Luis' bed, throwing his sheets on the floor. She puts on a wash and when she can no longer stand the quietness she goes downstairs and into the shop.

She's barely turned the open sign on the door when Frances the local vicar arrives. Frances says she's looking forward to the opening of the pub later that evening. 'But I'm really here on the off chance that you might be interested in buying some of my mother-in-law's furniture. Marjorie's had to go into a care home and I really don't know what to do with anything. I know I could call house clearance, but she really has some lovely pieces and I thought that perhaps you might have a look?'

Frances' eyes are sad.

'This must be hard for you; are you close to her?'

Frances smiles sadly. 'Yes. We're great friends but she needs so much care now that the doctor insists she has round-the-clock help. Although she lived near us and it was easy to pop in, it wasn't enough.' Frances grips her hands. Her knuckles are white. 'We just couldn't cope. Even the carers couldn't. I feel so inept - and I'll miss her.'

Carmen lays a hand on her arm. 'I understand. I took Luis to university this morning but at least Luis is starting his life. It's much worse for you with Marjorie now towards the end of hers.'

Frances smiles. 'That's why we must embrace each day.'

Carmen turns away. She's not quite ready for embracing the future but she will be glad of the pub opening tonight. It's the diversion she needs.

Frances continues, 'You'll miss Luis. Do you think Jack will join you? Or is that a nosy question? I don't want to pry.'

Carmen glances up. She hates it when virtual strangers ask about her private life or about her arrangement with Jack but Frances seems different. She actually seems to care - rather than being interested in gossip.

'He's in Australia at the moment.' Carmen is used to replying with information that could be gleaned from any social media site. 'He's on the dancing show over there.'

Frances' face lights up. 'How wonderful. Is he doing well?'

'He's dancing the waltz tomorrow.' Carmen grins.

'I hope he's fit.'

'Me too.' They both laugh.

'Paul has asked us to the opening at six; perhaps you could let me know then if you want to take a look at Marjorie's things—'

'I've decided, Frances. I will. Let me check my diary.'

Carmen heads to the counter where the book lies open. She uses it to mark the days working in the pub, the days in the shop and what Luis is doing. Now as she flicks the pages she realises all the dates looking forward are empty. How awful is that?

She smiles at Frances. 'When suits you?'

'I know tomorrow is Saturday but sooner rather than later as we're putting the house on the market.'

'Nine? I can pop in before I open the shop at ten.'

'Perfect.'

Frances gives her Marjorie's address and after she leaves Carmen walks over to the window. Harbour Street is quiet now. It's almost five and the shops are shutting. Harbour Café closed an hour ago. The butchers are locking their door and the Beauty Salon looks closed already. Carmen turns away but not before she sees Tracey standing on the corner, outside the pub looking in her direction. She has a scowl on her face and it sends a shiver down Carmen's spine. It's as if she's being spied on.

Chapter 12

The pub has been transformed into a harmonious blend of old-world charm and contemporary elegance. It's the reopening night and the townsfolk have gathered to marvel at the stunning makeover. There are candles on the tables, soft music playing in the background and although it isn't cold outside Paul has lit the fire for ambience.

Carmen mingles with the guests, enjoying the praise heaped on her.

Frances, Femi and Lawrence, Eva and Sanjay are all full of compliments and are in awe.

'You worked so quickly.'

'How did you come up with the idea for thatch over the bar?'

'I love the mantelpiece.'

'Paul says there's a secret compartment somewhere...'

Amidst the clinking of glasses and the laughter of patrons, Paul finds a moment alone with Carmen. 'You've truly outdone yourself, Carmen. This place looks incredible,' Paul's eyes reflect his admiration.

Carmen smiles with a glint of mischief in her eyes. 'Couldn't have done it without the charming pub owner's input and wit.'

Paul grins, a hint of bashfulness colouring his cheeks. 'Well, if you ever need a permanent advisor on wit, I'm your man.'

Their laughter mingles with the lively atmosphere of the pub. It's as if the walls themselves are celebrating the new-found harmony of tradition and modernity.

Carmen turns to Amber. 'I want to thank Ben for speaking to Luis.'

'He's in London tonight. We're just pleased it all worked out and that Luis went off okay.'

'Me too. Thank you.'

'You must focus on yourself now, Carmen.'

Carmen laughs. 'Me?'

'Yes, you need to meet some friends and have a social life.'

'I'm too busy. I'm trying to get my business sorted out.'

'That does take time,' Amber agrees. Then she nods at a couple heading in their direction and smiles. 'Have you met Sandrine and George? Your competition?'

Sandrine is a small, dark-haired French woman and George has white hair and a grey beard. After the introductions Sandrine raises her glass.

'Here's to your success, Carmen. It is lovely in here.'

'Thank you.' Carmen raises her own glass in response.

George taps her glass with his. 'You're lucky we had to go to our daughter in Devon. She had the baby early.'

Carmen frowns.

He smiles. 'We're your competition but we had to pull out of the tender—'

'Our daughter had a beautiful baby girl,' interrupts Sandrine, proudly. Her lips stretching into a wide smile. 'We had to leave quickly. The next day in fact.'

Carmen smiles automatically but her head is whirling. Paul had led her to believe she'd won this contract on merit not because her competition was called away.

Sandrine continues, 'It was such a coincidence. Paul had just phoned us to offer us the contract for the pub and it was literally just two minutes after our son-in-law phoned to say Emily's waters had broken. We were on grandparent duty for the older two children. So, we had no choice. We left immediately.'

'A month early! But what can you do?' George laughs 'But at least it's given you a foot in the door. You're very, very lucky, Carmen.'

Carmen's smile is fixed, her anger is bubbling inside like a cauldron on fire. Luck? She had worked so bloody hard and Paul had lied to her.

'Yes, I'm very lucky indeed,' she whispers.

'Next time, things will be different.' George puffs out his chest like a proud eagle. His eyes shining in the firelight like gleaming daggers. 'The fight is on.'

* * *

Frances's mother-in-law's house is two minutes from Harbour Street accessed by a narrow alleyway and only a few minutes walk to the beach.

'These alleyways are synonymous with Westbay. Smugglers used them all the time to run from the authorities and hide contraband,' Frances explains. 'This was one of the older houses in the town. It was owned by a wealthy merchant at the time - that's why it's detached.'

Carmen is enthralled with the character of the house; timber frames, worn flagged floors in the kitchen and oak floors through the lounge and dining room. She gasps with delight at the original stone fireplaces and old nooks and crannies.

'It's so charming.'

'It has so much character.' Frances beams back at her. 'Just like Marjorie! We love it. I'll be sorry to see it go. We miss her so much not living here.'

The lounge patio doors open onto the back garden and Carmen has an image of the old lady sitting under the shade of the twisted willow tree or perhaps in a deckchair under the awning in the shade at the side of the house.

'This part of the old coach house needs some repair,' Frances adds pointing at the stone outbuildings. 'You can imagine the old coaches being stored and looked after in here. I think work needs to be done on it all, and there's probably more to do than meets the eye.'

'It's beautiful.'

'It certainly has character,' replies Frances.

Carmen is thinking of her modern palatial prison in London and how different the two properties are; one so showy and obvious and this one so discreet and understated.

They walk around the house together and Frances points out various pieces of furniture.

'They're not that old. They're probably not even antiques and they might not fetch much but some pieces are so pretty. It would probably cost me more to pay to have them taken away. Call me nostalgic or emotional but I would really like these bits and pieces to find new homes and not be thrown onto some scrapheap.' She picks up a beautiful blue and silver Chinese vase. 'It's not Ming.' she smiles. 'It's not worth much but I have no use for these things. Graham is a typical man. He loves history but sorting out his mother's things is far too emotional for him.'

'Did he grow up in this house?'

She puts down the vase. 'His mother moved here after we did about ten years ago. She wanted to be near to him and I suppose some of these pieces might be from his family home - from years ago but he's not interested in sentimental things. I think I care more.' She gives an embarrassed laugh. 'She's been more of a mother to me than my own and everything here reminds me of her.'

'This dining table is lovely too.' Carmen runs her fingers across the mahogany wood and four matching chairs wondering about the history and stories that were talked about over long winter dinners.

'It's someone's life. It's *her* life and I don't know what to do with it all.'

'I'm not an expert.' Carmen runs her hand over a small lamp. 'But you're right. They're too lovely to be thrown away. It's as if they have a soul.'

Frances appears sad. 'There's all the soft furnishing too; the cushions and the curtains, and the bits and pieces...'

'It's timeless elegance and uniqueness.'

Frances smiles. 'You really do understand, Carmen. You've put my heart at peace.'

They spend the next hour or so making a list and discussing the logistics of getting the objects to Carmen's shop.

'I'll ask Ben. He'll help. He's got a cart and he'll be able to wheel them around for you then I'll get the estate agent round. Although nothing will probably happen before Christmas. Perhaps Graham is right and it won't sell now. He said I should probably leave it until the spring - but it's so awful thinking of everything here still in her home and Marjorie in a hospice knowing that time is precious...'

'Once people move out, they take the soul of the home with

them.' Carmen is thinking of Luis and her own flat. 'I'll do my best to find all of these lovely things a good home.'

'I know you will, Carmen. Thank you. I'm much happier now.'

* * *

Late on Saturday afternoon, Luis sends her a message with a link to a YouTube video.

Papi is loving his new life in Australia! Lxx

She opens her laptop to see him on the bigger screen. Jack and Shazzy B are dancing the waltz and although he makes a few mistakes there's no denying his agility or his passion for dancing. He doesn't seem to be having much problem with his knee either.

As they wait for their results Jack smiles at his dance partner. Their arms are entwined behind each other's back.

Carmen imagines Jack's muscular body against her. There's no mention of their waltz in Vienna. There's no nostalgia. Jack is living in the present and she isn't there to share it.

Carmen had hoped that he would be different. It would have been nice had there been some acknowledgement of her or his family back in England but there isn't. There's nothing. It's as if he's a single man again.

Jack is focused on himself and he can't take his eyes off Shazzy B. It's evident in his smile and twinkling blue eyes. That was how he used to gaze at her.

She slams the lid shut and closes her eyes.

* * *

Ben insists on carrying Frances' items inside the shop. 'This trolley is so handy. Where do you want this lamp?' Ben wheels everything inside with a cheerful countenance, going backwards and forwards to his cart outside.

'Thanks, Ben. I'll sort everything out later,' Carmen says. 'Pop it all in the corner over there.'

'How's Luis? Any news?' Ben asks, placing the last table at the back of the shop where she indicated.

'They've sent a few messages, and they seem okay, but I can't ask too much. I must give them room to flourish.'

Ben laughs. 'Strict instructions then?'

'Of course.'

He rubs a hand through his hair. 'It's tough, isn't it? I know with our foster kids how hard saying goodbye is. All we can say to ourselves is that we've done a good job. We've done our best. We've helped them with the foundations of their lives and that's all we can do.'

Carmen turns away. She places the blue and silver Chinese vase on the table. She's not ready for anyone else's emotions.

'Luis said they have a sister. You have a daughter? Perhaps she'll come and visit?'

'Elena's getting married just before Christmas.'

Ben's face lights up. 'Wonderful.'

Carmen doesn't say that she's marrying a controlling, narcissistic pilot and instead she smiles. 'We may have to go to Florida for it.'

'Really? Jack will be exhausted. Isn't he starting his book tour soon? I think I saw it in the paper the other day.'

'After the dance programme.'

'Will you fly over to Oz?'

Carmen shakes her head. 'My priority is to get my business sorted out.'

'Well, you're off to a good start with the pub. Are you going to pitch for the other big tender in town?'

Carmen regards him intently. 'Big tender?'

'Haven't you heard? That new development on the outskirts behind the supermarket needs three show homes and some furniture packages putting together. You should give them a ring and find out about it before Sandrine and George beat you to it.'

'I will.'

'The information should be on their website but let me know if you don't find it and I'll get the contact details for you.'

Carmen turns to him. 'Did you know they were Paul's first choice to refurbish the pub but then their daughter had a baby?'

'Well, they're local and they're more established,' Ben replies. 'I think they've had the monopoly on everything until now.'

Carmen's anger surges. 'Paul led me to believe that I had been their first choice for the pub. And to be honest I feel cheated. It seems I was the last resort...'

'Paul's a great guy but sometimes he's an idiot. Don't take it to heart.' Ben rubs his chin.

Carmen wanted to win on merit and not by default. If Paul had described the interior he wanted instead of teasing and flirting with her, then it might all have been different. She had changed her ideas to suit Paul and his partners - and lost.

Now it seems the whole of Harbour Street know she was the second choice - second best. And one thing that Carmen hated in life was to be second at anything. It just wasn't in her nature. It didn't happen to her.

* * *

On Monday evening Paul knocks on her front door.

'Carmen,' he calls.

Reluctantly, she lifts the sash window and shouts out, 'What do you want?'

'You haven't answered my messages or my calls.'

'I'm busy.'

'Come on, what's wrong? Open up.'

'I wasn't your first choice for the pub. You lied to me.'

'I didn't lie. You *were* my first choice. It was my associates who wanted Sandrine and George.'

'You never told me that.'

'What was the point? You got the tender. You've refurbished the pub, and everyone loves it. You've done an amazing job.'

'The point is,' Carmen says and then she hesitates. He is right. She has done it, and everyone knows what a good job she's done.

'Come and have dinner with me? Please, come on?'

Carmen checks her watch. It's barely six.

'Just for an hour?' He smiles.

The walls of the flat are closing in on her and besides she might need a reference from Paul for the next tender. It doesn't take Carmen long to pull on a coat.

For a Monday night, the Chinese restaurant is busy.

'It's Halloween,' says Paul. 'And the end of the month - payday.'

'I'd forgotten.'

They settle in the corner of the restaurant in the new part of town because Harbour Bistro is full, and they don't want a takeaway from Sanjay's Indian.

Paul orders a bottle of dry rosé, and they share Ginger Pork Pot Stickers, Black Pepper Chicken, Fried Rice, Beef and Broccoli Stir-Fry and Scallion Pancakes.

'This is a feast,' declares Carmen looking eagerly at the dishes.

'It's my favourite, so enjoy.'

Carmen eats slowly, savouring each dish, relishing the flavours on her tongue and the spices warming her mouth.

Paul is happy to speak about the pub and all the compliments he's received from everyone in the town. 'There's a feature about it in the local magazine this week and I've mentioned you and your business.'

'Thanks. I might need a reference for another job too, if that's okay?'

'No problem. I'm only too happy to help. How's Luis getting on?'

'Good, I think. I haven't heard from them today, but they were settling in over the weekend. How are things at home with the family?'

Paul shifts uncomfortably in his seat and speaks with his mouth full. In the lamp light, she notices that he's stopped shaving and there's a few days of stubble on his chin.

'Sandra likes the pub. She came in on Saturday with the kids. She couldn't come on Friday as she had a friend's baby shower.' He pauses to check Carmen's reaction, but she doesn't look at him, focusing instead on the food on the table. 'So, I was a bit pissed. It seemed her friend was more important than my business but I guess after everything that's happened, I wasn't going to come first.'

'Marriages need working at,' Carmen replies, helping herself to more ginger pork.

'Are you working at your marriage?' he asks.

'Of course.'

'So, you're happy with Jack?'

'Yes.'

'But you're living separate lives?'

'Only for a few weeks. Our diaries didn't coincide,' she says easily.

'So, Jack is going to come and live here after the book tour?'

Carmen flinches. She hasn't got to thinking about next year yet. It all seems so far away. 'It's only October, Paul. No one can plan their life to the nth degree.'

He frowns at her. 'Why would he go all that way to Australia and leave you here to start a new business on your own?'

'Because it's what I want to do.'

'And so next year?'

Carmen holds up her hand. 'Stop with the interrogation. Where will you and Sandra be next year? Will you have patched things up? Will you be happy?'

Paul blinks quickly taking her question seriously. 'She thinks I'm selfish. She thinks all I care about is the pub.'

'Is that true?'

'No!'

'Then you have to prove it to her.'

'How?'

Carmen shakes her head. 'Ask her?'

'I can't. She expects me to have all the answers. I mean, I don't make a fuss when she goes to visit her dad. He's not in great health and he's very lonely.'

'Where does he live?'

'Only ten miles away, but he's on his own. I think Sandra feels sorry for him and so every time there's a holiday he comes over to ours. Everything revolves around him and what he wants to do and what he's able to do...' Paul's voice trails off as he finishes the last of the rice on his plate. 'He's just so bloody lonely. She feels guilty and we don't get any peace together.'

'Then you need to find a solution, together. Where he gets company and you guys get family time away from the pub.'

Paul shakes his head. 'If only that were possible.'

'Do you love her?'

'Yes.'

'Then that's your answer.'

Paul pays for dinner and they head outside. Carmen pulls her woollen coat across her chest and Paul slips his arm through hers.

'Where now? Nightcap?'

'You go home to Sandra. You should have taken her out for dinner instead of me.'

'She went to the cinema with a friend.'

'It sounds like she's punishing you. Could that be possible?'

'Yeah. I was awful in the summer. We were so busy. Now it's quieter in the winter she says she's made a life for herself.'

'Then you need to schedule some dates together. Compromise.'

'It's going to be hard now with the Christmas season coming up.'

Carmen stops and she turns to face him. 'All I hear are excuses, Paul. If you want your marriage to work, then you have to communicate with your wife. Be honest with her.

Think about the children and their future - with and without you.'

'I love the kids.'

'Then sort yourself out.'

Paul stares at her. Under the streetlamp her eyes burn with passion. She's speaking from the heart. She listens. She cares. He leans toward her, but she steps back and unhooks her arm firmly from his.

'Goodnight, Paul.'

Behind them high heels are clicking on the pavement coming quickly toward them and a voice in the darkness calls out.

'I saw you two in the Chinese.' Tracey is breathless and she stops in front of them with a haughty smile on her face. Beside her is a stocky guy with a dark, Viking beard. His small eyes flick between Paul and Carmen watching their exchange with interest.

'Hello Tracey.'

'I saw you in the restaurant.'

Carmen nods. 'The food was delicious.'

Tracey stares at Paul. 'Didn't realise you had a date tonight.'

'Why would you?' Paul answers.

'It wasn't a date.' Carmen glares at him.

'You look very cosy to me.' Tracey tilts her head.

'Goodnight everyone.' Carmen moves away. Her gate is a few feet away - safety. She takes the key from her pocket.

Paul puts out a hand to stop her. 'Carmen—' he pleads.

'Bet Jack wouldn't be happy if he knew what you were up to.' Tracey smiles.

Carmen ignores her and unlatches the gate while placing her other hand against Paul's chest to stop him from following her.

'Imagine poor Jack. All sad and lonely in Australia while the local *married* publican is taking his wife out to dinner.'

Carmen turns at the gate. 'I'll have dinner with whoever I want.'

Paul adds laughing. 'He's hardly sad dancing with Shazzy B every day. I'm sure he's loving it!'

Carmen glares at him. They're both missing the point. She steps into her courtyard.

'Well, it shows how much you're in touch then, doesn't it?' Tracey raises her shoulders, like a tropical bird, as if preening herself.

'He's depressed. It says so on social media.'

'Then it must be true.' Paul laughs loudly.

Tracey is furious with him. She pulls her iPhone from her pocket and thrusts it in his face.

'He was booted off the show! Thought you might have known that.' She waves her phone at Carmen. 'I thought you might have spoken to him. After all you are married! Have you split up?'

Carmen closes the gate on them both. She can't wait to get away and to get upstairs to the comfort and security of her flat.

Jack's been booted off the show?

Why didn't Luis tell her?

More importantly, why didn't Jack tell her?

Chapter 13

Carmen throws her bag on the sofa and before she removes her coat she's already checking her phone. There are no messages from Jack, Luis or even Elena. She goes onto social media checking the sites carefully focusing her search on the dance show. Then she reads the headlines with growing worry.

Bailey Booted Off.

Bailey Bottled It.

Bailey Gets The Red Card.

Bailey Bites The Dust.

She spends the next few minutes phoning Jack's mobile but he doesn't reply. She doesn't leave a message.

There are photos of course. Jack smiling gracefully and there are quotes: 'Jack - grateful to have had the opportunity.' 'Shazzy B was the perfect dance partner' 'She's changed my life and the way I look at things.' 'My daily routine is going to be healthier.' 'Dancing will always be a part of my life.' 'Shazzy B is a friend for life!'

There are comments about their waltz from the judges: 'Poor performance', 'not light enough', 'tripped over on the basic turn' and 'it just wasn't his week.'

Carmen stares ahead at the sage feature wall.

This all happened three days ago in Australia.

She phones Luis but he doesn't answer either.

Where is Jack? She sends him a text.

Hey baby, haven't heard from you. Hope you're okay and not too disappointed? I'm proud of you. xxx

Then she texts Luis.

Hope you're having a good time? Didn't know that Papi got voted off?? Did you know???? Call me. Te quiero xxx

Then she texts Elena.

Hola cariño, hello darling, not sure where you are in the world? Can we meet when you fly back to London next? Even if it's just for a coffee? How are the wedding plans coming along? Would love to see you. Te quiero xxx

As she's removing her makeup her phone pings with a message.

Bloody Tracey! She's a nosy cow. Hope you're okay? Don't worry about her or what people think. Paul xx

Once she's in bed Carmen can't sleep. It was different with other celebrity programmes; the Jungle and SAS. But now Carmen stares at the ceiling, wondering if Jack's with Shazzy B and how she might be consoling him.

She turns on her side.

It's still strange with only one breast. She traces the scar with a finger. Maybe she should get surgery to look more normal and then Jack might come back to her? But that isn't why Jack left. Jack went to chase the money. He went to earn enough to save their house in London but he only lasted four weeks on the show. That won't be enough, not nearly enough, to save their house and the impending foreclosure on their property.

He'll be devastated.

And, as she drifts off to sleep, she says a silent prayer. *Please don't let him go off the rails again because I'm not there to pick up the pieces this time.*

* * *

The following morning Carmen recognises the client who'd come into the shop the first week she opened. The lady, tall with white hair, had been admiring the new wallpaper range, a very niche market of tropical birds; colourful, outrageous and eye catching.

'My name is Sheila,' she says.

'Of course, I remember you,' Carmen smiles. 'Would you like to take another look at the paper?'

'You've made the shop look very special,' Sheila says, looking around with appreciation. 'You have a natural eye for beauty.'

'That's kind of you.'

'You've worked hard.'

Carmen replies, 'It's been hard work getting it off the ground but I'm making progress.'

'Business isn't easy. And, when you're on your own it's ever harder.'

Sheila tells Carmen that she has been living in Westbay all her life. 'Never wanted to live anywhere else.' Sheila's brown eyes narrow at the memories. 'The town has changed but not so much that they've ruined it. It's still quite small and Harbour Street has managed to retain its uniqueness.' She walks toward the wallpaper display while tracing her hand lightly across Marjorie's mahogany dining table. 'I like buying locally sourced things.'

'This paper isn't sourced locally, I'm afraid. It's from a designer in Holland.'

Sheila grins. 'Well, sometimes you have to break the mould and do something different. I want to go wild. I want to do something excessive, and this is as daring as I'll ever get.' She laughs. 'Besides Tim, my husband, says he wants to embrace new things - and he's finally agreed to a new colour scheme.'

'Do you have someone to decorate?'

Sheila nods happily. 'I know a few builders who will help me.'

'That's great. If they're good, maybe you could mention me to them? It would be good to be able to recommend reliable decorators to my clients. It might make all the difference to a sale if I can offer my clients a reliable decorator who will do a good job in their home.'

'That's a good idea, Carmen. I'll give it some thought.' Sheila pulls out a small notebook. 'I've got all the measurements in here.'

They talk prices and work out approximate costs and delivery times. As Sheila pays the deposit she says, 'One of my sons or perhaps my husband, Tim, will collect it for me. Just let me know when it arrives and I'll ask one of them to come by and collect it.'

After she's gone, and Carmen has placed the order with the supplier, she checks her phone again.

There's a message from Luis.

Have you seen the papers????? LX

She's about to type back. She knows Jack was voted off the show but then her heart sinks. Is there more?

Instead of messaging, she scrolls through the popular social media sites and her eyes rest on a photo of Jack. He looks very drunk. He's sitting in a beach bar and in the background there's a golden, sandy beach.

She dials Luis' number.

He answers straight away. 'Mama? Are you alright?'

'Have you heard from him?' she asks.

'Papi hasn't answered my calls or messages.'

'Nor mine. Luis, I didn't know until last night that he was out of the competition.' She doesn't mention Tracey or the dinner she had with Paul. 'I was waiting for him to call me.'

'What shall we do, Mama? Have you seen the pictures of him?' Luis speaks quickly and with nervous energy.

'I've seen a few of him on the beach.'

'Jesus, Mama! He's hammered!'

'I know.'

'In public.'

'I know,' she whispers.

'What are you going to do?'

'What can I do?'

'Fly over there? Contact him?' Luis' tone is sarcastic and she recoils. She's unused to his caustic anger being aimed at her.

'He doesn't answer his phone.'

'Why did he bloody well have to go to Australia, anyway?'

Carmen takes a deep breath. 'We'll just have to ride out this storm like we have the others.'

'Others?'

Carmen frowns. Of course, Luis wouldn't remember. He was too young. 'We say nothing. Stick together. Just don't say anything negative - to anyone. We must give Papi our loyalty.'

'But what's he giving us?'

'He's trying to save our house in London. Besides, the world is round Luis. We are family. We all have different weaknesses and needs, and we should be there to support each other in our down times.' He doesn't reply. 'How are you getting on at uni? I haven't heard from you.'

'It's Freshers' week.'

'Of course, is it fun?'

'It's okay.'

'Have you met anyone on your course?'

'Yeah, there's one person...'

Carmen waits but Luis doesn't elaborate. She doesn't want to hound him for information. 'Well, have fun and let's speak soon.'

After she hangs up she dials Jack's number again. This time she leaves a message. Then, not having Simon's number, she looks up the name of Jack's agency and calls his number. He doesn't answer either so she leaves a terse message asking for the name of the hotel in Australia where Jack is staying.

Carmen wants to keep busy and her idea is to sort out Marjorie's things that Ben brought round to the shop. They are still packed up in one corner.

It's beginning to rain and Harbour Street is quiet so she takes her time sorting through the items, one by one, deciding if they should go into the shop or in the stock room. She decides to rotate them regularly until they sell.

Amber comes over later in the day. 'Are you alright?'

Carmen appears surprised. 'Of course.'

Amber frowns. 'Have you seen the memes on social media?'

Although Carmen's heart will not stop hammering she tries to appear nonchalant. 'He's just having a blow-out. You know. Disappointed at not getting through to the next round.'

Amber stares at her.

Carmen continues, 'Between you and me, it's what he does sometimes. It's just unfortunate that they got a picture of him looking worse for wear. He'll be alright—'

'What are you talking about?' Amber asks.

'Jack?'

'It's not Jack. It's you.'

'Me?' Carmen can't hide her surprise.

'Yes, you.' Amber pulls her phone from her pocket and shows her the screen. 'Haven't you seen this?'

'That's Paul.'

'With you,' says Amber. 'I'm sure it wasn't like that but the two of you are looking very intimate.'

'That was in the Chinese.' Carmen stares from the phone image to her friend. 'It was packed in there - we couldn't get into The Bistro.'

'It's not about *where* you were,' Amber says patiently. 'It's the fact that you're having dinner with Paul. I know it's not illegal but this picture is definitely giving off the wrong vibe in your relationship.'

'I'm allowed to go out for dinner.' Carmen moves away.

Amber stares at her. 'There's also reference to Luis being beaten up.'

Carmen turns back and this time she reads the script carefully. 'Who's done this?' she whispers.

Amber shrugs. 'I have no idea but it doesn't look good for

you or Luis.'

Carmen is stunned. 'Who would possibly...?'

'What was that about getting hammered?' asks Amber. 'Who were you talking about?'

Carmen sits down heavily on the chaise longue, realisation dawning on her. It looks to all the world that she and Jack have marital problems. But they've always been a team.

Carmen speaks slowly, 'Jack. I was talking about Jack. He's out of the dancing show. And there was a photo of him on the beach looking really drunk.'

Amber scrolls through her phone looking at the social media accounts and then she finds an unflattering photo of Jack. He's sitting in a bar with his arm around an attractive and much younger woman. 'Who's Shazzy B?'

'His dance partner from the show.'

'He doesn't look too good.'

Carmen looks away. 'I know.'

'Have you spoken to him?'

'I've been trying to contact him.'

'Keep trying.'

'The media might come here,' Carmen says. 'Now they know where I live and that Luis was beaten up. They often follow us and speak to neighbours – it was one advantage of living in our house in London. We had security. Big gates...'

'You'll be safe here.'

Carmen nods but she isn't convinced.

Amber places her hand on Carmen's shoulder. 'We won't say anything. We're your friends.'

Carmen raises a small grateful, smile. 'Thank you.'

'Do you want to close the shop for a few days?'

Carmen shakes her head. 'I have a wallpaper order I'm

expecting. I need to find out about the project at the new development and I'm still sorting through Marjorie's things that Ben brought around.'

Amber rubs her head. 'Okay, well, I'm just across the road. Call if you need help. Ben is down the road too.'

'Thanks Amber.'

'Phone Jack.'

'I'll try again now.'

***

It's an hour later when Simon phones. His tone is curt and he sounds busy. 'What is it?'

'I need to speak to Jack. Where is he?'

'You know he's in Australia.'

'Don't be an idiot, Simon. You know what I'm talking about. Where's he staying?'

'He's not answering.'

'Just because he's not talking to you doesn't mean he won't speak to me.'

'Well, then why hasn't he contacted you?' Simon replies quickly.

Carmen has never liked him but she's always been pleasant and polite because it means so much to Jack. But not today.

She hisses into the phone. 'YOU either give me his number or TELL him to call me - or there will be consequences. Jack will NEVER work with you again.'

'You don't know—'

'Jack is my husband! No one will come between us - and certainly NOT you. Now, you got him this work. You contact the producer or whoever you like in Australia or I will start creating hell in the press. And, if I go down, so will you and that shabby show and your poxy agency.'

When her phone rings five minutes later her heart is still racing and her hands are shaking.

'Mama?'

'Elena, my darl—'

'Have you seen social media?'

'Um, yes.'

'It's Papi. He's all over it!'

'Well, I wouldn't say all over. There are other more important things in the—'

'Mama, stop! Why is he doing this?'

Carmen pauses before answering quietly. 'I presume that he's upset.'

'Upset? That's an understatement. He'll ruin my wedding. It's everywhere. What will José's parents think?'

Carmen's body stiffens and she walks to the shop window where rain is beating solidly against the glass.

'I have no idea. But he's your father and we are a family. And, you can tell anyone who asks that they have no right to intervene. I am his wife, and I'm the only one who—'

'Fly over there. Go and get him. I'll get you a ticket.'

'No.'

'What? Why?'

'I am not his mother. I will not chase him.'

'Luis says you haven't spoken to him.'

'He won't return my calls.'

'He's such a loser. He's not coming to my wedding.'

'Elena, please wait. This will all blow over—'

'Not this time, Mama. You're just as bad. You can't keep covering for him.'

'I don't—'

'I have to go.'

Elena hangs up leaving Carmen staring at the rain dripping down the window. Across the road, Tracey's friend with the Viking beard leaves the Beauty Salon and walks toward the pub with a sly smile across his face.

* * *

To distract herself she searches for information on the website about the new development. She's so engrossed in her work that she doesn't realise the door opens until there's suddenly a draft around her legs.

A plump, homely, pale skinned, dark haired woman stares at her.

'Hello?' Carmen smiles.

'I had to see you for myself.'

'Pardon?'

'What sort of woman are you?'

Carmen stands up. 'I don't understand.'

'I'm not surprised considering what your husband is up to - you famous people think you can do anything you like and—'

'Who are you?' Carmen walks toward the stranger who hovers in the doorway.

'What do you care? He has children. He has a family. He has ME!'

Carmen's mouth drops open. It's not often she's taken by surprise but on top of everything else today this is surreal.

'Sandra?' she mutters.

'Yes. And you should be ashamed!'

'I have nothing to be ashamed of and I'm not having an

affair with your husband if that's what you think.'

Sandra blinks rapidly. 'Yes, you are.'

'Who said?'

She shakes her head. 'He wouldn't tell me the truth. Paul doesn't know what the truth is half the time.'

Carmen takes in the woman's demeanour. She's not glamorous. She's not dressed-up. In fact, she looks very ordinary and her face is creased in pain. She looks extremely tired. 'He loves you very much,' Carmen says softly.

'How do you know?'

'Because he told me.'

Sandra shakes her head in disbelief, tears welling up in her eyes. 'I can't take any more.'

'I understand. Look, it's quiet in the shop and I have a kettle in the back. We could chat?'

Sandra backs away. 'No. No...'

'He told me how hard you work. Juggling the twins and how you look after your father. You're very kind and Paul does appreciate you.'

Sandra seems unsure. 'He never tells me—'

Carmen smiles. 'That's men for you! But I can't say more than that. I can't judge Paul when my own husband is as drunk as a skunk in Australia, all over the papers and plastered across social media.'

'Is that why you went out with my husband?'

'I didn't go out with Paul. He led me to believe that I got the contract to refurbish the pub on merit when the truth is it was because my competitors backed out. I was furious with him. We went for dinner and he apologised—'

'He told you about me?'

'Yes. He said he wanted to make things right with you.'

Sandra rubs her nose and fumbles for a tissue. Carmen waits while she blows her nose.

'It's on social media,' she says stuffing the dirty tissue in her pocket.

'So, I believe.'

'It says your husband is with a younger woman.'

'I know.' Carmen sighs.

Sandra looks around the shop as if seeing it for the first time. 'What are you doing here?'

'This is my business.' She opens her palms. 'For my sins.'

'So, you're staying here?'

'This is home.'

'Will you stay away from Paul?'

'I'm not working in the pub now, so I probably won't even see him.'

'No more dinners?'

'No.'

'Promise?'

'Yes.'

'I can't compete with you. You're beautiful.'

'You don't have to compete with anyone. It's you he wants.'

Sandra offers a wry smile and then without another word she turns on her heels and walks out of the door.

Carmen watches her though the window walking toward the pub until she disappears. She's closing the shop when her phone rings.

'Cammy?'

'Madre de Dios, Jack? Are you alright?'

'Yeah, sort of, what about you?'

'This had better be good.'

Chapter 14

She turns the closed sign on the door and sits at the small table at the back of the shop where she's been googling the developers. Her phone is placed closely to her ear.

'Well?'

'It's all a mess,' Jack says.

'Where are you?'

'In the hotel.'

She imagines him leaning against the wall with his head in his hands, utterly ashamed. 'Alone?'

'I've always been alone.'

The silence is even more profound because of the distance.

'I promise, Cammy,' he adds.

'So, what happened?'

'It's been awful. It's so rigorous. I've barely had a moment to myself. Training all day, every day for weeks on end. I'd forgotten how fit you had to be - and my knee is buggered.'

'Is that why you didn't phone me for three days after you left the show?'

'No... I was. Christ, Cammy! I've had a terrible time.'

'It didn't look like that. You were grinning like a chimpanzee sitting in the beach bar.'

'Look, it's not how it looks. It never is.' He sounds

exhausted. 'The thing is Shazzy and I—'

'Yes?'

'It isn't what you think.'

'I hope not.'

'She hated me.'

'What?'

'Yeah, she's a ball-breaker. She was pushing me deliberately. She wanted to be with the young singer from that group, whatshisname? But she got stuck with me.'

'It looked like you were enjoying it.'

'It's all for show, you know what it's like. She was furious. Really pissed off and she pushed me hard to punish me.'

'Is that why you got hammered?'

'Partly. It's all just too much, Cammy.' He sighs and she hears the disappointment in his voice. 'So, yeah, once the show was finished on Saturday, I went out with a couple of the tech guys. The ones behind the scenes that do lighting and stuff. We went to the casino and one thing led to another.'

'Casino?'

'I didn't lose much.'

'Oh, Jack.' Disappointment echoes in her voice.

'It's nothing like the last time. I just wanted to hide. No one knew me in there. It was dark, there was food and company and—'

'Drink,' Carmen whispers.

'Yeah.'

'But the picture I saw you were on the beach?'

'I went for an early swim and then some people recognised me and insisted I had a drink with them. And I didn't say no. Look, I'm sorry.'

'Oh, Jack. I don't know what to say. It's all over social

media.'

'I know, I know. I spoke to Simon.'

'What are you going to do now? Come home?'

He pauses before answering. 'There's no point. Home isn't home without you.'

'Come here, to Westbay?'

'I can't.'

'Why?'

'Well, the thing is, Simon says the damage is pretty bad and he's told me to lie low for a while. You know, in the hotel, room service. Watch films, rest up. Then I'll reappear next week looking great again, and I'll be off on my book tour.'

'So, you're still going ahead with that?'

'I need to. It's about the money, you know it is. I have to save our home.'

'It's a house.'

'Oh, I know that, Cammy. Don't be angry...'

'Where are you going?'

'I'll send you the itinerary but Simon's managed to change it around, so I'll start in New Zealand now and then work my way back to the UK, in sequence, just like the fireworks at New Year.' There's a hint of laughter in his voice.

'Okay.'

'What do you think?'

'You seem to have a plan.' She taps the table with her index finger.

'Yeah. What about you? How's it been?'

'Not too bad. The people in Harbour Street are great and they're looking out for me.'

'Good.'

'I like it here.'

'So, the shop's going well?'

'I've refurbished the local pub. Now I'm hoping to put in a tender for some show homes on a new development.'

'That's great.'

She wishes he'd show more enthusiasm for her life and work.

'Look, can we talk again tomorrow?' he asks. 'I'm knackered.'

'Well, now that you're not allowed out you'll have more time to phone me everyday.' She smiles and Jack laughs. She adds, 'We need to talk about Elena and Luis.'

'I'll speak to them. I'll sort it.'

'Please do,' she replies. 'Please do, Jack. They're not happy.'

* * *

At the end of the week Carmen arranges for Sheila's husband or one of her sons to collect the wallpaper. She has also sold Marjorie's two lamps and an ornate mirror. Miraculously, she also finds the contact details for the developers. She phones them and she's surprised to be put through to one of the Directors - Martin.

He sounds charming and friendly. 'I've seen your shop in Harbour Street. I hear you've done a great job on the pub,' he says.

She's slightly overwhelmed by his enthusiasm and friendliness. 'Thank you. I'd like the outline specs for the show homes and the details of what needs to be submitted?'

'You're cutting it a bit fine. The deadline is next week.'

'I can do it.'

'Great. Then I'd like to see your work and the ideas you

have.'

'And my competitors?' she asks.

There's a teasing smile in his reply. 'What about them?'

'Do I have a chance?'

'This is a level playing field. Why do you ask?'

'Only because I'm new in town and I don't want to do all the work only to find that I'd never have got the contract anyway.'

'You mean, that we might have already given a nod and a wink to another company?'

'Yes.'

'Then let me assure you, Ms. Bailey. That is certainly *not* the case.'

Carmen is thrilled and by the time she hangs up, she's confident, but also aware that she'll have to up her game. This is a serious business.

She stares at the package on the table. It arrived earlier and she doesn't want to open it. It's the size and shape of a book. It's important to Jack, but she doesn't want to read the revealing secrets inside. She certainly doesn't want to be reminded of the past.

Ben puts his head around the shop door. 'Hi, Carmen. Got any plans for tonight?'

Carmen raises a smile. 'I intend opening a bottle of wine. I just spoke to one of the developers and I'm going to submit my proposal for the show homes but I only have one week.'

Ben laughs. 'You'll do it. Come on, close up the shop. Amber insists that you come to the Bistro for dinner.'

* * *

Carmen sits at the bar eating mussels in creamy white wine

with fluffy chips, drinking a cold glass of Albariño.

Amber is supervising the restaurant from behind the bar and occasionally leaves to speak to a customer but then Carmen is free to process her own thoughts and enjoy the ambiance of the restaurant. The tension in her shoulders subsides and she eats slowly and with pleasure.

Amber returns behind the bar. 'I think Ben might see Luis next week when he's in London.'

'Really?'

'How's Luis getting on?'

'I've only had a few text messages so I'm hoping it's because he's happy and busy.'

'And, how's Jack?' Amber asks out of earshot from other customers.

'He's holed up in his hotel. Getting ready for his book launch next weekend.'

'Have you read it?'

Carmen smiles. 'Not yet.'

Amber looks surprised. 'Why?'

'Why should I? I was there, remember? It's all about his early years and mostly about his football career and his injuries. It all seems a long time ago now. I can hardly believe people are still interested.'

'Jack's very popular.'

Carmen swallows a plump, orange mussel and smiles. 'Sadly, he's known by this generation as a celebrity and not a footballer.'

'It must have been hard for him having to give it all up?'

'It was.'

'And you?'

'Of course.'

Amber smiles at her. 'But I haven't invited you here for an interrogation on your life.'

Carmen raises her eyebrows. 'Really?'

'No, my reason is much more devious.' She laughs. 'The Christmas committee is meeting next Friday night at the vicarage and as a shop owner I'd like to ask you along. I'd love your support for our annual Harbour Street festivities. It's the strangest of events and no year has ever been the same. Last year, Ben and I weren't around for it but I'm hoping to be re-elected.'

'I'll vote for you. Especially after eating this delicious dinner.'

'That's what I was hoping. Bribery and corruption usually works.'

'I thought you used to be a lawyer.' Carmen grins.

'I'm speaking from experience.' Amber laughs.

* * *

Sunday is spent working on the project. There are three sizes of houses and each of them a different layout. The designs have to be adaptable for each house type.

Martin's secretary sent her a plan of the units, so she has the measurements. She checks colours, fabrics and textures knowing she has to come up with something spectacular.

Later that evening, after a light supper, Carmen's eyes begin to tire. She closes her laptop and reaches for the brown padded envelope. She removes the book from the packaging and stares at the cover.

Jack's Boots.

There are two superimposed images on the cover: one of the

West Ham stadium and the other of Jack's old football boots. Memories spring to life in her hand.

They were different people then. They had a different life. They had dreams and hopes and aspirations. Jack had craved fame while Carmen had wanted a family. Her children are still her proudest achievement.

On the back cover are five testimonials from authors, sports commentators and managers, but Carmen doesn't read them. Instead, she puts the book on the table and ignores it.

* * *

Jack phones her early on Monday morning. It's become their new routine that they speak each day before she works.

'Did you get the book?'

'Yes.'

'What do you think?'

'Great.'

'Did you read it?'

'Not yet.'

'Are you going to read it?'

'One day.'

'I'm swimming in the hotel pool,' he says.

'Thanks for the picture. You're looking much better.'

'Another week of this and all will be well. It's all died down here. What about over there?'

'It's all fine.' She tells him about her designs for the show homes.

'Send me a picture. It's hard for me to imagine.'

Carmen is pleased he's taking a genuine interest. After she comes off the phone, she's about to send her current ideas but there's an incoming call.

'Elena? Hola cariño. How are you, my darling?'

'I'm coming to see you.'

'Wonderful,' Carmen says automatically but already tensing. 'When?'

'Tomorrow.'

'Lovely. What a surprise! I'll make up the spare room.'

'Do you mean Luis' room?'

'Well, it's his when he's here but when he's not it's a guest room.'

'So, I'm a guest?'

Carmen takes a breath and smiles. 'My darling, you are family. My daughter. And I'm really looking forward to seeing you.'

'My plane gets in at three, so I'll be there about five.'

'I'll book a restaurant.'

'I'm flying in from Mumbai, so I'll be knackered. Can we have a takeaway?'

'Of course.'

'Hasta mañana, Mama.'

* * *

The following day, Carmen's project plans get shelved while she reorganises the flat. She hasn't bothered to employ a cleaner and she's found it strangely liberating to clean up and tidy each day. There's no one in her home to make it dirty. She makes up the double bed, puts fluffy towels in the bathroom, stocks the fridge and buys wine. She might even cook - depending on Elena, her mood and what she wants to eat.

Time seems to drag slowly. Carmen can't concentrate. She's excited about seeing Elena. Perhaps she should have offered to collect her.

She closes the shop early and waits upstairs looking constantly out of the window but there's no sign of her daughter. She opens her laptop and searches for flight arrivals from Mumbai. The three o'clock arrival is delayed until ten that evening. Carmen waits, unable to concentrate, in a state of limbo. Eventually her phone rings at eleven.

'Mama? The flight was delayed eight hours.'

'Are you okay?'

'Of course, but I won't make it tonight and now I won't have time before my next flight. My rota is rotten at the moment. I'll try and see you next week.'

'Alright.'

'Sorry, Mama. I'm really tired. I have to sleep. I'll call you.'

Carmen walks around the empty flat feeling let down and disillusioned. She knows it's not Elena's fault, but she had been so looking forward to seeing her. She wants to know that Elena is okay and that she's happy and that she's looking forward to the wedding. She hasn't mentioned it since she said she didn't want Jack there, but Carmen can't even begin to think about the wedding arrangements even though it's only five weeks away. There's so much going on.

Everyone is too busy.

Carmen undresses and removes her wig. Her hair has grown and now it sticks to her scalp in long, shapeless tufts with bald patches, like a barren dessert with scraggly patches of unruly tumble weed. Her face looks older at night without makeup and Carmen stares back into the sad eyes reflected in the mirror.

'Who are you?' she asks silently. 'Are you an imposter? Where's Carmen?'

* * *

While waiting for Elena, and being unable to concentrate, her project is behind schedule. She's sent photos to Jack who is now bored in the hotel and actually has time to look at them. Unfortunately, he gives her negative feedback.

It's a bit boring! A bit safe! Too mediocre for you!

Although she's annoyed with him. Carmen agrees. She needs to take a much bigger risk. She needs to do something bold and exciting so that they will remember her design.

She takes the bird-printed wallpaper sample upstairs to the flat and using a feature wall in the lounge for the show house she works her colour scheme around the various tropical birds.

On Thursday morning she's finished her designs and she sends them to Jack. She's excited by his reply.

Bright and bold! Perfect! You've nailed it baby. Talk soon xx

Carmen stays busy in the shop all day but something is niggling her. It had been annoying getting Jack's feedback, but she appreciates his honesty and she trusts his judgement.

But what if the developers didn't understand her thinking? Although the mood board is effective, how could they get a sense of what the actual rooms look like?

It's early evening when she searches the Internet looking for a design expert who will transform her drawings into 3D images. She needs pictures from different angles, so it looks as if you're walking through each room. That way, the developers will have a more immersive experience of the individual rooms.

She begins a live chat and the conversation goes backwards and forwards. Krish lives in India and he understands perfectly what she needs.

I need it now, she types.

I'll work with you and not stop until it's done. He messages back.

She sends him her designs and he converts them to 3D walk through images, but although they look good, and she's excited, some of the accessories she's chosen aren't perfect.

She sends different images for him to change: cushions, bed covers and chairs that are shaped better for each room. After six hours, Krish goes quiet.

Are you there? She types, stretching her neck and shoulders, checking her watch.

He replies after the longest ten minutes. *It's four in the morning here. I needed some water.*

She sends him more examples of different wallpaper, lamps and cushions for him to insert. She views the rooms from all angles using the light to create space and an illusion of the tropics. Then she has another idea. For another room: an underwater theme. She finds the pictures and uploads them to Krish. She instructs him where to put them and how to rearrange the furniture. He sends back a sample, and they continue working until the early hours of the morning in Westbay. It's eight in the morning in Mumbai when the final images are finished. She's excited and happy but also exhausted.

I can't thank you enough, Krish. She types and when she pays his invoice she adds a generous tip.

She sleeps for a few hours and is woken by Jack's phone call.

'Hello, sleepy,' he whispers. 'I've arrived in Auckland.'

'What? Already?' Carmen rubs her face and runs her fingers through her straggly hair. She's a complete mess and very groggy. Then she remembers Jack is starting his book tour.

'When is your first book signing?' she asks, throwing back the duvet.

'Saturday, but I'm here a day early as Simon wants some shots of me looking fitter and happier.'

'Great.'

'Did you see the final book cover? They changed it'

'Not yet.'

'I sent it to you a few minutes ago. Simon said the editors wanted to change it so they swapped a hazy image of my football boots and an old picture of West Ham stadium to a picture of just me.

'I'll look now.'

'No worries. I'll get him to send you a new hard copy. Gotta go. I just want to wish you good luck for today. I know what it means to you, Cammy.'

'Thanks, Jack.'

'Te quiero, I love you, baby.'

'Te quiero, cariño.'

* * *

Carmen delivers her presentation at two o'clock at the developers' office.

Martin is much younger than he sounds on the telephone,

probably early thirties. He has a casual demeanour and he wears a neat, grey suit and a warm smile.

She brings up her designs on a large screen in their boardroom. 'The wallpaper I've used consists not only of tropical birds but also underwater fish, pretty shoals of stingrays and everyone's favourite - smiling dolphins.'

There are four people present and although she's been allotted thirty minutes there are many questions and they seem genuinely interested in her 3D designs.

They appear surprised at the level of detail that she's included. 'There are matching colours in the aquamarine sofas, glass vases and glass coffee tables. It's high-end, imaginative and extremely original,' she adds.

As she comes to the end of her presentation, she spies Sandrine and George driving into the car park outside. She takes a breath then returns her attention to her audience and smiles.

'All of the designs are variable. I have used tropical birds and an underwater theme but there are more variations of animals, woodlands and beach scenes if you felt that a sea theme is more relevant.'

One of the ladies asks. 'What's the quality of the wallpaper like? Is it easy to hang?'

'I believe it's a very good quality. Judging from these samples,' Martin replies, rubbing the sample fabric between his fingers.

'Everything is high end. But, in this presentation folder that I'm leaving with you there are three furniture packages: white wood, mahogany and oak. The cost is reflected in the quality of the product so the buyer won't be intimidated by the price. It reflects a choice based on taste, rather than cost.'

Martin smiles.

After the presentation he walks with her to the door.

Sandrine and George are waiting in the reception. They wave and she smiles at them then she turns back to Martin.

'I forgot to ask. Do you know when you might have a decision?'

He grins. 'If we can all agree, hopefully in the next week or so. They need to be finished by the 20th of December.'

'Are you expecting a rush before Christmas?' Carmen smiles.

'Lots of people come and visit families here. Statistics tell us that many people make major decisions at Christmas time. You know the sort of thing. Let's move. Let's have a dog or a baby—'

'Let's get divorced.'

Martin laughs. 'Absolutely. Having been through it, I wouldn't wish that on anyone. But Christmas is the time when people often reevaluate their lives and decide what they want or don't want and that often involves moving or buying a home.'

'I'm sorry you've been through it.'

Martin smiles. 'I might get a dog this Christmas. Probably much less hassle.'

* * *

Walking back to the shop, Carmen crosses the square and is distracted by movement near the church. The doors are open and out of curiosity she steps inside.

It's been many months since she been into God's House. This is where Frances is vicar. There must have been a lunch or coffee morning as a few ladies are still whispering in the corner as they clean up.

Carmen strides down the aisle to the altar. She crosses herself and finds a candle to light. She says a prayer and leaves a pound coin. On her way out, she remembers that it's the Christmas Committee meeting at the vicarage that evening.

She's about to open her shop when Tracey hails her from across the road. She isn't quick enough to pretend she didn't see or hear her so she waits impatiently for Tracey to walk over.

'What have I done?' Tracey asks.

'I don't know what you mean?'

'Luis isn't texting me.'

Carmen smiles. 'Join the group.'

'It's not funny. It's rude.'

'I think they're busy. They're settling in and making new friends.' Carmen opens the door eager to escape.

'You don't like me, do you?' Tracey asks.

'I don't know you.' Carmen tries to hide her distaste.

'I know you don't!'

Carmen shrugs. 'I've got a phone call to make.'

* * *

The vicarage is charming. There's the same vibe, quaint English, chintz sofas, fire in the hearth, lots of books and warm lamps as there was in Marjorie's home.

'It will probably be noisy later with all the fireworks,' Frances says by way of greeting. 'Let me get you a glass of wine.'

Derek the butcher and Ian the grocer are both already

nursing glasses of red wine.

'Tommy is looking after Coral,' Jane says to Carmen as she sits beside her. 'He took her in last year. She was tied up outside the pet shop.'

'That was kind of him.'

Luke and Mario who are sitting side by side on the opposite sofa, remember the incident well.

'He was such a cute puppy.'

'We didn't want to give him up.'

'A dog wouldn't fit in with our lifestyle.'

They're interrupted as Amber and Ben then Eva and Sanjay arrive. They all agree that the puppy was and still is - very cute.

Frances bustles around offering wine or tea and when the door opens again, there are exclamations of delight when Yusef and Ozan appear.

'This is a surprise!' exclaims Frances.

'It's about time.' Ben laughs. 'It's only been four years since our first meeting!'

Yusef grins and struts across the room wiggling his hips suggestively. 'We are here, guys. The main team is here now. Me and my bro' Ozan are about to spice things up! Things are goin' to be buzzin' this Christmas in Harbour Street.'

Ozan grins and shakes his head in fake exasperation and Carmen smiles as the energy in the room escalates.

'Right,' says Amber. 'I think we're ready. Who's missing?'

'Tracey bought the salon from Pamela last year so she might come.' Frances checks her list. 'She changed the name from Step Ahead to Beauty Salon.'

'So original.' Yusef claps while raising his eyes to the ceiling.

'Marion's missing,' calls Derek. 'Although she'd have a

cheek showing her face after last year.'

Frances looks up. 'Her cousin is running the boutique. But I checked. She's not coming.'

'Kit and Jenna.' Ben rubs his hands together. 'They've taken the kids to the bonfire party but they've given me their vote.'

The doorbell chimes and within a few minutes Tracey bustles in. Once again, the atmosphere in the room changes. She pushes past everyone, without a hello, and plonks herself on a seat at the table. 'I'm a shop owner this year,' she says loudly. 'I'm allowed to vote.'

'You can indeed, Tracey. Welcome!' Frances smiles. 'Everyone is very welcome. Let's get the first thing out of the way. 'Let's elect the Committee Chairperson. I suggest Amber. Are there any other suggestions?'

There are nods of agreements. 'No.'

'Let's vote all vote for Amber,' cries Yusef.

'Is there anyone else who wants to be it?' Tracey looks around the room.

'No!' Jane's face clouds over. 'Let's not mess around after last years' fiasco, Tracey.' She stares meaningfully. 'It was a disaster last year and Carmen, if you want to know more you'll find it all over social media.'

Carmen smiles. 'Thanks. But, for various reasons I'm not a fan of social media. I'm also happy to vote for Amber.'

Yusef whoops and pats her amicably on the shoulder.

Frances nods. 'Good. That's settled. Over to you Amber.'

Amber smiles. 'Thanks everyone. I won't let you down. Firstly, welcome Carmen to your first Christmas in Harbour Street.' There's a smattering of applause and Carmen smiles. 'The idea of this meeting is to get organised so that we do something special this year for the locals and also for the numerous visitors. Harbour Street thrives on people spending money and I believe we all want to build on this each year. After our initial investment of Christmas lights a few years ago, this reduces the cost of whatever it is we decide to do this year. So, I'll open it up now and ask for suggestions.'

There's a pause before Sanjay speaks. 'Do we have a date?'

'Probably the first weekend of December. Let's have a show of hands?'

Amber makes a note. 'Great that's decided. That's the first weekend in December. We can easily get our marketing materials printed and distributed by then. Now some ideas, please...'

'Christmas market.'

'Carols'

'Snow machine.'

'Santa on motorbikes,' adds Yusef. 'I loved that.' Everyone laughs at his enthusiasm.

'Will Kit be Santa?' asks Derek.

'He said he would,' Ben confirms.

'We need a theme.' Amber frowns. We need something a little bit special and different this year.

The room falls silent.

Tracey says, 'I could make up some beauty products in pretty bags to sell.'

Amber nods and makes a note. 'Good.'

'We can all do individual things to promote our own shop but what about something together?' Jane says.

'A raffle?' suggests Eva.

'Good idea but it's not really a theme.'

Jane leans forward and speaks quietly, 'I have a suggestion.' She makes sure she has everyone's attention before continuing. 'After the events of last year, I've been very appreciative of all of you here in Harbour Street. You all know that Tommy and I—'

Yusef whistles and everyone laughs.

'Tommy and I are grateful to you all. And we've come up with an idea. With the help of the fishermen, and with the advice of the RNLI, Santa could arrive by sea. I know this doesn't actually take place in Harbour Street but a few years ago we used the art gallery as Santa's grotto and that worked really well. So, if Santa arrives in the harbour, he could bring everyone - all the children and families - with him back into Harbour Street.'

'Like the Pied Piper?' says Yusef clapping excitedly.

'I love that idea,' says Frances.

Amber smiles. 'Brilliant!'

Jane continues, 'I will bear all of those costs as a thank you to all of you for last Christmas.'

There are protests. 'You don't need to do that.' 'It's not necessary.' But Jane holds up her hand. 'Tommy and I insist.'

They spend a few happy minutes going over the details and then Tracey speaks up.

'I think we should aim to get it all out on social media. That's what will make people come here to Westbay. If we take videos, add reels and posts we can post it all on TikTok.'

Jane shakes her head.

Ozan frowns warily.

Yusef looks unsure.

'After last year, we need to be careful that we're not crushed with the wrong sort of people.' Amber looks at Tracey. 'We want families and children here. People have to feel safe.'

Tracey glares at her but everyone agrees and as the meeting

begins to close Carmen stands up. She wants to make a quick exit. She's exhausted from the presentation earlier and she wants a hot bath.

'Thank you, Amber,' she says making her way to the door. 'Bye Frances, bye everyone. Thanks for including me this year.'

Tracey's voice is loud behind her. 'What's wrong with social media? I think it's a good idea. And why don't we get Jack Bailey onboard for Christmas now that his wife lives here.'

'That's an idea,' agrees Derek. 'I watched him a few times at West Ham.'

Carmen turns around slowly.

The room is still.

'I'm sorry. That's not an option,' she speaks quietly and firmly.

'I don't see why?' Tracey says. 'This is a community. This is Harbour Street, and we all give what we can. Why can't he be involved?' Tracey stands up and faces her.

Carmen's cheeks begin to redden at the deliberate challenge. She hates any form of public confrontation and she holds her breath before replying quietly.

'Jack's away on a book tour.'

'He could do some social media posts for us. You can do them anywhere in the world.' Tracey's smile is smug.

'For various reasons, neither Jack nor I like social media.'

'Well, he's always on it. Preening and posing with young girls - or maybe it's because you've separated and he's not coming here for Christmas...?'

'That's none of your business,' Amber interrupts quickly.

Tracey continues, 'Maybe you and your family are too stuck up for this town. Luis is a user, and he dresses like he's looking for attention - all that makeup. He looks like a tart! That's what happened that night he was attacked. Luis provoked those blokes and that's why they beat him up.'

'Tracey!' Jane shouts.

Amber grabs her but she won't shut up.

Tracey pulls her arm roughly away, her voice growing louder. 'You walk around town with your nose stuck in the air. You're sleeping with Paul, and you think you're above everyone else because you think you're still a top model and you're perfect but you're not, you're a...'

Carmen raises her hand and shakes her index finger. Her accent growing stronger. 'It's people like you who ruin lives. It was you who posted an innocent picture of me and Paul having dinner last week. It's caused him terrible problems. His poor wife Sandra is very upset! You should be ashamed of yourself.' She turns away, her shoulders straight, her head held high. Carmen's almost at the front door when Tracey's voice floats over her shoulder:

'You're not a nice person. You're cold. You have no feelings and that's why Jack's consoling himself with a younger, sexier woman in Australia.'

Carmen calls over her shoulder. 'And that's why you can't trust social media because people like you twist the truth then call everyone else liars. Get a life, Tracey.' She raises her chin in defiance, angry and humiliated.

There's a scuffle behind her. Suddenly there's a sharp pain between her shoulders as she's shoved forward. She hits her head on the door frame and then it all happens in slow motion; Tracey pulls on her hair and rips the wig from her head. Instinctively Carmen raises her hands to cover herself. Her wig is dangling from Tracey's fingers. The shocked faces of the people in the room adds to the deathly silence as they all stare aghast.

Flinging open the front door, Carmen propels herself out of the house and she begins running down the street with tears streaming down her cheeks.

Chapter 15

It's eight o'clock in the morning when Jack phones but Carmen doesn't answer. Instead, she burrows her head under the duvet. The scene from last night is still replaying itself over and over, in slow motion, on repeat as it has all night. She registers the individual shock on each persons' face and like most memories, Carmen fills in the missing pieces, exaggerating reactions and making up snatches of conversation so that multiple voices are now buzzing in her head.

There's a knock on the front door. She stiffens, gripping the duvet tighter around her neck.

Her phone rings but she doesn't answer it.

It pings with a message.

She ignores it.

The front doorbell rings again.

She throws on a dressing gown. Although she has another wig, she can't bear the thought that everyone knows. She looks in the mirror and her eyes are swollen. Dark circles cover her hollow eyes and her nose is mottled and red. She looks old.

She wanders into the kitchen and puts on the kettle.

Her phone pings repeatedly.

She picks it up. There is one message after another with the same text every few seconds - all from Amber.

The first message reads:

I'm sitting on your doorstep and not moving until you answer.

Ping.

Still here.

Ping.

Still here.

Carmen glances out of the window into the alleyway and her front door.

Amber waves up at her. 'Let me in, Carmen. Please!'

She ignores her. She makes coffee and sits on the sofa. She's outlasted the media for years so this is nothing. She's hidden behind her home, her gates, inside the palatial prison of her London house on so many occasions that this will be easy by comparison. Amber will give up soon.

She sips her coffee.

Ping.

I'm your friend. xx

Carmen wipes her eyes.

Ping.

I'm your friend. xx

Carmen finds steely resolve and stares at the feature wall.

Ping.

It's bloody freezing out here. I'm turning into an ice statue.

Ping

Throw a bucket of hot water over me?

Carmen stands up and flings open the window. 'Go away, Amber.'

'Let me in.'

Carmen sighs. 'Why?'

'I told you.'

'You're not my friend.'

'It's bloody freezing out here!'

'Go home.'

'And I thought Ben was stubborn. He'll be thrilled you're much worse than him. Come on, open up!'

Carmen grins. 'Oh... okay. Hang on.'

* * *

Carmen opens the front door. As she climbs the stairs she's aware of Amber's eyes on her scruffy hair poking out of her head. In the lounge Carmen turns to face her. 'There, now you've seen me without my wig, as have the whole street, you can all laugh.'

Amber shakes her head and pushes past her to the kitchen. 'No one is laughing, Carmen. Come on, where do you hide the coffee? I need to thaw out.'

Carmen's shoulders ease and her stomach stops contracting in nervous cramps.

'I thought Ben was bad!' Amber grumbles. 'It took months for him to trust me.'

'But he did in the end?'

'Yes. And for good reason.' Amber's voice softens. 'I hope you'll be as sensible.'

They take their coffee to the lounge and sit companionably on the sofa.

'So?' asks Carmen. 'I bet they all thought it was funny.'

'Would you? If it had happened to me?'

Carmen frowns. 'No, of course not.'

'Exactly.'

'But—'

'But what? Because it's not the same? Because I wasn't a top model or married to a famous football celebrity?'

'Well, no—'

'Does that make it more powerful because of your public image? Or would it be just as awful for anyone?'

Carmen sips her coffee. Slowly she says, 'It's awful for anyone. I had breast cancer.'

Amber's voice softens. 'I'm sorry,' she pauses. 'But that's like so many, many women. You're amazing, Carmen. You should be very proud of yourself coping the way you do.'

Carmen inhales deeply. 'When you're in the public eye there's often an image that goes with it. I admire the celebrities who go public. The ones who share all and bare all but I'm not like them.'

'You don't have to be.'

'Unless you've lived in the public eye and your life has been scrutinised, analysed, and then picked apart - you wouldn't understand.'

'Tracey might argue that Jack looks for publicity.'

Carmen's nostrils flare. 'Jack might, but never me.'

'Ah.' Amber sits silently digesting the information then she asks, 'Are you alright, health wise?'

'Fortunately, yes.'

'Good. I'm pleased.'

Carmen stares at her coffee. She's never spoken to anyone about her breast cancer before. 'I'm a very private person,' she explains. 'I didn't speak to anyone. I didn't want to worry my mother or sister.'

'But you had nurses?'

'I didn't speak to them because sadly, everyone has a price.'

'Price?'

'People sell stories.'

Amber smiles. 'Not me.'

Carmen stares silently into her coffee before answering. 'I've never really had many friends... I've been self-sufficient in that way. I think that's why it's been so hard for Luis and Elena. They take after me. They're very private. We're all paranoid about people finding out about us.'

'Finding what out?'

'Personal details. About us. The fact that we are very ordinary.'

'It must be hard.' Amber stretches out her legs and crosses her ankles. 'To live in the public eye.'

'When I was diagnosed my life fell apart. I didn't want to tell Jack. Not because I thought he would leave me, but probably - more vainly - because I was frightened he wouldn't be attracted to me anymore. Then when I did tell him he was incredible. Supportive and kind. I don't know what I would have done without him. After the operation we agreed that I'd get a wig and that things would be back to normal, but...'

'But?'

'Well, I didn't feel like me. Even before the mastectomy, I changed. Thinking about death, losing my family, not breathing, not being here with them to share their lives. I was frightened. And it was this fear that brought us all closer. After that initial diagnosis, when your life is literally in the hands of the experts and you're at God's mercy I realised what was important to me. And I didn't like what I saw.'

'What did you see?'

'I saw a vain and empty woman who indulged her spoilt husband and children. And, I didn't like her.'

Amber regards Carmen over her coffee mug. 'What changed?'

'I love my family. We've led a privileged life. Jack earned lots of money. But it wasn't about any of that. I realised that I'd given up my modelling career for Jack and to have a family. And, when I thought I might die, I regretted all the things I hadn't done - for me. How selfish is that?'

'That's not selfish. They were just choices you made at the time and then suddenly you look up and think where did those years go? What about me?'

Carmen blinks rapidly. 'You understand?'

'Of course.'

'It's not as if the children are small or Jack needs me now. If I died, Elena would still work as cabin crew. Luis would still go to university and Jack would still look for celebrity work.'

Amber grins. 'I think they would miss you.'

Carmen smiles. 'Claro, of course - but they would move on. They all have a purpose, and I decided that if I lived, then I too would have a purpose. I needed to be free.'

'Free?'

'Well, I had to give them all the opportunity to live without me so that I could be selfish. For Elena and Luis their lives would continue but it was Jack I had to set free. So, I decided against reconstructive surgery. I told him I didn't want a bit of plastic shoved under my pectoral muscle.'

'That's a bit harsh, isn't it?'

'The oncoplastic surgeon said immediate construction may help me move on with my life more quickly. I could have used parts of my own body - they could mould a new breast from fat - normally the tummy - but I felt that breasts were sexualising who I was, so I told Jack about Kintsugi. It's the Japanese art of putting broken pottery back together with gold.'

Amber nods. 'Ben was in Tokyo before I met him and he experimented with that type of art.'

'I told Jack that my scar would be a flaw, and this imperfection would make me more beautiful. I lied to him. It's a philosophy, I suppose, rather than art, but I hoped that Jack would find it repulsive and that he wouldn't want me. I wanted to free him. I wanted him to leave me. But he didn't.'

'That plan backfired then.' Amber smiles. 'I think I like Jack.'

'He even loved me when I paraded my ugly body in front of him, when I was bald and then when my hair started growing back in these ugly tufts and I was too embarrassed to get it cut. So, it turned out that it was me who left in the end.'

'You left?'

'I wanted to follow my dream. I'd furnished many properties, some that we'd owned and I loved it. I'd designed so many interiors and it's what made me happy. I had a purpose other than being a model at an early age, then wife, and then mother. I could learn and teach myself things and I realised I could evolve as a person. I'd always harboured a dream that I could live anonymously by the sea and that I could have my own interior design shop. I wanted to make my dreams happen instead of sitting back and watching everyone else fulfil theirs,' she pauses. 'You must think I'm an awful person?'

Amber smiles. 'So, far so good. You're pretty normal.'

'I'm a terrible wife.'

'No worse than many other women.'

'But think about it.' Carmen is agitated. Amber isn't understanding how awful she really is. 'Knowing I was going to live. Knowing I had survived cancer - instead of looking after Jack and being with my husband - I chose to move away.'

'But you love him.'

'Yes, of course.'

'Then think of it as a new beginning. It's like a building and after it's built the concrete settles and cracks appear. It doesn't make it a terrible house. Cracks can be repaired or they just become part of the character of the house, and everyone learns to live with them.'

'Yes but—'

'What I'm saying Carmen is that after your diagnosis and treatment - it's life changing. Everyone behaves differently and given your lifestyle and restrictions, I'd say it's quite normal that you feel this way.'

'Really?'

'Yes.'

'But I feel so ashamed. I'm an imposter in my own body.'

Amber shrugs. 'Are you still in touch with Jack?'

'Everyday.'

Amber laughs. 'Then that's more than most wives after they've separated.'

'I don't want a separation. I love Jack. But I can't lead his life anymore. I can't live in a perfect home that has no soul. It was a prison.'

'You don't strike me as the sort of person who wallows in the past or wants people to feel sorry for them.'

'I don't!'

'Good. So, what are we going to do?'

Carmen shrugs. She can't think about her missing wig or Tracey or the reaction of the people in Harbour Street. 'Carry on, I suppose. Pretend it never happened?'

Amber smiles and leans forward. 'I have a better idea.'

Carmen blinks quickly taken aback by Amber's radiant smile. 'You have a very pretty face and I'll be honest. Short hair suits you much better than that long wig.'

Carmen tugs at the ugly strands plastered to her head. 'It's a mess. I didn't want to go to a hairdresser. I felt too ashamed. I don't care that I'm ugly to look at.'

'You're certainly not ugly. Will you let me help you?'

'How?'

'Will you trust me?'

Carmen shrugs and Amber laughs.

'Well, let's be honest, Carmen. You haven't anything to lose right now, have you?'

* * *

Carmen watches Amber texting. Her fingers fly over the keys, then as agreed, she goes upstairs and showers. When she comes downstairs, Yusef is sitting on her sofa. She holds her hands to her head self-consciously. 'What's he doing here?'

Yusef smiles. 'Hello, Carmen. I've washed your wig for you.' He nods at her false hair all brushed, cleaned and gleaming. 'I had to wrestle it off Tracey,' he jokes.

'I asked him to come here,' Amber says. 'He's the best hairdresser you'll ever meet and he's brilliantly creative for people with short hair. He has flair and creativity—'

Yusef laughs and holds up his palm. 'Now, now, my beautiful Amber. Don't get carried away girl or I'll begin to think you fancy me.'

'Dream on.' Amber nudges him and winks.

Yusef turns his attention to Carmen. His voice is serious and his tone practical and caring. 'I'm sorry that Tracey did that to you, but to be honest, I think she's done you a favour. Look at you! You're a dark horse. You're absolutely beautiful.'

Yusef moves around her studying her cheeks, her nose, her lips and then her hair. 'So, you gorgeous lady. You have two choices.' He smiles. 'You can put on that boring, old-fashioned wig or I can transform you into the ravishing beauty that you deserve to be.'

Carmen laughs. 'You really do have all the chat, Yusef.'

'I can see what Shelley sees in you,' agrees Amber.

'Calm down ladies. It's just as well I'm spoken for and that I'm madly in love. Now, let me get my scissors.'

Chapter 16

Yusef cuts Carmen's hair short and he gives her a fringe that sweeps across her forehead making her smoky eyes look large and alluring.

'Once I cut off the dead ends, it's quite long in places,' he says looking at her closely. 'Some of it is actually quite thick,' he adds.

'The grey strands have all disappeared,' Amber says.

'They're still there.' Carmen leans toward the mirror for a closer look.

'Very few,' agrees Yusef. 'But baby, we can add colour. Any colour you like. You can be as funky as you want.' He stands back to admire his handiwork and points with his comb to her discarded wig. 'It's better than that old style. It's taken years off you.'

'Do you think?' Carmen peers more closely at the stranger staring back at her. She's trying to get used to the younger looking woman in the reflection - if only she'd stop frowning and looking so serious.

'Smile!' orders Amber.

Carmen bares her teeth and they all laugh. But magically, Carmen's smile transforms her face. The worry lines disappear and the anxiety in her eyes fades.

'That's the secret, baby. Smile more!' Yusef claps his hands in delight and begins to pack up his hairdressing bag. 'You're going to be the biggest hit in Harbour Street.'

'Thank you, Yusef. What do I owe you?' Carmen asks, reaching for her purse.

'Nothing my beauty Queen. Although I will ask that when you see me or think of me - that you smile. That will be payment enough.'

'Don't be crazy.' Carmen laughs.

Before leaving Yusef kisses her on the cheek. 'Now, you need to walk around town with your head held high. Show everyonc how truly beautiful you are.'

'He's got a point.' Amber picks up her coat. 'Come on, let's go for a walk. We need some fresh air.'

Suddenly, Carmen doesn't feel so confident. In the confines and security of her home she's feeling more comfortable but going outside was a very different matter.

'We need to show you off. Let's give all the people in Harbour Street the chance to help you get over your embarrassment. They'll be cheering you on.' Amber waits patiently.

'Maybe not today.'

Amber holds out her hand. 'Give me your phone. I'm taking a photo and you can send it to Jack.'

'I don't know what he'll say.'

'It's too late for him to say anything. Smile!' She snaps a few photos then hands the camera back to Carmen.

'Come on.' Amber selects a jacket from the hook and holds it out. 'We'll start with Ben and then work our way down the street. Eva wanted to come with me this morning. She's very protective of you and I thought Jane was going to punch Tracey.' Amber laughs.

'That's the last thing I'd want to happen.'

'The worst is over. What more can anyone find to write about?'

Carmen pulls on her jacket. Amber is right. The worst is over.

They walk along Harbour Street as if they have a purpose in mind and at first people don't recognise her.

'Wow! You were beautiful before but now you look amazing,' says Eva.

'I love it!' Ben smiles.

'Out of everything bad comes something good.' Frances beams at her. 'You look so much better - happier.'

'Beautiful, says Sanjay.

'Stunning,' cries Jane. 'I'm so proud of Yusef.'

'He's done an incredible job,' agrees Shelly. 'You look amazing.'

At the RNLI station Femi's mouth falls open. 'Gosh! You look so young and gorgeous.'

With growing confidence Carmen's soul is restored and invigorated and she spends the rest of the day sorting out Marjorie's soft furnishings and rearranging the shop.

Jack phones out of the blue and she's pleased to hear from him.

'Did you see the picture, I sent?' she asks him.

'Yeah.'

'What do you think?'

'When were you going to tell me about that bloke?'

'What bloke?'

'The one you were having dinner with?'

'Paul? Have you only just seen it? It wasn't a date. I was furious with him. Besides we spent most of the evening talking about his relationship with his wife.'

Jack sighs loudly. 'Is that why you had your hair cut?'

Carmen laughs. 'No! It's because Tracey from the Beauty Salon across the road got angry with me and she pulled my wig off—'

'What?'

'I was at the Christmas committee meeting and—'

'Look, we need to think about Christmas and Elena's wedding. She said she's coming to see you this week. Can you try and talk her out of marrying that plonker?'

'How?'

'I don't know. Have a chat with her. You know, women's talk. Tell her marriage is rubbish and that it's not worth it.'

'Isn't it? Is that what you believe after all these years?'

'No, no, I don't!'

'Good.'

'I'm not talking about us, Cammy. We're different. We understand each other, but it's bloody hard work sometimes.'

Carmen smiles. 'I'll speak to Elena, but I won't tell her *not* to get married. She must decide the same as we did. It's her life. Anyway, tell me, how's the book tour going?'

They spend a while talking about his book signing. They're talking as friends, and she's interested in Jack and how it's all going. Afterwards, she wonders if she's more relaxed because she can now finally be herself. Maybe her wig was a metaphor for hiding her real character - her real thoughts and her real personality. She has no idea what journey she's on, but as she falls asleep, she sighs deeply. Her heart is much lighter as if some of her darker emotions have taken flight. Somehow, she's managed to take a big step closer to becoming the person she's always been destined to be.

* * *

Elena arrives on Tuesday evening. 'I'm a bit jet lagged. I'm just back from Tokyo.' She kisses her mother on both cheeks and Carmen resists the urge to hang on to her daughter and smother her in a hug.

She has dusty-blonde hair, like Jack, but neatly tied in a ponytail, showing off the long nose and broad forehead she shares with her father, Elena is smaller than Carmen, but her shoulders are broader. She's still wearing her smart navy and maroon uniform.

Elena steps back to look more closely at her mother. 'Your wig's gone?'

'Do you like it?'

Elena frowns. 'It doesn't look like you yet. You've always had long hair.'

'It makes a change for me.' Carmen smiles and touches the back of her head, but Elena turns abruptly. 'Would you like a shower? Tea? Dinner? Drink?'

'So, this is home now, is it?' Elena wanders around the flat picking up a vase and looking at a purple orchid with intensity. 'It's very small.'

'It's not that bad.' Carmen laughs. It's past seven o'clock, so she pours a glass of Rioja. 'Wine?'

Elena nods. 'I see you have Papi's book. Have you read it?'

'No. Not yet.'

'You have the new cover version? It's a good picture of Papi but it looks like it's been airbrushed. He looks ten years younger in this photo.' She turns the book over in her hands to look at the back cover. 'Thank God they got rid of his awful boots.'

'Yes.'

Elena places it back onto the side table. 'Will you read it?'

'Probably.' Carmen hands her a wine glass. 'Salud, my darling. It's so lovely to see you cariño.'

'Salud.' Elena won't look at her. She gazes at the sage wall and the sash window. 'I thought it would be... I don't know... different.'

Carmen frowns. 'It's homely, no?'

'It's above a shop, Mama. You live above a shop.'

'Sí, my darling. Yes, but the shop is mine too.'

Elena sits and crosses her legs. 'This isn't right. How are you managing here when you could be at home?'

'This is home.'

Elena shakes her head. 'Luis warned me but they were complimentary by comparison.'

Carmen regards her daughter thinking how easily she referred to Luis as they, if only she could teach Jack.

'I'm settling in well and I like it here. I've refurbished the pub - we can go and have a drink there later if you like and you can see what I've done.'

Elena sips her wine and stares at the floor.

Carmen continues, 'I'm making some lovely friends. One of them owns Harbour Bistro and she's saved a table for us for tonight, but only if you'd like to go out. I also have chicken if you prefer to stay at home?'

'I'll have to shower.' Elena puts her glass on the table. 'Show me my room, and where the bathroom is, and I'll be ready in thirty minutes.'

* * *

The pub is busy and Paul does a double take when he sees Carmen.

'I didn't recognise you.' He smiles.

'This is my daughter, Elena.'

Elena beams at him. It's her professional smile. One that she saves for passengers. It's a smile that Carmen knows well. It doesn't quite reach her eyes.

He pours them two glasses of wine.

'Do you like the pub?' Carmen asks after Paul walks away and they've settled near the fire.

'It's nice. It's got a good vibe to it.' Elena looks around.

'I think Paul wants to have some live music a few nights a week,' Carmen explains.

'Is he the guy that you had dinner with?'

Carmen sighs. 'Yes, it was on social media. But you can see why? We'd done up the pub and we spent the whole night talking about him and his wife.' She doesn't tell Elena how angry she was that he'd misled her. It all seems so trivial now and she really wants to know more about Elena. She's more interested in speaking to her daughter about more important things.

'So, enough about me, how are you?'

'Fine.'

'And José?'

'I'm meeting him tomorrow. He's flying in from Qatar and we're going to sort out the final plans for the wedding.'

'That sounds exciting.' Carmen hopes her voice sounds more enthusiastic than she feels. 'So where are you up to with it all?'

'His mum and sister have the venue sorted. There's a hotel near his dad's golf club. We're flying over to look at it and to finalise the details at the end of the month. But we need to get numbers sorted. I want to find out what's going on with you and Papi.'

Carmen's face remains neutral, her eyes engaged with her daughter's. She's enthralled at how similar her eyes are to Jack's, but Elena's don't twinkle like they used to when she was happy and excited. Although she's twenty-five, her forehead is furrowed with deep tram lines between her eyes and she looks very serious.

'So, are you getting divorced?' Elena asks.

Carmen looks aghast. 'Who's mentioned divorce? Papi?'

'No.' Elena' stammers. 'No, but I just thought...'

'Thought what?'

'Well, it's not normal that you've moved here and you're living in a cramped flat when you have a lovely comfortable home—'

'Has Papi told you that we may lose the house?'

Elena stares at her. 'Why would we lose it? It's our home?'

'It's not our home. You left four years ago and Luis is at university now.'

'I know but you and Papi...?'

'Papi said he was going to tell you. Didn't he?'

'He said you have until the 24th of December to find the money but you've gone and bought this place? How is that possible?'

'I cashed in an insurance policy.'

'And you didn't put the money into our London home?'

'It wasn't nearly enough. Besides Papi said *he* wanted to get the money to pay off the debt. He's the one who has arranged the loans on the mortgages and he will feel responsible if the banks foreclose on the house.'

Elena shakes her head. 'If he was relying on that dancing programme for money then he won't have got much. Will it be enough?'

'I don't know.'

'You haven't asked?'

Carmen shakes her head.

Elena leans forward. 'Mama, what's happened? Why don't you care about our home? Papi has a custom-made jukebox, there's a pool table and a garden big enough for a football pitch with a swimming pool. He loves that house. What will he do?'

'Home is where you're happy. Luis is at uni and you're flying. Papi is travelling. It's like a mausoleum when I'm there on my own.'

Elena looks shocked. 'It's our *home.*'

'It *was* our home when you came home with friends or Luis was there or even when Papi had parties for all his show business friends but, then more recently, it's not been a home.'

'Since you had cancer?' Elena asks abruptly.

'I think that has something to do with it, yes. Will we go to the restaurant? You must be hungry. I know I am.' Carmen drains her glass and stands up. She's finding her daughter's inquisition quite disturbing.

* * *

Amber has saved them a window table in Harbour Bistro and after they've studied the menu and ordered a bottle of Merlot, Carmen leans forward in anticipation.

'Let's talk about the wedding. Are you excited?'

Elena shrugs. 'I would be if I knew what was happening with you and Papi.'

'We'll be there,' she replies with certainty.

'Papi said it's a few days before our home is being repossessed. He says he'll have to fly home and sort everything out - empty it and everything.'

'His book tour should be over by then.'

'He said he'll have to pack up the house as you're so busy. It was like he was telling me that he couldn't come to the wedding. Seemingly, packing up our home that's about to be repossessed is more important than me getting married.' She pouts. 'And Luis is no better. They said they might still be at university doing some project work. It's like no one wants to come to Florida to see me get married. No one cares.'

'Of course we do, cariño.'

The conversation pauses while the waitress places in front of them fresh salmon on a bed of spinach.

'This looks delicious.' Elena sounds surprised.

Carmen watches Elena savour the flavours as she eats with relish. She smiles.

'My friend Amber owns the restaurant and also the café across the road.' She tells Elena more about the people in Harbour Street: Eva and Sanjay, Jane and Tommy, and Frances the vicar and their plans for the Christmas lights switch on.

'It's a shame Amber's not working tonight, but we might pop over to the café for breakfast in the morning. I'd like you to meet her.'

'I'm leaving early. José's flying in at twelve.' She covers her mouth to yawn.

Carmen nods. 'You look tired. I hope you'll get some rest.'

'I have to work, Mama.'

'I know, but all these hours, flying into different times zones—'

'It's what I do, Mama. It's my job.'

'What happens after you get married? Will you still fly?'

'For a little while. José is keen to have a family.'

'What about his other children? Will they come to the wedding?' Carmen knows that José is divorced but Elena has always been scant on any details.

'He wants them to be there, but his ex is being a bitch. She's being difficult. They only live down the road. Very near to his mum and dad.'

This was news to Carmen. 'So, you've met his children?'

'Once. But that's why he's keen for us to have a family soon. So that the children's ages will be close.'

'How old are they again?'

'Sky is two and Matt is four.'

'Very young then.' Carmen finishes her salmon, trying not to sound judgemental. Elena had started dating José shortly after Carmen was diagnosed a year ago.

'José wants his children to be close. That's why we'll buy a house in Florida and settle there.'

Carmen looks up sharply. 'You'll live in Florida?'

'Of course. He's close to his mum and sister and with Sky and Matt nearby - he's keen for all the family to get on.'

Carmen digests this information slowly. This is news to her and she's shocked to think her daughter will live so far away. 'Did you tell Papi?'

'Not yet. We're going to sort out all the details in the next few weeks. That's partly why we're flying over there at the end of the month. We're going to look at houses. José wants to make sure we live close enough to his family so that I have support when he's not around.'

'Will you be happy living in Florida?'

'There's not a lot here for me now, is there? You and Papi's example of marriage is hardly an advertisement for a happy family. José is on social media all the time and he shows me what's going on between you both. Papi's behaviour with Shazzy B was so embarrassing and then he saw the pictures of you and Paul out for dinner. You're hardly going to be a role model for my kids, are you?'

Carmen replies slowly, 'I think there's someone in Westbay who is overly interested in my life. They were a fan of Papi's and they've been posting on social media—'

'I read about Luis too. They seem to think it was a person they'd met here?'

'Tracey.' Carmen remembers her last encounter and instinctively she raises a hand to her head. 'I think she was involved.'

'Well then you need to speak to Tracey and tell her to back-off.'

Carmen looks away.

Elena looks at her plate and then places her fork and knife together. 'I want a home, Mama. You and Papi are being ridiculous and it's exhausting. I need a home of my own for *my* family.'

'We are your family.'

'It doesn't feel like it. We don't even have a place to call home.'

'Florida is a long way away.'

'Mama, flights are so easy now. Besides, you can come and stay whenever you want. We'll have a spare room.'

'Is it definite then?'

'José has asked for a transfer. He's going to be based in Florida. I'll do the same.'

Elena looks tired. In the glow of the table lamps, she looks exhausted, and Carmen has a desire to hug her close and to whisper, 'think carefully'. Instead she asks.

'Would you like a dessert?'

'Impossible. I can barely keep my eyes open.'

* * *

Back in the flat Elena goes upstairs to bed while Carmen checks her iPhone. She texts a message to Jack with a brief resumé of her evening and as she's texting, a message comes through from Luis.

Elena tells me you've cut your hair. She said you're behaving differently??

Carmen smiles. Elena must be texting Luis upstairs. She finds the photo Amber took and texts back.

Hope you like it? I'm still me. (smiley face).

Luis texts back immediately.

Guapa! Hope you told her I'm not going to her wedding to that poxy pilot???

Carmen shakes her head and yawns. She's exhausted from them all.

No, that's your job. xx

Luis replies.

I'll text her now so be prepared for the fallout tomorrow. xx

***

Elena's face is like thunder. She's dressed in jeans and a casual navy and beige jumper when she comes downstairs with her small suitcase already packed.

'Did you know?' she says by way of greeting.

'Hola cariño, did you sleep well?'

'Did Luis tell you they weren't coming to my wedding? They say they're too busy.'

'I'm sure they'll change their mind.'

'What is wrong with everyone?' Elena's voice rises.

'Let's go for breakfast in the café and talk about it?'

'Don't you have to open the shop?'

'I'll open at ten thirty.'

Elena sniffs. 'I suppose I'm lucky you're giving me the time.'

Carmen smiles and holds her arms out to Elena, but she moves away and out of reach. 'My darling, everyone is busy, but none of us are too busy to come to your wedding.'

Elena looks slightly mollified and by the time they're seated in the café, Elena looks considerably brighter.

'I'll just have a black coffee,' she says.

'You've lost a lot of weight,' says Carmen. 'I hadn't noticed until I saw you in jeans this morning.'

'I want to get into my wedding dress.'

'Do you have any photos?' Carmen orders coffee and a croissant for herself from Karl and a black coffee. Fortunately, he's too busy to have a long conversation but he winks at her and takes their order straight away.

Elena scrolls through the photos in her phone uninterested in the waiter. She turns her phone around for Carmen to see.

'How beautiful. So, it's a white wedding?' Carmen smiles.

'These are the dresses that José's mother has picked out for me. I'll try them on when I'm over there. There will still be time for any alterations.'

Carmen's heart grows heavier. She had hoped that she would help in the wedding arrangements or be involved in choosing the dress or even the venue, but she's been cast aside. She wonders if it's because she's moved to Westbay or if it might have happened anyway.

'What's wrong, Mama? It won't be expensive. I'll tell Papi how much it will all cost.'

'It's not about the cost.'

'You look upset with me.'

A waitress places their coffee and croissant on the table and Carmen looks at the food. Her stomach is churning. She's so distant from her daughter. Would they ever be friends?

'I suppose,' Carmen says slowly. 'I had hoped that you might get married in England and that Papi and I would be more involved.'

Elena stares at her, open-mouthed.

Carmen continues, 'I would have liked to have helped you choose a dress. We could have met in London, gone for lunch, gone to the bridal shops together? Perhaps had time to talk in more detail about your wedding—'

'That's rich coming from you when Papi calls my future husband a control-freak.'

Carmen tries to regulate her breathing. Elena's eyes are burning with passion. They're on fire. She's ready to fight her corner and defend her husband-to-be and his family.

'We are here for you.' Carmen places her hand on Elena's, but she snatches it away.

'Papi is more concerned about launching his bloody book

and you have mysteriously gone off grid as if you're searching for something - or someone. Are you having an affair?'

'No, and I'm not searching for anyone. I love Papi.'

'Then why aren't you living together?'

'He's working away.'

'And when he comes back? What then? Where will you both live? I can't imagine him living in that bloody flat.'

Carmen regards her daughter. Elena has perceptively and so cleverly stated what Carmen has been thinking and she doesn't have the answer. Her heart is trembling with wild emotion.

'Carmen?' Amber appears at their table. 'Hello, I'm Amber. You must be Elena. Gosh, I can see you're mother and daughter!'

Elena smiles. It's the professional smile. Her eyes are still angry.

'Are you staying long?' asks Amber.

'I'm leaving now. After breakfast.'

'A flying visit.' Carmen smiles but her heart is breaking.

'To discuss my wedding'

'Oh, wow, you're getting married. Here in Westbay?' Amber smiles at Carmen.

'No, in Florida.'

Amber clearly knows nothing about the wedding arrangements and Elena explains quickly what her intentions are but Karl beckons her from behind the counter and Amber is called away.

Elena leans across the table. 'So, Amber is your best friend here?'

'Yes.' Carmen smiles. 'Isn't she lovely?'

'That's interesting because she clearly knows nothing about

me or my wedding. That's great, Mama. How amazing is that? Your best friend knows nothing about me or my fiancé or anything about my wedding next month in Florida. That pretty much shows what you think about me, doesn't it? You have the cheek to say you want to be involved in my wedding plans, yet you've clearly kept it all a secret as if you're ashamed of me.' Elena stands up.

'I'm not ashamed of you.' Carmen gathers her coat and follows her daughter to the door and out onto the street.

'All you do is to think of yourself, Mama. It's always about you.'

'That's not true.' Carmen crosses the road stretching her stride to keep up with her daughter.

'It is true,' Elena calls over her shoulder and waves an arm down the street. 'Look at this place? Who'd want to live here?'

'I love it here.'

In the flat, it takes Elena only a few minutes to grab her case and head for the door.

'I cannot tell you how upset I am, Mama. You've left our home. You've abandoned Luis and Papi. You've cut your hair and now you're living in this place that—'

'NO!' Carmen waves her index finger. 'Do not say anything that is not true! I am always here for you but life changes and life moves on. It doesn't always work out how you want it to and sometimes life throws you an opportunity—'

'Is that what this is? An opportunity while our family is in ruins?'

'We are not in ruins—'

'We are not a family.'

Carmen straightens her shoulders as Elena attempts to push past her through the door and down the stairs.

'Please don't leave here angry, Elena. I was so looking forward to seeing you and spending time with you—'

'Well, we've done that now, Mama. I've seen your flat and your new haircut and I've met your best friend. I've told you about my wedding plans and when they're finalised, I'll get José's mother or sister to send you all the details. Then it's up to you all if any of you can be bothered to turn up.'

'I'll be there.'

'You can tell Papi that we've chosen the venue as they have good security and we can keep the paparazzi out.'

'That won't be necessary.'

'We all know that Papi tells everyone where he is all the time so they can get pictures of him.'

'He knows how important your wedding is.'

Elena leans toward her. He eyes burning with resentment. 'It is important to *me* and José. Quite honestly, I don't care if any of you turn up.'

Chapter 17

The video on social media goes viral.

'All you do is to think of yourself, Mama. It's always about you.'

'That's not true.' Carmen crosses the road stretching her stride to keep up with her daughter.

'It is true,' Elena calls over her shoulder and waves an arm down the street. 'Look at this place? Who'd want to live here?'

They are clearly arguing. Elena's face is screwed up in anger as she crosses the road. The person taking the video must have been outside the art gallery or near Eva's flower shop. The meme's heading: *RECOGNISE HER?* and the caption reads: *New hair, new life... but same old family fights.*

Carmen stares at her image and at her daughter's angry and dismissive wave, all caught on camera. Elena's words still echo in the shop. *Who'd want to live here?*

The filmmaker didn't record Carmen's answer. In fact, Carmen didn't recall even answering.

The events of the past twenty-four hours were challenging enough but now Elena's angry accusations are splashed across the media. Unlike a photo or some scandalous quote this video is brutal and, although it's been taken out of context, it's clearly true and can't be denied.

* * *

The Beauty Salon is quiet and a mousy haired girl looks up. She wears false eyelashes, thick foundation and has colourful, pointed nails and a fake smile that's probably cost a lot of money. But it's the size of her lips and her pout that makes Carmen sad for her. The filler inside her lips makes her look cheap and quite ugly.

'Is Tracey here?'

'She's with someone.'

'How long will she be?'

The girl looks at the clock then the register open in front of her and then the clock on the wall again. She cracks the gum in her mouth loudly. 'Not sure.'

'Please ask her to come to my shop when she's free?' Carmen is about to leave when Tracey comes hurrying down the narrow corridor from the treatment rooms. She slows her pace when she sees Carmen and she looks terrified.

Carmen speaks slowly. 'The photo of Paul and me, in the Chinese. The images of Luis being beaten up and what happened in the vicarage last Friday was humiliating enough.' Carmen holds up her iPhone. 'But this is unacceptable. I'm going to the police.'

'It wasn't me.'

'None of it?'

Tracey stares at her unable to speak.

Carmen's smoky eyes are dark and angry. Her voice hisses with anger. 'I will not have you ruin my life. Consider this your last warning.'

'I didn't post it. Not this time.'

'I don't care. I'm going to hold you accountable for anything posted about me again on social media.'

'You can't.'

'I can and I have witnesses from the night in the vicarage.'

'I'm sorry about that. I told Amber and Frances it was an accident.'

'I don't believe you and certainly not now.'

'I wasn't even there yesterday.'

'I'm holding you responsible.'

'You can't threaten me!' Tracey shouts.

'This is not a threat.' Carmen leans closer to her and Tracey backs away. 'This is a promise. Next time it's the police.'

* * *

Frances comes into her shop with a beautiful bouquet of sunflowers.

'I would have come earlier but I knew you had your daughter visiting. I want to apologise. I know this won't make up for what happened at my house but I want you to know how brave you are.'

Carmen finds a vase for them.

'I appreciate this, thank you, Frances. But it wasn't your fault.'

'I also want to tell you that we spoke to Tracey about all this social media business and she's promised that she won't speak to anyone or do anything. I'm not on social media but I'm sure she will keep her word.'

'Something else was posted yesterday.'

Frances looks shocked. 'Did she?'

'I went to see her. She said it wasn't her.'

Frances nods with satisfaction but doesn't look convinced.

'She's a silly girl. It will land her in so much trouble if she's not careful.'

Carmen arranges the sunflowers with care and stands back to admire them. 'How is your mother-in-law? How is Marjorie?'

'She's taken a bad turn. It's upsetting for her and for all of us. Graham is not coping well. Especially at this time of year. They loved Christmas together. They're a close family.'

Carmen doesn't look up. Her heart is heavy.

'I've put her house on the market.' Frances looks around the shop as if trying to identify Marjorie's things.

'Any interest?'

'Not yet.'

'I've sold a few pieces,' Carmen says answering the unasked question.

'I'm pleased we didn't throw them out. Someone will get some enjoyment from her things. Did I tell you that Graham has ordered a copy of Jack's book? He's always been a fan and he supported West Ham when we lived in London.'

Carmen smiles. 'You'll have to come and have dinner with us when Jack gets back.'

'Is Jack coming here?'

'Of course.'

'Oh?'

Carmen laughs. 'You seem surprised.'

'I suppose... I thought you'd have a more permanent home in London.'

'I like it here. This is more like home to me already.'

'Great. Then let's hope Jack likes it as much as you.' Frances beams at her.

'There's always hope,' says Carmen, wondering if Frances

will detect the irony in her voice.

* * *

Elena's words still echo in her head. It's been over a week since her visit and now Carmen strides along Harbour Street toward the harbour. Her head is reliving her daughter's visit and she's having imaginary conversations - wondering where everything went wrong and wishing everything had ended happily.

It's the middle of November and a blustery cold day. It's strange for Carmen's head to be so cold. She hadn't realised how much the wig kept her warm, but now, as the wind whips across her face„ she makes a mental note to buy a hat. Striding out along the promenade, with her body leaning into the wind, she makes a mental note of everything: Jack's book launch seems okay. He's happy. Ben saw Luis in London last week and he's enjoying university. Elena sent a text to say she was sorry about the argument and that it would all blow over on social media. She also told Carmen that she needed to go to the police.

Elena had asked what would happen when Jack finished his tour? Where would they live? But Carmen hadn't got that far in her thinking. Each day has been a challenge, planning something, moving forward - either for the shop or for Luis - or for her.

Black-headed gulls swoop overhead and their screeches are lost on the wind. Time has flown but now Carmen realises she must think about the future. She puts distance between her and the town trying to narrow down what's really bothering her. She'd hoped to hear from Martin by now. If the show homes were to be furnished before Christmas, then she had five weeks. She'd been crazy saying at her presentation that she could have them all furnished in four weeks. What had she been thinking of?

Her pace slows and she pauses on the boardwalk to watch a boat out at sea navigate their route back to the safety of the harbour, bouncing on the waves, never seeming to get closer.

'I know how you feel,' she mumbles. It's getting dark and she needs to buy some milk. It's getting much colder but as she turns around to head home, she realises it's none of these things that are really bothering her.

It's something else.

She ducks down the alleyway to get to the shop and glances into the houses. Lights are coming on around her and she glances through the windows at couples making dinner, children watching TV and people arriving home from work.

She ducks through another alleyway and past Marjorie's house where, there's now a For Sale sign in the garden, and into the high street to the supermarket. She picks up milk and heads home, where she sees a text message on her iPhone.

Congratulations! Call me tomorrow and we'll discuss details. Martin.

* * *

The next few days pass in a whirl. Carmen opens the shop but she's also managing her regular on-site meetings with Martin. They go over the details and requirements for each show house and then the technicalities of delivery, unpacking, assembly and final details for the official opening.

Carmen notes down the dates and times then at home she

places orders and matches dates and times of delivery. It's a complicated timetable – a juggling process. When one supplier can't deliver, Carmen must improvise and use a different supplier or come up with an alternative plan.

One evening she's scheduling and rescheduling her timetable when Jack calls. 'How's it going?

'It's busy. You sound exhausted,' she says.

'It's gruelling but it's the literary festival in Seattle next week. This is the big one that will gain real interest in the book.'

'You're getting closer to coming home.' She smiles. 'I've forgotten what you look like.'

She hears him grinning back and the laughter in his voice. 'I'll send you a photo.'

'I'd prefer to see you.'

'Cammy, I really miss you too. Look, have you read the book yet?'

Carmen glances where it lies unopened on the table. 'Not yet.'

'Oh?'

'It's been crazy here and now I've got the contract for the show homes I'm going to be flat out until Christmas.'

'What about the wedding? Did you see Elena's email?'

'Yes. She's booked flights for the three of us on the 19th.' Carmen rubs her short hair. It's beginning to seem more normal now that she's used to her bare neck. It may also need another cut before the wedding. 'I've emailed you and Luis the schedule.'

'She wants us to stay for Christmas,' he moans. 'What do you think?'

'A nightmare,' replies Carmen grinning.

Jack laughs. 'What can we do?'

'You have to sort out the finances on the house in London. I have to furnish show homes. You need to finish your book tour and Luis is coming home from uni. But we must all be ready to leave on the 19th.'

'That's four weeks time, Cammy. Can we do it?'

'Will we be able to save the house in London?' she asks.

Jack clears his throat. 'Book sales aren't as good as I thought they might be. I'm worried.'

'Why is Simon sending you over to the States to promote it when you're more well-known over here? Surely the book will sell better here?'

Jack replies slowly, 'I'm not sure.'

'Well, it will be what it will be, Jack. When do you plan on being back in England?'

'The second week of December.'

'You'll have a week to sort out the house?'

'I don't think I can raise enough money to save it.'

'It's not important, Jack. It's our family that's important.'

'Will I sell our things or put them in storage?'

Carmen looks at the material and swatches surrounding her. 'Jack, we can make a home anywhere. It's all just stuff. Maybe we have too much of it?'

'Really?'

'Maybe it's time to move on and begin again.'

'A fresh start and all that?' He sounds hopeful and Carmen's spirits rise.

'Marriage is about us,' she says. 'I always said I could live in an envelope with you just as long as we're happy.'

Jack laughs. 'That takes me back. Yes, you did! The problem is that I've been used to living in a gift-wrapped box and I'm not sure an envelope will fit me again.'

* * *

At the end of November there's a final meeting for the Harbour Street Christmas Committee and this time Amber holds it in the café. Carmen wonders if it is because of what happened in the vicarage but either way she's pleased to see everyone together.

She settles around the table, squeezing in between Kit and Eva and noticing that Tracey isn't present.

'You look great,' says Eva.

Carmen touches her hair. 'I think it might need another trim soon.'

Sanjay pours her a glass of Merlot and sits beside her. 'It suits you,' he whispers as Amber opens the meeting.

'So, you'll definitely be Santa?' confirms Amber looking at Kit.

Yusef interrupts and claps loudly. 'He's our main man. The only Santa for the job.'

Amber raises her voice. 'Christmas lights go up on Saturday. That's Sanjay, Kit, Ben, Derek and Ian.'

They all nod and give murmurs of approval.

'The lights switch on is the first weekend of December. It's all confirmed.'

'Yay!' Yusef grins. 'I love Christmas.'

'Jane has confirmed the fishermen, the fishing boats and tides. So, we're all set for Santa's arrival on the Saturday at four. He'll be escorted into the harbour by two fishing boats and the RNLI.'

Jane nods in confirmation and Tommy smiles proudly at her

side.

'I'll be on the boat too,' Yusef calls. 'Me and my bro'. Won't we Ozan?'

Ozan's face lights up. 'That's the plan.'

Amber continues, 'Frances has confirmed the choir will be there. They'll be singing carols before Santa docks and then once Santa arrives it will be Christmas music. Frances is going to liaise with the choir master.'

'Perfect,' Luke and Mario say in unison, and they clap their hands together in delight.

Amber grins and holds up her hand. 'Then Santa will walk up the high street following the choir to the art gallery. It will be turned into Santa's grotto the night before by Ben, and me, and anyone else who wants to help. Then Kit, as Santa, will switch on the lights.'

'After last year's fiasco we're not having anyone famous.' Jane's face clouds over. 'It will be a relief to have the whole event a lot more low-key.'

'Exactly,' agree Luke and Mario.

Carmen studies the excited faces around the table. Everyone is involved. Everyone is looking out for each other and volunteering to help. Nothing is too much trouble and there's a general air of good will. It's a very special and humble community and Carmen experiences a sudden sense of warmth toward these wonderful people who have been so kind to her.

'We'll have the barrows out for the Christmas market again,' says Amber checking her list. 'The snow machine.... what else? Have we forgotten anything?'

Everyone looks around and when Carmen speaks all eyes focus on her.

'I'm so honoured to be part of this wonderful community but I'm not contributing anything. What can I do?'

The room falls silent.

Sanjay says, 'We're going to hang lights up along the top of your shop, and—'

Ben interrupts. 'I have a spare barrow if you need it? To put outside your shop?'

'I don't know if the shop will even be open. I got the contract for the show homes in the new development and I haven't got anyone to help in the shop.'

Amber replies, 'That's alright. You just come by whenever you can.'

'But I want to help.'

Ben laughs. 'Then come and help set up the grotto in the gallery on Friday night. You can help me and Sanjay.'

* * *

Luis is furious.

'Where does she get off telling me I've got to spend Christmas in Florida? I'm not going. But if I do, I'm coming straight back afterwards. I don't want Christmas over there with him and his poxy family.'

'You might like them.' Carmen throws her bag on the sofa and kicks off her shoes. Her nose is cold from crossing the road from the café and she's still buzzing from the happy atmosphere and the bonhomie from her neighbours.

She pours a glass of wine as she speaks on the speaker phone. 'He might have a very nice family. They may be very nice people.'

'Tell me honestly, Mama. Do you like José?'

'I don't know him very well but if Elena likes him...'

'Can't you talk her out of it? He's a plonker. He smiled at me like I was a slug that he wanted to put a knife into. What does she see in him?'

'I don't know,' Carmen replies honestly. 'But, like it or not we must plan for her wedding.'

'Plan what? Two days that's all she's getting and then I'm coming home.'

Chapter 18

Martin is considerably younger than Carmen. He doesn't look much older than Luis although she guesses he must be early thirties. Very young to be divorced. He stirs his coffee and looks out of the Harbour Café window. His short hair and neatly trimmed beard make him seem older, but he also appears more relaxed now than when she last saw him. He's taken to visiting her in the shop and he often seeks her out when he knows she's on site. She assumes it's because it's the first time they've worked together and he's probably unsure of her work ethic. This is his first commercial build, and he must be anxious, but he never hassles her or makes a fuss of the timetable. He prefers to listen and watch and he helps with suggestions for installation and building furniture.

'Your hair is lovely much shorter,' he says. 'It suits you.'

Carmen returns his smile. She's knows he's not flirting with her. It's a genuine comment such as she'd get from Luis or, on a good day, from Elena.

'I was diagnosed with breast cancer at the beginning of the year.'

'I'm sorry. I hope you're okay now?'

She touches the wooden table. 'I'm fine.'

'Mum had it five years ago and you'd never know. Although

at the time it's harrowing, isn't it?'

She smiles. 'I'm very lucky.'

He adds sugar and stirs his coffee. 'Is Harry looking after you?'

Harry is the site manager who has a miraculous way of getting her units built and organised.

'He is, thanks. He's incredible.'

'Don't tell him that! He's my younger brother and it will go to his head.'

'So, it's a family business?'

'You didn't know?'

Carmen shakes her head.

Martin continues. 'Didn't you google it.'

'I should have done but I was too busy finding the specs for the presentation.'

'You did well to complete in such a short space of time.'

'I was lucky that Sandrine and George didn't win.'

Martin turns down the corners of his mouth. 'It wasn't luck. They're talented but to be honest they don't take risks. I knew what I'd get with them and I suppose, because this is my first project, I wanted something different. I was looking for more originality, something that would push the boundaries and get everyone talking.'

Carmen laughs. 'I didn't know it was that controversial.'

Martin grins. 'So, let's take a look and see where you are and if we're on schedule?'

Carmen turns her timetable toward him, and they spend an hour going over the details of what can't be sourced, what looks better, offering substitutions and talking timelines. 'Using pale colours doesn't necessarily mean it will make the place look chilly,' she explains. 'It will be effective if I create a cosy backdrop using well-placed lights but there's no need to over accessorise.' She pulls out some designs to show him. 'There's also no need to spend a fortune but upholstered headboards are key - we could use faux leather or even suede they're both very popular.' She turns the pages of her scrapbook. 'We can ditch the heavy drapes - we can go for taupe or stonewashed linen. What do you think?'

He turns the pages. 'Fantastic. I like the way you're happy to be flexible now they're almost finished.'

She smiles. 'Just because something is soft it doesn't make it cosy. It's all about the layers of textures: rugs, tiles, laminate - all of these give balance to the rooms.'

'What about ornaments?'

'They can be understated especially in a show house in case of inquisitive children.' She laughs. 'But if you want to go high-end, we can do sheepskin throws and blown glass vases.'

'I like your thinking.'

Afterwards Martin leans back and crosses his legs. 'So, we're on schedule and I can definitely arrange the opening for the 22nd of December?'

Carmen nods. 'I aim to have them finished by the 18th. My daughter is getting married.'

Martin looks surprised. 'Here in Westbay?' he asks.

'In Florida.'

Martin regards her with interest and Carmen continues.

'We're all flying over on the 19th. She's getting married just before Christmas.'

'How wonderful.'

Carmen packs the scrapbook, mood board and notes into her bag. It was time to get back to the shop and she certainly didn't want to talk to him about her daughter's impending wedding to a narcissist – she could hardly call Martin a friend. She looks into his eyes. 'I'd like to thank you for giving me this opportunity. I really appreciate it, Martin.'

'You're welcome and now I'd like to ask you something and if it's not appropriate please tell me. This is just an idea.'

Carmen holds her breath and regards him as he continues speaking.

'You don't trade or market yourself very well. You're married to a very prominent man – a footballer and celebrity and you could easily capitalise on that.' He draws an imaginary headline in the air. 'Footballer's Wife Leads Interior Fashion or Wife of International Star Breaks into Interiors. What do you think?'

Carmen shakes her head. 'No.' She knows he means well but she finds it hard to explain.

He scratches his chin. 'Sorry, Carmen. It's just an idea. I'm thinking that if you milked it then you could get into some of the glossy magazines and that would raise your profile...'

'You have a point but to be honest—'

'You want to do it all on your own?' he finishes for her.

Carmen smiles. 'Exactly.'

'Well, you have the talent and I think I can help you.'

'How?' Carmen tilts her head wondering what more this boy who could probably be her son, can possibly suggest.

'My dad is also a developer in Surrey. I think that after he's seen these show homes he'll be blown away.'

'Really?'

'I'd like you to meet him. I've planned the opening for the 22nd but if you're not going to be here—'

'Perhaps another time?'

'He doesn't come here very often since my mum remarried.'

Martin frowns and then grins. 'You have worked it out, haven't you? You do know who my mother is?'

Bewildered Carmen shakes her head and that makes Martin laugh louder.

'It's Sheila. She bought the tropical wallpaper from you. Didn't Tim, her husband, collect it one day?'

Carmen remembers one of her first clients. Sheila had said her sons were developers or decorators. She must have meant Martin and his brother Harry. 'Tim is your stepfather?'

Martin nods. 'Fortunately, we all get on. And, when Harry put up Mum's wallpaper, we were all blown away. I couldn't believe it when you applied for the tender and I kept my fingers crossed hoping that you'd pull it out of the bag - and you did.'

Carmen grins. 'Does your mother know?'

Martin nods. 'She spoke very highly of you. That was another reason I wanted to go with you. I figured that, like me, you're starting a new business and I was hoping it might be the start of a mutually beneficial project.'

'I don't know what to say,' Carmen replies. Her heart is soaring. She got this job on merit. It was her achievement.

'Well, let's hope dad likes it because he's building a massive development next year.'

* * *

Carmen is mentally doing the maths in her head. With the current sales in the shop plus what she earned from the pub and now the show homes, she's earning a tidy profit. And, if she were to meet Martin's dad and get a bigger contract with him, then the world would open up for her. She could employ an assistant in the shop and that would leave her free for more design work. But it didn't have to stop there. She could help renovate, design and project manage all sorts of things. Her world is finally changing. Her dream job is becoming a reality, but at what price?

* * *

On the first Friday in December, she closes the shop early and heads to Ben's art gallery. He has already cleared a lot of the space. The walls are bare and the desk and counter have been removed. They are moving fake cardboard walls into place to build Santa's grotto.

'Here's Santa's other helper.' Sanjay greets her with a big smile.

'The grotto was calling me.' She laughs pulling off her coat. She helps Sanjay move the boards into place. 'I need to pull my weight around here.'

'We're keeping the space in the gallery restricted for Santa and his elves or else the children run around and cause havoc.' Ben shakes his head in mock exasperation. 'Anyone would think it's Christmas.'

Sanjay offers Carmen a bag of fluffy white cotton wool.

'Snow?' Carmen observes dryly. 'Anyone would think it's winter.'

'It's cold enough for snow.' Ben rubs his hands.

They work companionably and then Sanjay asks, 'What are your plans for Christmas, Carmen?'

She doesn't stop working. She's on her knees placing the cotton wool padding around Santa's throne. 'We're going to Florida for my daughter's wedding.'

Ben grins. 'That's a treat. Some winter sunshine.'

'Plus, a family wedding,' adds Sanjay. 'How joyful.'

Carmen doesn't reply, and she squirms under Ben's gaze.

'Are you looking forward to it?' he asks.

She won't look at him. 'There's a lot to do before I go.'

'Are you organising it all from here?'

'Elena's future in-laws are sorting everything out.'

Ben stands up. 'Are you all going?'

Carmen regards him carefully before asking, 'Has Luis spoken to you about it?'

Ben nods. 'Yes, sort of.'

'So, you know they don't want to go?'

'It might help if Jack's more onboard with the idea,' Ben replies.

Carmen frowns. 'Really?'

'I think Luis holds him in high regard and if Jack were happier about it, then maybe Luis would be more willing?' He holds up his hand. 'I don't want to interfere but it's just an inkling.'

'Thanks for letting me know. I'll speak to Jack.'

'Do you have any idea what Jack will do when he gets back to the UK?'

Carmen frowns. This is something that's now keeping her awake at night. How will they live in the flat above the shop and, more importantly, what will Jack do every day?'

Carmen doesn't answer him. She walks over to where Sanjay is pushing more snow against the boards to help him.

'I'll put a shelter - a roof - over Santa's head which will bring the space down,' says Ben. 'It will make it more exciting for the kids. We can balance it on these poles here like we've done before.'

***

Amber and Eva join them in decorating the grotto and when it's finished Sanjay rubs his hands together. 'Got to dash. Opening now.'

'How about I invite you to a takeaway and we go back to my flat?' Carmen suggests to the others. 'It's been such fun.'

A little later they're in Carmen's flat and they're sitting around the table in the kitchen.

'This curry is a lifesaver,' says Amber. 'I haven't eaten all day.'

Eva opens the wine she's bought from the off licence. A rich red from the banks of the Duero River. 'I swear your taste in décor gets better every time I'm in here, Carmen. It's like walking into a Pinterest board!'

'Thanks, Eva! That's high praise coming from you.'

'These look interesting.' Amber eyes the fabric books.

'They are the samples for the show homes.' Carmen nods at the swatches on the chair beside them and Eva takes a cheeky look at the designs.

'Amazing. You're so talented.'

Carmen grins. 'So, what's new in the world of flowers and design? Are you ready for Christmas?'

'Everyone suddenly wants roses in every possible shade, shape and form. It's a whirlwind but I love it. What about you, Amber?'

'Christmas parties - ordering wine and juggling staff shifts. It's a nightmare. Not something you have to worry about Carmen. Do you think you'll need any help in the shop?'

'I'm managing at the moment, juggling colour schemes and deliveries. But I had this fantastic idea for a new project - a fusion of modern minimalism with a touch of vintage charm and I'm eager to try it. Especially if the right project comes along. Martin, the developer, is lovely and his father has a building project in Surrey next year. So, I'm hoping to meet him.'

'I heard they're having an opening of the show homes before Christmas.'

'It's on the 20th.' Carmen then explains how she will miss it because of Elena's wedding in Florida.

'She seemed very stressed when she was here.' Amber helps herself to more chicken curry. 'I wasn't sure if I'd upset her when you both came for breakfast.'

'It wasn't you. Elena's very nervous. I put the stress down to her wedding but Jack and Luis blame her boyfriend – they say he's controlling.'

'Is he?' asks Eva.

Carmen shrugs. She doesn't want to speak badly about her future son-in-law. 'I've only met him a couple of times and he seemed charming. His family are helping with the wedding arrangements which is kind. He's a pilot and he wants Elena to relocate to Florida so he can be near his two children from his previous marriage.'

'Is that normal?' says Eva.

'They're two and four years old.'

Eva frowns. 'That's not so good.' She wipes her chin with her napkin. 'Marriage is hard enough let alone when you move to a foreign country. I'm speaking from experience. My husband was so awful I don't know what I'd have done without Amber – and then Sanjay.' She smiles gratefully. 'I think friendship is the most important thing. If we can support and help each other that's important. I think Harbour Street has been good for me and the sense of community is incredible.'

'The trouble is,' Amber says, polishing off the egg fried rice, 'Is that we have no control over social media. It happened at Christmas last year when Westbay was invaded. Now, I see it on a more personal level with you, Carmen. Including that last post of you and Elena in the street.'

'I did ask Tracey, but she said it wasn't her.' Carmen sips her wine.

'It wasn't,' Eva says, and they all turn to stare at her. 'It's that boyfriend. The one with the Viking beard - Eric. He's an influencer and they hooked up online. He's been here a few times to Westbay recently.'

'That makes sense because she was upset when I accused her.' Carmen frowns at the recollection.

'We'll have to keep an eye on him. I don't want any problems tomorrow with Santa's arrival and the lights switch on.' Amber bites her lip. 'No more accidents or tragedies like last year.'

'No,' agrees Eva.

They tell Carmen what happened in more detail and how Jane made a good recovery and is now happy living with Tommy.

'It was Shelley who kept me up to date with what's going on, on social media.' Amber pours more wine. 'She's really keeping on top of it so we can protect you, Carmen.'

Eva adds, 'She thinks it's Eric who's making trouble. But Tracey doesn't seem to see him now. In fact, I heard she's selling the Beauty Salon.'

Amber raises her eyebrows. 'Why? We've supported Tracey. It's up to her what she wants to do but Eric shouldn't ruin it for her.'

Carmen shakes her head. 'I'll stay away tomorrow or come in disguise so that no one will recognise me. I certainly don't want to upset the plans or ruin anything.' Carmen enjoys the wine and helps herself to the last of the chicken korma.

'You won't ruin anything.' Eva reaches over to place her hand on Carmen's arm. 'It will all be fine.'

'Talking of weddings,' says Amber with a naughty glint in her eye. 'When are you and Sanjay getting married?'

Eva laughs and covers her mouth with her hand. 'Who knows? Maybe about the same time as you and Ben.'

Amber giggles. 'We're far too busy. Ben works so hard with his charity now. He's sometimes in London for days. I wish he had some help.'

'What sort of help?' asks Eva.

'Someone to help him with the children.' She explains to them. 'They're often homeless and they have social problems. Ben's charity helps them with woodwork classes. They love it but it's exhausting for him and it's not enough. They need something else.'

'There's no time for marriage,' says Eva.

'Like with you and Sanjay. We are all too busy.' Amber sits back and sips her wine with satisfaction. 'I've eaten too much. I couldn't even wear Kit's Santa suit tomorrow. I'd burst.'

They laugh.

'Do you think marriage is important, Carmen?' Eva asks.

Carmen thinks carefully before answering knowing she's with friends and her answer is safe. 'For me it's very important. I honestly don't know what I would do if I wasn't married to Jack.'

'I don't know what I would do if I *was* married to Jack.' Frowns Eva.

Their laughter fills the room as they enjoy the camaraderie, a blend of fun, banter and the deeper connections that weave through their lives and which bind them together.

For the first time Carmen has friends. These are friendships she's made on her own, not because of who she is or who she married. This bond is genuinely growing through care, warmth, trust and dare she say, love?

Amber pulls a piece of garlic naan and pops it in her mouth. 'I've been brainstorming some new coffee blends, experimenting with flavours and getting some Christmas gift boxes. What do you think if…'

* * *

The morning of Santa's arrival bodes well. There's a clear blue sky and a soft, chilled wind. Carmen has decorated the shop tastefully with large red baubles, classic holly with berries and Christmas wreaths from Eva's shop and she feels simmering excitement with the thought of Santa's parade and the lights switch-on.

Although it's early, the other shop owners are already placing barrows in the street and decorating them with their goods.

Ian, the grocer, has an incredible display of vegetables and fruits. Derek, the butcher, is preparing to cook hot dogs and hamburgers and there's already the smell of frying onions wafting down the street.

Carmen pops across the road to get a coffee from the café and on her way back she deliberately loiters in Harbour Street marvelling at the colourful displays and the vast array of independent shops offering a variety of wares.

It's all incredibly pretty and she sighs with pleasure. It's a dream. Her dream.

By lunchtime the town is heaving with visitors from out of town. They come with children's buggies, an assortment of dogs and wearing expensively designed hats and coats, and their excited babble fills the street.

Carmen remembers when all her clothes had been from a well-known designer, and she smiles. She hasn't bought clothes for months. This triggers an alert that she must now think about a wedding outfit and as she stands staring out of the window of her shop she's wondering what the temperature might be in Florida and how many outfits she will need.

At three o'clock she closes the shop and makes her way through Harbour Street weaving between couples, side-stepping children and dodging older people pushing strollers.

The harbour is packed. The choir is singing, *Joy to The World*, and Carmen is happy to stand in the background listening to the music and the snatches of strangers' conversations.

She has to stand on tiptoe to see Santa arriving on the RNLI boat and waving frantically at the children, the horns of the fishing vessels heralding his arrival. She smiles when the choir breaks into a medley of Mariah Carey's *All I Want for Christmas Is You* and she follows the crowd as they gather around Santa and begin to follow him toward Harbour Street.

Behind Santa Yusef and Ozan are dressed as elves. They have green and red costumes, pointed ears and shoes that curl up at the toes. They throw sweets high up in the air that land amongst the crowds who reach out to catch the rainfall of treats. The golden colourful paper catches the fading sunlight before being caught by tiny hands and screams of joy.

Jane the jeweller and Shelley, Yusef's girlfriend, applaud

loudly. Shelley's wearing yellow and red bumble bee dungarees, and they both fall into step with Carmen.

Shelley waves at Yusef following Santa. 'He's been so excited about this.'

'He loves Christmas,' agrees Jane.

'He's been looking forward to this since last August.' Shelley giggles. They reach the middle of Harbour Street and she pulls out her iPhone to film Yusef and the procession.

The crowd are clapping in time with the choir who are now singing a medley of Michael Bublé Christmas songs and Carmen finds herself humming and clapping along. She has never felt this relaxed, happy or part of such a wonderful community in her entire life except perhaps in the small Spanish village in the Andalusian hills where she was born. Everyone knew their neighbours and no one ventured very far.

But here it is different. She has the sea, she has friends and she also has her business.

The crowd separates her from Jane and Shelley and she ducks down an alleyway into the familiar street between her shop and the sea.

Marjorie's old merchant's house is empty.

Around it all the other houses have been decorated with pretty Christmas lights, but this house is set back from the road and it looks forlorn, as if it needs new life. Carmen pauses to stare and then she's distracted by the countdown to the Christmas lights switch on in Harbour Street.

'Ten - nine - eight - seven...'

Carmen ducks back up the alleyway and into the busy street pushing herself away from the crowd and against the wall and straining to see Kit, dressed as Santa, shouting with the crowd.

'Three-two-ONE!'

The lights come on all along Harbour Street. There are cries of delight, cheers and exclamations of joy. The crowd claps spontaneously in awe. Suddenly she's beside Jane and Shelley again and Jane is beaming happily. She's clapping and cheering loudly. 'Brilliant! So different from last year. This is wonderful.'

The choir busts into song, *O Holy Night* and a hush falls over the street.

Shelley looks up from her phone with a worried look on her face. 'Oh God, Carmen. I'm really sorry but you might want to see this.'

'What is it?'

'You might need to speak to Jack.' Shelley turns her iPhone for Carmen to read the social media newsfeed.

Book Bombs. One Step Too Far for Faded Footballer. Bailey Needs Bailing Out.

Carmen's instant good humour vanishes and she freezes. She stares at the smiling picture of Jack dressed in jeans and his favourite brown jacket looking relaxed and happy.

Carmen scans the article: *Revealing the Truth. Jack Stands by Every Word. More Secrets Than Stones Unturned. Family Confessions.*

'Have you read the book?' asks Jane, looking over her shoulder.

'Not yet.'

'If I can do anything,' says Shelley. 'Please let me know.'

But Carmen is already pushing herself in the direction of her shop and the safety of her flat. She covers her face with her scarf, wishing she were invisible. She wishes the ground would open up and she could disappear forever, then she would never have to face the inquisition of the braying public.

Family Confessions?

How could such a perfect day turn into such an awful nightmare?

The phone in her pocket starts to vibrate. It rings. Then it pings with constant messages. As she puts the key in the front door Carmen is wound like a tightly coiled spring, her stomach a knot of twisted emotions and memories.

What has he written?

Once safe upstairs in the flat she checks her messages.

Both Luis and Elena are trying to reach her.

She picks up Jack's book from the table and strides into the kitchen where she dumps it unceremoniously into the bin. 'What have you done, Jack?' she whispers.

Chapter 19

Fighting fires. It's one thing after another. Carmen has three missed calls from Elena plus a demand to call immediately and five separate messages from Luis:

Is he for real?

WTF is he playing at?

Doesn't he understand privacy?

I'll never talk to him again.

I hate him.

She also has one message from Jack sent an hour ago.

Hello Cammy, it's about to hit the fan so please call me so I can explain. I love you. Always remember that. xx

There's hammering on her front door.

'Mrs Bailey? Can we speak to you?' A voice shouts. 'We know you're in there.'

Carmen's heart is hammering but she grits her teeth and slides open the sash window. There's a man with a grey beard and a woman in a red bobble hat standing outside her front door. She's seen their type before. The press is her worst nightmare.

'Get off my property or I'll call the police.' She points to

Harbour Street on the other side of the gate.

'Did you know Jack was going to tell all in his book?'

'What do your children think of his book?'

'Did he release the book in Australia because of the revelations—?'

'Get off my property.' Carmen slams the window shut.

She closes her eyes. Is it possible to have PTSD about being hunted by the press?

Carmen blanks out all the Christmas festivities in Harbour Street but the choir are now singing a medley of songs from musicals: *Cats*, *Les Miserable* and *Joseph*.

On any other occasion Carmen would have joined in. She'd been having a wonderful day but now she studies the messages on her iPhone. Very calmly she pours herself a whiskey and dials Jack's number.

'Hello?' His voice is rough and scratchy. It sounds like she's woken him.

'It's all hitting the fan as you predicted.'

'Oh, no. Christ!'

Was he asleep? She can hear him ruffling the duvet. Clearing his throat. She imagines him fumbling for the light wondering what time it is.

'Are you alright?' he asks.

'They're outside the flat.'

'Oh no.'

'Tell me what's happened.'

'The book's bombed.'

'But it hasn't been released here in the UK yet, has it?'

She hears him sighing and imagines him running his hands through his hair. He takes a deep gulp of air. 'It's not going well.'

'Why?'

'Don't be angry, Cammy.'

'Then tell me the truth.'

'That's the truth. I don't know what's going.'

'What did you say in the book? What revelations?'

'You mean, you haven't read it? Simon said he sent you an advance reader copy.'

'I have a copy but I didn't read it. I trusted you.'

'I thought you'd read it. I assumed you were okay with everything.'

'You told me it was about football and the early days and...'

'It was, but then...' Jack coughs. 'I don't know what to say.'

'Begin with the truth and we can take it from there.' Carmen places her legs on the coffee table and crosses her ankles. She won't be going anywhere soon. Outside in Harbour Street the noise is joyous. People are laughing, singing, clapping and all enjoying the festive lights switch on. Just a few doors away Santa's handing out presents to small children in his grotto.

It's dark, but she doesn't switch on the lights. She watches the Christmas streetlights dancing across her ceiling like multi coloured alien invaders.

'I don't understand what's so shocking,' he says. 'Simon assured me it would all be alright and now I can't get hold of him.'

Carmen's waited fifteen years to say this and she savours the words on her tongue. 'He's a snake.'

'Ow, come on. Simon's been good to me.'

'Perhaps in the past. But a long time ago.'

'Well, it was all his idea to change tactic in the book. He said that it would be better received by the public and we'd earn more money if I spoke more about the family and what happened rather than when... you know, I had my injury.'

'So, your book isn't about football and the early years?'

'That's where it starts but when Simon and the agents read it they said it was banal - not exciting or interesting.'

'Interesting?'

'They wanted something new from me.'

'Is that why they changed the book cover?'

'I know, it's crazy isn't it?'

Carmen rubs her eyes then sips her whiskey. 'None of this makes sense.'

'They wanted me to write about the aftermath.'

'The aftermath?'

'Yeah, when I met you, our romance and the early years—'

'The early years include me, Elena and Luis.'

'Exactly.'

'You mean they wanted information about our *family*?'

'Well... sort of...'

'Oh, Jack! It's no wonder they've left me messages tonight. Elena and Luis are furious. What on earth have you said?'

'Only the truth. Nothing else.'

'You know how we all value our privacy. Especially our kids!'

'I know. But it's all positive. I wanted to make it up to them. I wanted to be honest and speak from the heart. People see me as this has-been, an ex-footballer and now a would-be-celebrity. I wanted them to take me seriously. This was all Simon's idea,' he grumbles.

'What was?'

'He said if we release the book in Australia and America then if it did bomb, it wouldn't be so bad in England. But I think he underestimated the power of social media.'

'If it's bombed, why all the interest?'

'Because it's so bad. That's the irony. It becomes more talked about.'

'So, this is worldwide,' says Carmen. 'Elena can't fly away from the embarrassment of her family anymore and Luis is probably hiding in his room at university.'

'But you must know I love you - and the kids. I wouldn't do anything to harm or upset any of you.'

'I can't believe it, Jack. I really thought your book was about football.'

'Simon said that was boring and people wanted to know more about our personal life.'

'You haven't...?'

'No. Well, sort of...'

'You've told them about my cancer?'

'Well, yes, but I thought you knew. I thought you'd read the book.'

'But you didn't even discuss it with me!'

'I thought that's why you got rid of the wig - I thought you were embracing it all.'

'What did you say about Elena and Luis?'

He remains quiet.

'Jack? What did you say?'

'Well, I did mention that Luis is non-binary and that Elena works as cabin crew to get away from us.'

Carmen hears the laughter in the street. It brings her back to the reality of her life, the implications of Jack's story and how it will affect them all forever.

'Oh, my God, Jack! How did you think this book was ever going to be a success?'

'It's from the heart.'

'When you haven't even spoken to me or the kids?'

'I'm getting a flight tonight. I'll arrive back tomorrow,' Jack says. 'Will you meet me at home? In London?'

'No, Jack. I'm not going to just drop everything for you again. I'm sick of dealing with the fallout from your mistakes.' Carmen looks around the flat and sips her whiskey. 'This is my home.'

'Don't be mad at me, Cammy. It's bad enough that the kids hate me.'

'I'm sure they don't.'

'They do! It's any excuse. They've never really...'

Carmen's iPhone rings, there's another incoming call. 'It's Elena on the other line. I have to go.'

'Yeah, speak to her. Tell her we're all coming to the wedding. Play it all down - you know the book thing. It will all blow over and I'll see you tomorrow.'

* * *

Elena isn't playing anything down. She's furious.

'He's not taking my calls,' she complains.

'He's flying back later. You can speak to him when he's home tomorrow.'

'How could he do this?'

Carmen's voice is calm even though her heart is hammering in her ears as if she's drowning. 'It will all work out.'

'Our family is in the spotlight again. None of us will *ever* live this down. He's made a fool of himself and all of us. José is furious. My fiancé is embarrassed! His family can't believe it. They don't know what to say to their friends and they certainly don't want all this fuss at my wedding. It's two weeks away,

Mama. The press is bound to find out that I'm getting married - who have you told?'

'Families stand by each other.'

'How can you say that? We're a laughing stock! Have you actually read what he's said in his book?'

'Not yet.' Carmen stands up and retrieves the book from the bin. She wipes grease from the glossy hard back cover and stares at Jack's smiling face. She wants to punch him in the eye.

'What are you doing?' asks Elena.

'I've just got home from the Christmas lights switch on. It was beautiful.'

'Well, you'll probably want to barricade yourself into your flat because the paparazzi will be like vultures.'

She doesn't tell her daughter that they've already arrived or that she's hiding in the flat.

Elena continues, 'I can't imagine why he's done this, Mama. What good could possibly come from any of it? And you can tell him from me, I wanted to work as cabin crew because I like flying and travelling. How dare he accuse me of abandoning the family.'

Carmen breaths slowly and evenly. She's angry with Jack but upset for Elena. 'He loves you.'

'I don't think he loves any of us.' Elena speaks quickly. 'It's so horrendous. Wait until you read about losing your hair.'

'What?'

'He's told them everything. He's talked about you not wanting reconstructive surgery. Literally everything.'

* * *

Luis is incensed. 'He's a liability, Mama. Is he on drugs?'

'No.'

'What possessed him to speak about me? How does he know how I feel and the person I am? When did he become such an authority on transgender, gay, lesbian and bi people? How can he understand gender neutral when he constantly gets my pronouns wrong?'

'I'll speak to him.'

'It's a bit late now—'

'I know but—'

'Just so long as he doesn't do any more interviews trying to justify the crap he's written. You know what he's like! He'll milk it all - and worse - he'll revel in the limelight.'

'He's flying home tomorrow.'

'Well, I'm never speaking to him again. I don't want to see him. He's betrayed our trust, Mama. He's betrayed me. What will my friends say?'

Carmen breathes in slowly. 'He loves you.'

'That's not what he says in the book.'

This takes Carmen by surprise. What has Jack written? What could he have been thinking when he wrote it all? 'We'll sort this all out. We are a family.'

'Mama, are you stupid? This is why they released the book in Australia and America first. In case it caused this upset. The book is crap, but he's sensationalised our lives to hype himself up,' Luis cries.

'I'm sure —'

'Mama, please don't defend him or it will make you look pathetic. He's written a whole chapter on me, my sexuality, gender discrimination and how hard it is for him to call me *they*. How do you think that makes me feel? Everyone is laughing at me. And, besides, what does he really know about me and how I feel? He's always been so dismissive. He hates me.'

'Will I come and collect you?'

'Mama, stay at home. He describes in the book how you've hidden behind our palatial home for years and the most secure things in your life were our electronic gates. This book is brutal, Mama. And worse, I think the press will be all over us - especially you. And because of social media they will find you so be careful.'

Carmen stands up and glances out of the side window. The grey-bearded man and the woman with the red bobble hat are not at her back door. She moves to the front window and checks the main street. Although Harbour Café is now closed, they are standing outside, nursing a coffee and stomping their feet with the cold.

'Mama? Will you be alright?'

'Yes. What will you do, Luis?'

'I have a project to finish by Friday.'

'That's five days away. I can come and collect you?'

'I spoke to Ben earlier and he has a room at the charity for me if I need it. But Elena is furious about her wedding. Have you spoken to her? She says José is furious with her. He calls Jack a parasite. She's very upset, Mama. You need to speak to her.'

'I just did.'

'And?'

'She's very upset.'

'What will we do? The book is now for sale in the shops here and because of all this publicity it will be a nightmare. Mama. It's so bad - everyone wants to read it!'

'Yes, but we will get through it all.'

'Why did he have to write about us?'

'I think that Simon, his agent, persuaded him because there are no more stories that Papi can tell about his football career that he hasn't already told. It was such a long time ago. I suppose that being a celebrity has brought him back into the public eye and people want to read about his personal stuff.'

'I'll tell you, Mama. I wish he'd never been a famous footballer. I wish we'd never lived in that big house or had all that money. I'd have sacrificed everything to have a simple life in an ordinary home - even to live in someone else's home. I wouldn't care.'

Carmen has a sudden urge to hold her child. It all seems so unfair that he has to go through all this. 'I understand, cariño. Look, you have one more week. I'll collect you for the holidays.'

'I'll speak to Ben.'

'Okay.' Carmen is upset to think he'd go to Ben instead of her but she's grateful. She knows Ben will help them both.

'And you can tell Papi from me that I never want to speak to him again.'

* * *

Social media stirs up an avalanche of questions and videos and by Saturday night there are more paparazzi outside the house waiting in Harbour Street.

Amber phones. 'Have you spotted them?'

'Yes. I'm so sorry.'

'It's not your fault.'

'I mean, I'm sorry for the town. This year with Santa's

parade I didn't want to ruin it all.'

'You haven't. It's all over and it was a great success. Now, we have to work out a way of getting rid of these bloody photographers for you.'

Frances phones next.

'Are you alright? I can get the choir to stand outside your shop and sing for two hours. That should get them running for cover.' She laughs.

Jane the jeweller calls. 'We're here for you. Shelley is keeping us up to date with social media if you need any information. Just say the word and Yusef will be outside the shop, cutting hair and making the most of the publicity.' Jane laughs. 'Believe me, he's enough to drive away a saint.'

Eva phones. 'Let me know if you're hungry and Sanjay will send over some food.'

Carmen is overwhelmed.

Then she receives a text from Martin. 'You've got this. It will blow over. All will be okay.'

Then Paul, pushes past the group outside her gate and leaves a basket on the doorstep. She collects it half an hour later. It contains nuts, grapes, chocolates, crackers and cheese. There's a note.

It's the Christmas hamper for the raffle. It's all I had in the bar. I'll replace it. Let me know if you need anything else. Px.

Ben phones about ten o'clock just as Carmen pours her second whiskey.

'I spoke to Luis. I'm going to London in the morning and I said that if they need a safe space then Luis can come to the charity at Kings Cross. I can bring them back to Westbay if they want. Anything you want or need Carmen. Just let me or

Amber know.'

'Thank you, Ben. I really don't know what to say. Jack said he's going to our London house when he lands tomorrow and Elena is in Dubai at the moment.'

'I'll be backwards and forwards to London between now and Christmas almost everyday because of the charity, so I can sneak any of them in when it's dark,' he says.

'Thanks Ben, but I don't think any of them want to come here. They don't consider this to be their home. At this rate, I'll probably be lucky if I see any of them again.'

* * *

Carmen hasn't slept. She considers going for an early morning walk but when she sees photographers still hanging around in Harbour Street she moves away from the blinds. Her life is forever repeating itself. At least in her last home she could swim in the pool. There was space to sit in the garden and she could walk around the house undetected. Here she's cramped, but completely safe.

Occasionally her front doorbell rings, but she ignores it. She's not hungry. She puts on the TV and it's loud enough for her to block out the morning noises in Harbour Street. The shops are opening and it's probably one of the busiest Sundays before Christmas. Although she's exhausted, she can't sleep. She picks up Jack's book and begins to scan read. The details are all too familiar.

It was her but it was a different life. She was a different person. Reading all the sad details, the difficulties of Jack's numerous operations to restore his knee and how guilty he is that she gave up her modelling career for him is excruciating.

She doesn't need to be reminded about those days. Her modelling days are better forgotten. It appeared glamorous on the outside but behind the scenes she was a young, innocent and vulnerable girl. She was almost seduced by designer drugs and by influential men with inflamed egos and false promises. It had been a narrow escape. And there are dark memories. She shivers as if an icy wind has travelled across her path. She flicks through each chapter: Jack's drinking, his gambling losses, their bad investments, the financial losses. She can't bear to read about their children. It's too brutal. Too detailed. Unfinished she tosses the book aside.

How could he?

She was carving out a lovely life here with good friends, helping Ben and Sanjay decorate the grotto and having Amber and Eva up here for dinner then watching Santa's arrival. She'd felt part of the community. She felt that she belonged. People liked her for her and not for who Jack was or what size house they had.

She stays in her dressing gown, walking from room to room, realising how small the flat is compared to her last house. It's no wonder that Elena and Luis were derogatory about it. They would never stay here for long. How could she have ever imagined that Jack would settle here?

She hadn't asked what flight he was on or what time he would arrive. She calls his number and it flicks straight to voicemail. Then she calls Elena, but there's no answer, she doesn't leave a message. Then she calls Luis.

No answer.

She's alone.

By lunchtime Carmen is feeling claustrophobic and angry. She's indignant that she's been forced into this situation. She refuses to be a victim.

She showers. Then using the back stairs she goes down into the shop. The blinds are drawn at the front so she works methodically, preparing her samples to take to the show home tomorrow. She mixes and matches, changes her mind, googles different ideas and alternative materials and uses soft furnishings that she finds in the storeroom. She places a new order for a stack of glass tables for one of the show homes and by six o'clock the town is quiet. She goes upstairs. There are three photographers hanging around outside including Red Bobble-Hat and Grey Beard.

There are missed calls and messages on her mobile from daily newspapers asking for interviews, but nothing from her family. She's bereft, abandoned.

* * *

After a better night's sleep, Carmen wakes on Monday morning with new resolve and ternacity. She dresses in a smart navy Chanel suit and checks her reflection in the mirror. She looks tired, her face is gaunt and her eyes are swollen - but she's determined.

She isn't hiding any more. She opens the front door of her shop and stands motionless while cameras flash in her face. It's all so reminiscent of her modelling days but now they're photographing her for different reasons.

There's the Red Bobble-Hat and Grey Beard but also Eric, Tracey's boyfriend with the Viking beard. Although that surprises her, she speaks in a loud, clear and controlled voice.

'I have a job to do today. This is my home and this is my shop. I have nothing to say. So, you may as well go home. But if you desperately need a quote for your paper then this is it. *I love my family. They are my world. This is our home. Please respect us at this time. Thank you.*'

She returns inside with her heart hammering and closes the door. She begins packing the soft furnishing into large bags. There's a scuffle outside and then the shop door opens.

'They're a pain in the neck! I guessed you'd need to take the soft furnishings today so I've come to help.' Martin is rubbing his hands. 'It's freezing out there. They must be nuts hanging around.'

Carmen smiles gratefully, relieved to see a friendly face. 'That's kind of you.'

'Mum said you'd need help and we can keep them away from you on site. We'll block them from coming in. Harry is waiting in the van outside. We're here to support you so don't worry. What shall I carry out first?'

They spend the next twenty minutes loading the van and during this time, Amber arrives and ignoring the photographers, she hands coffee to Martin, Harry and Carmen.

'I think they're probably hoping Jack will turn up,' Carmen whispers to Amber and nods across the street. 'He's flying into England today. Even Tracey's boyfriend is hanging around as if he knows something.'

'I'll tell her to get rid of him.'

'I think they'll soon get fed up waiting.'

'Do you think Jack will come here?'

Carmen shrugs. 'I've given up wondering what he'll do. He's got to sort the house out and he's only got two weeks left.'

'Give him Ben's number and tell him to go to the charity at any time and Ben can always bring him here.'

Carmen nods. 'Thank you.' She takes out her phone and messages Jack, then she spends the rest of the morning working at the show homes. They do an inventory check of the items missing and Carmen makes a note to order fresh flowers from Eva for the opening. At lunchtime Martin buys sandwiches and they sit companionably talking quietly.

'Are you ready for the wedding?' Martin asks, 'When do you leave?'

'Next week. And, no – I'm not at all ready.'

'Have you booked flights?'

'Elena was supposed to be sorting them out.'

Martin laughs. 'I love how you're so cool with it all.'

'I'm like a duck. I'm splashing around frantically underneath.'

Martin's laugh is loud and infectious and soon Carmen is giggling too.

'You wouldn't believe it, Martin. I don't even have an outfit. I haven't bought any gifts for José's family and I haven't even begun to think about Christmas presents for my family here or my family in Spain.'

Martin bites into his cheese and ham sandwich. 'I love Christmas here. I wouldn't want to be in the sun.'

Carmen regards him carefully. 'Will it be a difficult Christmas now that you're divorced?'

Martin looks surprised and then frowns. 'I'm far happier now. I know what I want. Looks aren't everything, Carmen. My ex was stunning and she knew it. She flirted with everyone, and when she had an affair with her personal trainer, she wasn't even sorry for the hurt she caused.'

'You deserve better.'

He grins. 'You're right! And I'll enjoy Christmas with my

family here in Westbay.'

Carmen looks around the show home. 'I'd prefer to be here too. I'd like to be at the opening of this development and be a part of all this.'

'You are a part of it all. You're making these homes what they are. You're turning these houses in someone else's home. You have an incredible talent. My mum spotted it immediately.'

Carmen makes a mental note to buy a Christmas gift for her loyal clients including Sheila and all her friends in Westbay. But where would she get the time?

'Come on.' She stands up. 'We can't sit around here all day. We've got the three-bed to sort out now.'

Later that afternoon, Martin drives her back to Harbour Street and drops her outside the shop.

'You look exhausted. Get some sleep,' he says.

Carmen is dizzy with tiredness. She regards Harbour Street with disappointment. 'There are only two photographers now,' she mumbles.

They snap quick pictures as she climbs from her car and opens her gate. Once inside the alleyway she gasps. A man in a thick coat and black beanie hat sits on her step. He's holding his head in his hands and there's a large box beside him.

'You can't sit here. You're on private property. Get out!' She points at the gate.

The man looks wearily up at her. 'Cammy? Thank, God you're back! It's bloody Baltic out here.'

* * *

Upstairs, in the privacy of the flat, Carmen closes the blinds.

She goes into the kitchen and switches on the kettle. Jack follows her shaking with the cold. He leaves the box in the hallway.

'I thought you'd be at home. You normally don't go out when the paparazzi are...'

'I'm not going to be intimidated, Jack. This is my home.'

He regards her wordlessly.

'That coat looks massive on you,' she says.

'It's Ben's. I got your message and I went straight to that place where he looks after all those kids. The charity.'

'So you've met Ben?'

'He drove me here. He left me outside the gate so I could duck inside. He pretended there was a delivery and he carried that box in while I slipped out of the passenger door. No one saw me.'

'What's in the box?'

'Nothing. It was a ploy. He's a clever bloke.' Jack's face breaks into a grin. 'He's a decent guy. We had a great chat on the way down and we really bonded, you know?'

Carmen doesn't want to know. She can't believe Jack is here standing in front of her telling her how nice her friend is.

'You look exhausted,' she says. 'Go and have a hot shower and I'll make tea.'

'I'd prefer a whiskey. Have you got any? I'm knackered.' He throws himself onto the sofa.

Carmen pulls the bottle from the cupboard and finds a glass. Then she follows Jack into the living room where he's kicked off his shoes and is snoring quietly.

Chapter 20

It's almost ten o'clock when he wakes and he sits up quickly, appearing disoriented and surprised to see Carmen sitting on the chair opposite with her laptop open.

'Hi,' he whispers, rubbing his cheeks, making a rasping noise. 'Sorry. I fell asleep.'

Carmen regards him carefully. She's spent the past few hours watching him sleep and wondering about her future - life with and without him.

'Are you alright?' he asks swinging his legs off the sofa. 'What are you doing?'

'Buying presents.'

'Who for?'

'José's family - the wedding in Florida, remember?'

'What are you buying?'

'I've ordered some expensive royal cushions with William and Catherine on them.'

Jack laughs. 'Have you got enough money?'

'Yes, thanks.'

'I don't know if they'll want me there now.'

'Why did you do this, Jack? Why did you have to write that book?'

'Cammy, please. I was just being honest.'

'Why?' she cries.

'I wanted to be able to pay the bills and save the house.'

'Like you'd earn enough with the dancing programme?'

'Yeah.'

'Well, that worked, didn't it?' Her sarcasm cuts through the air.

'I wasn't to know it would all go so wrong. We needed the advance payment for the mortgage.'

'But it wasn't enough!'

'No!'

'Why couldn't you just write about football? Was it revenge?'

'Revenge for what?'

'You tell me.'

'What's that supposed to mean?' His eyes darken.

'Because I wanted something new. Something different. Somewhere different. I wanted a new life?'

'No, it's not that—'

'So, there's another reason why you sold out your family?'

'I didn't sell anyone out! It's the truth. Don't you remember? I said to you, after the book was finished that it was cathartic. I said I felt better.'

'Yes, but—'

'I mean it, Cammy. Please baby, listen to me. It just seemed the right thing to do.'

Carmen stands up. She's surprised that it's quiet outside, and when she checks the photographers have gone.

Jack leans forward and pours a glass of whiskey and they sit looking at each other.

'We never really spoke about any of it, did we? I mean, we just got on with life. In the beginning it was all about me and football. I never thought about you and what you'd given up to marry me. I never really considered you or what it was like being an international model and then to be stuck at home raising two children.' He refills his glass. 'I was the one who did everything wrong and you always picked up the pieces. That's what I'm trying to say in the book.'

'You could have just spoken to me.'

'I tried but you block me out. Once you got cancer it was like you were fighting your own battle that had nothing to do with me. You made your own choices about your body and it made me feel helpless.' He raises his glass. 'But it also made me realise that's how I'd treated *you*. I bought the house in London without ever asking you if you liked it or if you wanted to live there. I assumed that because it had everything - security and luxury - that you would love it.'

'It was a prison.'

Jack shakes his head. 'I had no idea.'

Carmen reaches for a glass, pours whiskey and drinks deeply. The liquid burns her throat but she's alive.

'I'm happy here. I can be me,' she says quietly. 'I can't live with all the celebrity attention. The constant reels on social media and the paparazzi sleeping outside my house. I've had enough.'

'I know.'

'Jack.' She leans forward. 'If you want to go on all the celebrity shows and have the ups and downs of public opinion thrown in your face, then do it. But please keep me and Elena and Luis out of it. They are so distraught.'

'But they don't need to be...'

'Jack! You've splashed the details of their lives all over your book!'

'But, if they read it properly, and in context, and not just the salacious parts that the media have hooked into then they'd realise how much I love them.'

'Jack—'

'You haven't read it all, have you?'

'No.'

'Then please, read it. It's an apology. To all of you.' Jack stands up. 'I'm going for a shower and then to bed. I've got an early lift back to London tomorrow morning with Ben. I'm going to sort out the house.'

* * *

Jack is up early. He's slept in Luis' room and Carmen is disappointed that he didn't come to seek her out in the night. She's upset to think that she's pushed him away. But she doesn't look like she used to. Jack had loved her long hair and marvelled over her beautiful body. But that was before her cancer. His words still echo in her head. *She'd made all the decisions about her body.* That was true. She'd decided that she wasn't having a breast implant. Breasts didn't define who she was.

'I'll phone, you.' Jack pulls on Ben's heavy coat. 'There might be things that you want from the house. I'll check with you first.'

'Luis and Elena still have their things there too.'

'I'll box them up. I can put them into storage.'

'Will you be okay?'

Jack looks up. His normally twinkling blue eyes are sad and he looks lost. 'I just want us to be alright,' he says. 'I'll do anything.'

'Can you live here?'

Jack looks around the flat and then scratches the stubble on his cheek. 'It's small.'

'Yes.'

'There's no pool.'

'There's the sea.'

'There's no garden.'

'There are woods all around us.'

Jack pulls his beanie hat down low over his eyes. 'Do you think they'll forgive me?'

'You need to speak to them.

'We'll need to speak about next week - you know, the arrangements for the wedding and all that. Do you want any clothes from the house? Suitcases? I mean what about—'

'Let's take one day at a time, Jack. Now you're home and we're on the same timeframe, we can talk more easily. We could video call.'

'Be honest with me, Cammy. Do you even like José?'

She thinks carefully before answering. 'I don't have to marry him.'

'I know but when Elena was growing up, do you remember? She was always strong willed and we said she'd have to marry a lion-tamer.' He gives a small grin. 'But José? I mean, he's still got young kids - the youngest is only two and Elena's been dating him for a year...'

'What are you trying to say?'

'What if he gets her to move over to Florida and then he's flying all over the world having affairs?'

'We don't know he'll do that.'

'Come on, Cammy—'

'People could say the same about you.'

'What?'

'With Shazzy B— '

'She's a ball-breaker. And, I'll tell you something else, the press love her over there and she leaked a story that we'd had a fight.'

'Had you?'

'We fought all the time and then smiled for the cameras. She was a demon trainer. I'm twenty years older than her and no one took that into consideration. Besides, she couldn't hold a candle to you, baby.'

'I was jealous when you did the waltz. That was always our dance.'

Jack grins. 'I think that's why we fell out. She wasn't dancing it as elegantly as you.'

Carmen smiles, she's flattered he still cares to pay her a compliment.

'There's no one, like you, Cammy. No one at all. Look, I'll sort out the house. I promise. I'm going to fight for us.'

Carmen fights back her tears. 'Is that what you want?' Her voice is husky with emotion.

'More than anything.'

Carmen reaches out to him. She needs his touch and he pulls her into his arms. She rests her head on his shoulder and tears begin falling down her cheeks. His heart is thumping rapidly and the familiarity of his touch and the smell of his skin fills her with desire. He pulls away and very gently he wipes away her tears. 'I'm sorry, Cammy.'

Chapter 21

By Wednesday evening the paparazzi have disappeared and the only person still hanging around in Harbour Street is Eric.

'Who's the guy with the Viking beard?' asks Martin, looking out of the shop window.

'That's Tracey's boyfriend. I think he sells stories to the press or puts videos up on social media.'

Martin groans. 'What a loser! Come on, let's go for something to eat in the pub. I'm starving.'

'You want to have dinner with me?'

'Why not?'

'I could be your mother.'

'I also have dinner with my mother.' He grins. 'She's great fun and much more interesting than half the women I meet.'

'Don't you have a girlfriend to go home to?'

'No. I'm single.'

'Happily single?'

'That's a good question. Most people at this point ask if I'm gay.' He laughs. He holds up his hand. 'I have nothing against gay people but I'm perfectly straight. Come on, get your coat.'

Carmen frowns and glances anxiously out of the window.

'Ignore Eric. I'm with you. I'll protect you,' he says.

'Then he'll post a video of us in the pub and it will go viral.'

'So what? You're allowed to have friends. You're allowed to live. You can't hide away forever.' Martin's smile is full of youthful confidence.

Carmen straightens her shoulders. 'You're right.'

'Come on, hold my arm. Let's give him something to video.'

* * *

They settle in the quieter corner of the busy pub and they both order steak and chips. Martin has a pint of local ale and Carmen opts for a gin and tonic. He buys her a double.

'We won't be able to do this next week. You'll be in sunny Florida. When do you leave?'

'The day after tomorrow.'

'Are you all ready?'

Carmen blows air heavily from her cheeks. 'I've bought gifts but don't have my outfit sorted yet.'

'You work better under pressure.' He grins.

They talk about what she needs to finish the show homes while waiting for their dinner.

'It has come together quickly, Carmen. I'm impressed that you've managed to bring it in on time - under the circumstances. The homes look amazing.'

'I've really enjoyed it, Martin. It's been great working with you and Harry.'

'Thanks for all your help. It's a shame you won't be here for the opening.'

'If there are no sales I'll have to come up with some more designs.' She laughs.

'You have natural expertise, Carmen You have an eye for it all. It's like you have a vision for interiors. Just look at what you've done in here. This pub is totally transformed and it's all done with such good taste.'

Paul brings over their food and he's smiling happily. 'It's good to see you, Carmen. And, if you're on a date, Martin, then good luck to you.' Paul pats Martin on the shoulder and they all laugh, but Carmen waggles her index finger in mock anger. 'No! No! No! You know me better than that, Paul.'

Paul replies, 'I know you still love that husband of yours and I can't wait for him to come in here one day so that I can tell him how bloody lucky he is.'

'Hear, hear.' Martin raises his glass in agreement.

'I'll tell you something, Carmen. You were right about me putting more effort into my marriage and understanding Sandra and what she's going through with her dad. I know he's lonely and she feels guilty if she's not with him. I was thinking that Christmas is going to be a nightmare for us, but then I had this brainwave.' He smiles expectantly. 'I'm opening the pub on Christmas Day for a special lunch and I'm inviting anyone who is on their own to join us. Free of charge. I'd hadn't realised until I spoke to Sandra, just how many people are on their own at Christmas. So many families get caught up with their children they forget about the older and lonelier members of the family.'

Martin says, 'There's probably a lot of lonely people at Christmas who would welcome some company.'

'I'll be doing some publicity in the coming week so if you know of anyone who's on their own, they'll be a place for them at the table here in The Ship.'

'That's a brilliant idea, Paul. Well done.' Martin raises his glass.

Carmen smiles. 'If I wasn't in Florida for Christmas I'd be

here.'

'And you'd be very welcome. You've saved our marriage. You've got Sandra and I agreeing on Christmas - which is a great start. We're very happy.' He grins. 'Enjoy your meal.'

After Paul leaves, they eat their meal chatting comfortably. Martin is impressed that Carmen helped Paul sort out his marriage.

'It's because you're so easy to talk to,' Martin adds.

'I wish you'd tell my kids that.' She jokes.

'Have you heard from them?'

'Not since last weekend. Not since parts of Jack's book were serialised in the tabloids. 'They're furious with him and probably with me by default.'

'The wedding's going to be challenging then,' Martin says.

Carmen nods. 'If only Jack hadn't written that bloody book!'

Martin laughs.

Carmen is enjoying Martin's company. The pub is warm and friendly and she's relaxed.

'To be honest,' Martin says, a little later, returning from the bar with more drinks. 'I didn't think it was that bad - it wasn't that damaging.'

'You mean, Jack's book?' Carmen can't hide her surprise. 'It was awful.'

'It's no worse than lots of other celebrities and if you break it down...'

'He told everyone I had breast cancer...' her voice trails off.

'Why was it such a secret?' Martin wipes froth from his top lip. 'I know I haven't had it and I'm not famous. But so what? I mean, look at you. You're a survivor. You're gorgeous and your hair looks fabulous.'

'I have Yusef to thank for that.' Carmen rubs the back of her bare neck. She enjoys the freedom of short hair. 'It's much easier to manage each morning in the shower.'

'So what if people know?'

Carmen shrugs. 'I suppose it's not important now because I've changed. I'm not so uptight about everything. I used to defend our privacy, our private lives, and it was easier to hide everything back then.'

'Behind the big closed palatial gates.'

'You know?'

'He says that in the book.'

'You've read it all?'

Martin grins. 'Haven't you?'

'I scanned the first few chapters. I saw what he wrote about Luis and Elena and they're furious.'

'You didn't read it all?'

Carmen shakes her head and sips her gin and tonic. 'I couldn't.'

Martin continues, 'He starts off by saying how different your two children are. Elena is headstrong and stubborn and she wants to eat life as if she's been starved. He feels responsible for that. He says it's his fault that he's fed her this diet of never being satisfied and always wanting more, but that it's made her into a fiercely independent woman. He says he's proud of that. And Luis, he thinks is naturally more cautious and more afraid and he's created a different persona to help him deal with the stresses of life.'

'To help *them*.'

Martin smiles. 'Jack says in the book how he constantly gets the pronouns wrong. He blames himself but he makes a good argument from a father's viewpoint about gender recognition. He also says the word *they* is plural for him and to others of his generation. That's why *they* find it so hard. By the end of the book he says he knows he's not perfect, but he's determined to nail it. His love for both his children comes through.'

'So, it's all his fault, is it?'

Martin scratches his chin. 'He does blame himself for pretty much everything.'

'I can't bear self-pity.'

'I know.'

Carmen stares at him and Martin continues, 'He says that in the book too. The hardest thing he's ever been through is when you were diagnosed with breast cancer. He felt shut out.'

'He wasn't—'

'But.' Martin holds up his hand. 'He puts a good point forward that for the first time in your life together, it wasn't about him. He had to play the supporting role and he admits he was pants at it!' Martin grins.

'He wasn't pants. He just had to adapt, and he did.'

Martin takes a deep gulp of beer. 'It seems to me that in his book he's trying to apologise to everyone. The problem is that he doesn't actually say how sorry he is and how so many things were his fault - until the final chapter. That's the most positive part of the book where it all comes together. Did Luis and Elena read it all - right to the end?'

Carmen shrugs. 'I don't know. I can't believe you did!'

'How can you decide or have an opinion unless you have all the information? At the end, he takes responsibility for everything and he's determined to make things right.He seems like a decent bloke to me and I'd be very proud if he were my dad.'

Carmen places her hand on his. 'Thanks Martin. That's a lovely thing to say.'

Martin smiles. He places his other hand on hers and he squeezes it reassuringly. 'I hope it's helped, Carmen. Please read it.'

'What the hell are you doing?' A shadow comes over their table and they break apart. Elena's face is screwed up in anger. Her eyes are blazing. 'Who the hell is he?'

'Elena,' Carmen gasps.

'What are you playing at, Mama?'

'This is Martin. He's my friend.'

'I can see that. You're bloody holding hands in public!' she hisses.

Martin laughs. 'Ah, you must be Elena. Can I get you a drink?'

Elena ignores him and glares furiously at her mother. 'I came in here to keep warm because you weren't in the flat. You're never at home and I didn't know where you were. You didn't answer my messages. You're not answering your phone.'

'I wasn't expecting yo—'

'Clearly, Mama! I thought you would be hiding upstairs in your flat. You always do when things get...'

'She's not hiding any more.' Martin stands up and smiles. 'Gin and tonic, Elena?'

* * *

As Martin goes to the bar, Carmen indicates for Elena to sit beside her. She tries to give her a hug but Elena leans away before sitting beside her grudgingly.

'I'm only having a drink because I'm so bloody cold!'

'It's so lovely to see you.'

'What's going on?' asks Elena.

'We've just had dinner. Are you hungry?'

Elena shakes her head and pulls off her scarf. She looks around the pub and her eyes fix on Martin's back. 'Who's Martin?'

'My boss.'

'But you have your own shop.'

'He's the developer with the show homes that I'm decorating.'

'He's young.' Elena stares at his back and it gives Carmen a chance to take a good look at her daughter. She looks exhausted. There are dark circles around her blood-shot eyes and deep hollows in her cheeks as if she hasn't eaten or slept in weeks.

'You've lost weight,' Carmen says.

Elena is about to speak when Martin returns and places her drink on the table.

'I bought you the menu.' He waves it in the air. 'Are you hungry?'

Elena looks at the menu and licks her lips. 'I am actually.'

'What can I get you?' Martin asks gently.

'Something small, maybe calamari?'

'Good choice. They're lovely in here.'

Martin returns to the bar and Elena looks from him to her mother. 'What about Papi, have you seen him?'

'He was here a few days ago. He's sorting out the house.' Then she changes the subject. 'It's so lovely to see you, Elena. This is a wonderful surprise.' It wasn't in Elena's schedule to visit her in Westbay and Carmen can only assume that she's here to make sure everything is organised for the wedding trip. Carmen's pleased she has ordered the gifts for José's family.

'How are the show homes going?' Elena asks.

'I just need to add the final details, but everything is on time and Martin seems pleased.'

As if on cue he returns to the table and smiles politely at them both.

'What does he know?' Elena asks nodding at Martin.

Carmen shrugs and smiles. 'Probably just about everything. He's the only person I know who's read Papi's book from cover to cover.'

Elena frowns at him. 'You have?'

Martin grins.

'Why?'

Fearing that Martin is about to be subjected to an inquisition, Carmen interrupts and smiles brightly. 'We're very excited about the wedding and the trip to Florida.'

'That's a lie, Mama.'

Carmen blinks. 'Well...'

'No one wants to go...'

'It's only for a few days and I have bought gifts for José's family and...'

'Well, you'll have to send them back.'

'Why?'

'The wedding's off.'

'Que?' Instinctively Carmen leans forward and takes Elena's hand. 'Oh, cariño, I'm so sorry.'

'Mama, don't be sorry. It was me who called it off. And besides I don't think you ever really liked José anyway, did you?'

Carmen's mouth falls open and Martin grins.

Elena raises her glass. 'Here's to being single.'

Martin taps his glass against hers. 'I'll drink to that.'

***

Carmen is elated. She's had far too much gin, but Elena is home and the wedding is off. Upstairs in the flat, Elena kicks off her shoes and curls up on the sofa. She sips coffee and she's less aggressive than she's been in recent months. Her hostility is thawing.

Carmen eyes the stack of gift boxes in the corner. 'They'll have to go back then.'

'Sorry, Mama.'

'I just want you to be happy, my darling.'

'I'm happy now.' Elena leans against Carmen's shoulder. 'He was horrible.'

'Do you want to tell me what happened?'

'He was furious when Papi's book came out. He said it made him look foolish. I said he wasn't even in the book. Then he said I would have to distance myself from Papi and from you and all the family - including Luis. He said that you were an awful family and terrible people and that once we moved to Florida things would be very different but....'

'Isn't that what you wanted?'

Elena sighs. 'Mama, I've been so tired. I've been working extra shifts to take time off for the wedding, but when we went to Florida to sort out the wedding details, his mother and sister took over. It was all done. It was all organised. I had nothing to do. These people were all strangers. They were making decisions for me about my hair, the flowers, the dress and even bridesmaids. They said it would be a small wedding but there were so many of his family....' her voice trails off.

'You're exhausted.'

Elena reaches for her mother's hand. 'I realised then that

I'd always wanted you and Papi with me when I got married.'

Carmen's heart soars, but it breaks again at the sight of her daughter's exhaustion. 'You need a good night's sleep and a proper rest.'

'Can I stay?'

'You can stay for as long as you like. This is home.'

'I'll have to tell Papi.'

'It's late now. We'll call him tomorrow.'

'And Luis?'

'And Luis,' Carmen agrees. 'Come on, time to sleep and you can have a lie in. There's no need for you to get up tomorrow.'

'Where will you be?'

'I'll be in the shop and then I'll go for an hour to check the final details of the show homes. The opening is on Saturday.' Carmen realises that she will be here now for the opening of the development on Saturday night. Her heart skips with an excited beat of happiness. Perhaps her luck is finally changing.

* * *

'You mean Elena is there in the flat?' Jack can't hide his surprise. 'And the wedding's cancelled.'

'Isn't that great?' Carmen's head is thumping from too much gin last night but she can't stop smiling. She's in the shop preparing to leave for the development and she wanders over to gaze out of the window into Harbour Street.

'Is she alright?' he asks.

'She's exhausted. I've told her to sleep in.'

'And she's staying for a few days?'

'It seems like it.'

'So, what about Florida?'

'We're clearly not going.'

'Then what about Christmas? I found the tree decorations yesterday.'

'I'll speak to her later and see what she's doing for Christmas. She needs a good rest.'

'What about Luis?'

'I'll speak to them later when Elena's awake.'

'No, I mean what will we all do for Christmas? It's next Tuesday.'

'Let's take one day at a time, Jack.'

Jack sighs. 'I need to have the house empty by Monday, so I've packed a lot of things and I've organised storage.'

'Well done.'

'You sound different?' he says. 'Are you alright?'

'Fine.'

'You sound happier. Is that because Elena's home?'

Carmen thinks for a minute. She's happier. Her heart is lighter because the wedding is off and Elena isn't going to live in Florida but there's something else and she's not sure what it is.

'Yes.' It's the simple answer and it gives her time to think.

'Right. Good.'

'We'll call again when Elena is awake.'

'Maybe she'd like to come home tomorrow?' Jack says. 'Before the house goes.'

Carmen is suddenly winded. Her daughter is only just back and last night she felt they were closer than they had been in years. She doesn't want to let her go now. She wants more special time with Elena. 'Maybe.'

Jack's voice sounds brighter. 'I'll ask her. It will be good for us to spend some time together and perhaps she might even forgive me. You know, about the book.'

* * *

The morning flies by and there's no sign of Elena. Carmen drives over to the show homes and finishes the final details. Although she doesn't need him, she's surprised that Martin isn't around on her last day to finalise everything.

She hands her keys back to Harry.

'I'll be able to come to the party on Saturday now,' she says. 'I'll also be here to supervise the flowers that Eva will bring over in the morning.'

'The caterers are setting up in the teepee tomorrow,' confirms Harry. 'You should keep the keys if you're not going away, just in case.'

'Exciting times.' Carmen pockets the keys and rubs her hands in nervous excitement. 'I'm so pleased I'm not missing it.'

'Me too,' agrees Harry, 'and I know Martin will be thrilled.

Martin has clearly not told Harry that they were out together last night or that Elena's wedding had been cancelled. She wonders where he is. Perhaps he's in bed with a hangover?

* * *

When Elena gets up, Carmen is already back and she takes a great interest in the shop.

'This is lovely.' Elena picks up Marjorie's blue and silver Chinese vase.

'I have to find it a special home.'

They spend the afternoon together looking at stock and

changing things around: swapping vases, hanging mirrors and different paintings. There are a few customers buying last minute gifts for Christmas and although Elena fades into the background, Carmen is pleased she's making an effort to stay with her.

Just before closing time Sheila comes in.

'I hadn't realised that Martin is your son.' Carmen smiles. 'You must be so proud of him.'

Sheila smiles. 'I'm looking forward to Saturday. He tells me that you'll be here now for the opening.'

Carmen covers her surprise with a smile. Martin certainly communicates with his mother.

'Now, he said, he saw a lovely Chinese-looking vase in here?' Sheila looks around the shop.

'Is this it?' Elena calls, pointing to the vase in the corner of the room. 'It's one of my favourite pieces.'

Sheila smiles. 'It's very pretty but I was actually looking for the green and yellow one.'

'This is my daughter, Elena,' says Carmen.

'Yes, Martin said he met you, last night.' Sheila smiles.

Elena's cheeks flush. 'Here's the vase you want.' She takes it from the corner table and lifts it onto the counter.

'Will you come to the opening on Saturday?' Sheila asks.

Elena smiles. 'Maybe.'

As Carmen wraps the vase they speak about Christmas. After Sheila pays she says, 'I'll see you both at the opening. I'm really looking forward to seeing your designs, Carmen. Martin's been very naughty and he's kept me in suspense. Even Harry has been forbidden to tell me anything about your designs.' She casts her eyes to the ceiling and smiles. 'I guess that's men for you.'

* * *

Carmen manages to get a booking for an early dinner sitting at the bar in Harbour Bistro. But before that, she links her arm through Elena's.

'Come with me. You must see Harbour Street at night. It's one of the prettiest streets I've ever seen.'

Muffled up with hats and scarves, they venture along the street, window shopping and browsing companionably.

'Ben owns the art gallery. He's Amber's partner. Isn't Eva's flower shop beautiful? She's arranging the flowers for the show homes on Saturday. This is Jane's jewellery shop. She has some lovely designs.' She points across the road. 'That's Yusef and Ozan's Grooming Salon. It was Yusef who cut my hair. That's Derek in the butcher's shop and Ian who has the grocers. Kit from the gift shop was Santa, and Frances the vicar organised the choir to sing in the harbour.' They duck down the alleyway and into the quiet street leading to the sea.

'The blue and silver Chinese vase came from that house.' Carmen points to the Merchant's house. 'It belonged to Frances' mother-in-law, Marjorie, but she went into a home a few months ago. There's an old coach house in the garden where the merchant would have kept his carriage, many years ago.'

They walk along the boardwalk, past the sailing boats, and return through the archway of Harbour Street to the warmth of the Bistro. It's decorated with warm yellow lights, leafy poinsettias and fragrant candles. Christmas music plays in the background and the smell of rosemary, garlic and tasty spices hangs in the air.

Amber hugs them both. 'Welcome back, Elena. A glass of

fizz on the house?'

When Carmen booked earlier, she had told Amber the wedding was off. Now Amber hands them menus and pours the bubbles into chilled glasses. 'It's busy tonight. Christmas celebrations are in full swing.'

Elena beams back at her. 'Everything smells delicious.'

Amber leans forward and with a conspiratorial wink she says, 'The rack of lamb is incredible.'

Carmen grins. 'Two of those, please.'

Amber goes to serve other customers, and Elena turns to her mother.

'I'm sorry, Mama. I couldn't marry that control freak. I need my freedom.'

'There's no need to apologise. At least you found out before we all trekked over to Florida.' She grins.

'But now I have to face the judgment of the entire family.'

Carmen laughs. 'As we all do, cariño. Think of poor Papi.'

Elena sips slowly from her glass. 'He's asked me to go home, back to London tomorrow, to sort out my things before they go into storage.'

'Ah.' Carmen pauses. The thought of losing her daughter tears at her stomach and the dead weight of dread returns to her soul. She can't bear to think about it. She had wanted Elena to come to the opening with her tomorrow night and she certainly doesn't want to spoil tonight.

'Let's make a toast to your freedom from Captain control freak.'

Elena giggles. 'You know how to make me better, Mama. Besides, why do I need a pilot when I can soar through life on my own terms?'

They clink glasses.

'The best journeys in life are the ones you take with a sense of humour and a touch of rebellion,' says Carmen.

'I'm in the mood to rebel, Mama. Cheers!' Elena laughs and Carmen smiles back at her daughter. She's reassured that Elena's healing. She has her whole life ahead of her to find love.

They sit at the bar sharing stories and enjoying roasted rack of lamb with fresh pea shoots and mash that looks like fluffy cotton wool. It tastes delicious. The past few years of acrimony and blame seem to have evaporated and Elena has reverted to the young woman she was before she met José. She's full of warmth, laughter and wicked humour.

'Now I know now that I want to live in England, Mama. I want to be near you and Papi.'

Then without warning, Carmen's vision goes suddenly black.

* * *

She pulls the cold hands away from her eyes and there is laughter all around her. Still holding the familiar fingers, she turns, blinks and gasps.

'Luis?'

'Surprise!' He folds her into a big hug. 'So, this is where you're hanging out.' Luis leans over and Elena throws her arms around his neck.

'Hello, stranger.' She giggles. 'Crikey, you look amazing. Better than me.'

'Thanks, Sis. Although in fairness that wouldn't be hard.' He laughs and preens, flicking long hair from his shoulders as Carmen used to do. His eyes are heavily made up with colourful pinks and purples and his face seems fuller and rosier.

Carmen realises it's been two months since she's seen Luis.

He rubs her shoulder. 'I love your hair, Mama. You look different. So beautiful.'

Carmen smiles, unable to remove her arm from Luis' waist. 'What a surprise. I'm so lucky to have my two beautiful children with me.'

Luis raises his eyes to the ceiling. 'Hardly children, Mama.'

'How did you get here?" asks Elena.

'I drove down with Ben. He dropped me at the front as the Viking is hanging around and I ducked in here without being seen.'

Through the kitchen window Ben is hugging Amber and laughing. Carmen is thankful that he's so kind and supportive and is helping them all.

She sighs happily. 'Are you hungry, Luis?'

'We had a burger on the way down. How are you, Sis?'

'Good. Getting slightly drunk with Mama.'

'Celebrating your freedom?'

'Of course.'

'It was definitely your decision?'

'Definitely.'

'So, can I say what I like?'

Elena giggles. 'Go on, we've already done Captain cruise-control.'

'From Narcissistic Airways,' quips Luis. 'Plonker the Pilot.'

'Enough.' Carmen laughs. 'Why didn't you tell us you were coming home?'

'I wanted to surprise you. Then Ben said you and Elena were eating in here tonight and I knew I had to get back.' He looks at Elena. 'You look really pale and your make-up needs sorting out. I'll help you if you like?' He teases.

'I've managed for twenty-six years, thanks.'

'Yeah, but now you're Elena-no-mates again. Elena-on-the-shelf and I'm thinking about dating sites for you. You'll probably have to go on the old ones now. You may meet a bloke who's divorced and looking for love the second time around. You've missed the young ones now...'

Elena reaches inside Luis' jacket and tickles him as she used to when he was younger. Carmen watches their interaction with delight. Luis giggles and pushes Elena gently away.

Carmen smiles. Everything's going to be alright.

'What did you say, Mama?' asks Luis, turning serious.

'Nothing. It's just lovely having you both here with me.'

'Well make the most of us. I've already told Ben that Elena and I are going back to London with him in the morning.'

'Really? Why?' Disappointment floods through her veins.

'You think I'm letting Papi sort through my things? You've got to be joking. Knowing him he'll probably sell everything on eBay.... *Luis Bailey's Life for Sale,*' he quips.

'He wouldn't—'

'I'm not taking the chance, Mama. And I know that Elena feels the same way. She doesn't want Papi rifling through all her private things either.'

'He's not rifling...'

Luis holds up his hand. 'Mama, stop! It's already decided. We're leaving at eight. Ben needs to be in town for a ten o'clock meeting.'

Carmen stares. They won't be here for her big opening tomorrow night.

Chapter 22

Carmen is the last to leave the restaurant and as Elena and Luis head out into the street she settles the bill and thanks Ben who is with Amber behind the bar.

'I don't know how I'll ever repay you for all your kindness, ferrying my family around.'

'You don't need to repay me, Carmen. I'm always going backwards and forwards at this time of year. There are so many homeless kids and the more we find, the more we can help. I just wish there were more hours in the day.'

'It's such a responsibility, Ben.'

'We need to give these kids a chance. They're having a rotten time and we have to try and get some normality in their lives. They deserve to have some enjoyment. To know there's hope.'

Outside, in Harbour Street, there's a piercing scream. Instinctively Carmen is at the door and Ben is right behind her. They rush out into the street. Elena and Luis are across the road and they have the Viking pinned against the wall.

'WAIT!' Ben shouts and rushes over. 'What's going on?'

It's taking both Elena and Luis to hold him.

'Eric? What's going on?' demands Ben. His solid frame is back up for Luis and Elena. 'Let him go.'

'He's been taking videos,' shouts Luis. 'He's ruining our

lives.'

'You don't need me for that. With a dad like yours—'

Luis raises his fist and punches Eric in the face. His lip splits open and blood runs down his coat. 'That's for my broken ribs last September. It was you that followed me. I remember you.' He raises his hand again.

'Luis! Stop!' cries Elena.

Ben steps forward, pushing Luis away and grabbing Eric's collar. 'Is this true?'

'No.'

'It is true! Paul has the CCTV from the pub to prove it.' Carmen stares defiantly at Eric.

'What?' cries Luis.

'Why haven't you done anything then?' asks Elena, her tone accusatory.

Carmen doesn't like to say that the images were too grainy or that it couldn't be proved in a court of law, but she remembers the two figures hurrying after Luis on the screen after he'd got off the bus with Tracey.

Now the angry stares from her two children make her uncomfortable.

Ben takes Eric by the collar and snatches his iPhone from his grasp. 'You won't be needing this.' He throws it on the floor and stamps on it with his heel, grinding it into the pavement. 'You've caused enough trouble around here. Tracey is too embarrassed to show her face in Harbour Street because of you. No one wants you here so get out. Get away from here because next time you won't be so lucky!' He thrusts him into the street and Eric stumbles, trying to stay on his feet and wiping his bloody face.

'Stay away from Westbay or there will be a price to pay,' Ben shouts.

'The press are paying me.'

'They won't want anything to do with you once I've been in touch with the editors. They have to be very careful with litigation. It costs them a fortune now in court. And, just for the record– there's no story here. Not now! Not ever!'

Eric stumbles up the road, pulling his coat around his shoulders and wiping his bloody lip with the back of his hand.

'Alright, everyone?' Ben asks looking around.

Luis grins. 'Thanks, Ben. See you at eight. I've only just arrived and can't wait to get out of this bloody place.' Luis stalks off across the road in the direction of the shop and Carmen's flat.

Elena follows him. 'Thanks, Ben. See you tomorrow.'

Only Carmen and Ben are left standing in the street looking at each other.

'It will be alright,' says Ben.

'Not this time,' replies Carmen. 'And it's all my fault.'

* * *

The atmosphere inside the flat is icy and almost hostile.

'I didn't say anything because the images on the CCTV weren't good enough,' Carmen explains.

'Where's a spare duvet?' Luis ignores her. 'I'll sleep on the sofa.'

'You can have the bedroom,' says Elena. 'It's yours.'

'It's not mine. This isn't my home. I live at uni now.'

'Please,' begs Carmen almost in tears. 'Please don't be like this.'

'Like this?' fumes Luis. 'With the parents we have? A father who plasters his feelings all over social media and a mother who has spent her whole life hiding away and never standing up for us.'

'I'm going to sleep.' Elena turns her back on them both. 'The one good thing I've learnt from you and Papi is that I never want to get married. It's a crap life.'

Carmen listens to her daughter's footsteps going up the stairs.

'Luis...?'

He holds up his hands in defence. 'Go to bed, Mama. You and Elena are both drunk and I want nothing to do with you.'

* * *

Drunk?

Carmen lays in bed in the dark staring up at the ceiling. She isn't drunk. Maybe a little merry but she and Elena had been having so much fun. They had really been laughing and speaking properly for the first time in years. Then Luis had surprised them and it was perfect.

Now her heart has palpations and her mouth is dry. She wants to weep. She wants to shout and rant and rave at God and anyone else who will listen. Everything is so unfair. She loves her family more than anything. She's devoted her life to them all and they can't see it.

What more could she have done?

What more can she do?

This is worse than any of Jack's mistakes. This is far worse than leaving him to begin a new life here in Westbay. This is worse than her cancer diagnosis. The loss of her children is worse than the loss of life itself. The sacrifices, the energy, the diplomacy and all the strength she's ever had has evaporated tonight leaving her hollow and empty.

She has no more strength.

She has nothing left to give.

For the first time in her life, she's completely exhausted. She buries her head in her pillow so that they won't hear her smothered howls and uncontrollable sobbing.

* * *

The next morning Carmen makes coffee and prepares toast. She hears the murmur of their voices upstairs that would normally make her smile, but today she senses their conspiracy.

Luis has folded the duvet and placed it with the pillow at the end of the sofa and when there's no sign of them, she calls up the stairs.

'I've made coffee.'

There's no answer.

At five minutes to eight, they come down the stairs and they barely look at her.

'Bye, Mama.' Luis calls from the front door.

'Don't you want coffee?'

'Can't keep Ben waiting. Come on, Elena.' He disappears.

Elena stands at the door and regards her mother. Her face is pinched with anger. 'How much more hurt do we have to go through, Mama?'

Carmen raises her tired head and stares defiantly at her daughter. 'It's not what you go through. It's how you deal with it.'

Elena shakes her head with exasperation and bangs the door behind her. Carmen listens to their feet going downstairs, the front door slamming, the gate opening and closing and then they're gone.

Carmen sits on the sofa and stares at the feature wall.

She's all alone again.

* * *

Carmen goes down early and opens she shop. She needs to keep occupied and it gives her something to do. She should have been in Florida and this should have been her daughter's wedding weekend.

Given how things have all worked out, Carmen can barely think straight. The past few months have been an emotional roller-coaster. She's refurbished the local pub and won the contract for the show homes. She's opened the shop and worked to deadlines. She's turned her life around. Aside from the family traumas she's actually been happier than she has been for years. For the first time she's been in charge of her own destiny and made decisions based on her own wants and needs.

It's mid-morning when Eva arrives with the most beautiful arrangement of fresh flowers in a Christmas wreath filled with holly and mistletoe.

'This is for you. All the others are ready to go to the show homes.'

'It's beautiful.' Carmen admires the wreath and moves Marjorie's blue and silver Chinese vase. 'I'll put it on the front door later.'

'That's a beautiful vase. I've never seen one like that before.' Eva touches the china gently, before turning her attention to Carmen.

'You look exhausted.'

Carmen grins. 'Thanks for the compliment.'

'I mean it. What happened?'

'Elena cancelled her wedding and came here last night. It was great. Then Luis came home as a surprise...'

'And?'

And Carmen tells her what happened in the street with the Viking, and how unfriendly they were this morning. 'So, now they've gone back to London.'

'It will be alright,' Eva says smiling. 'Or it won't.'

Carmen grins. 'The simplicity of life.'

'I've been through similar things with my twins and either way,' continues Eva, 'You have to ask yourself if you're happy here in Harbour Street and if you're doing the right thing - for you.'

'Wise words my friend. Come on, let's go to the show homes.' Carmen grabs her car keys. 'We've saved the best until last.'

That afternoon when she's back in her shop, an older couple come in and buy Marjorie's elegant mahogany dining table and four chairs. 'We've an extended family coming for Christmas,' the lady explains. 'Family coming home from Brazil that we haven't seen since before Covid.'

Carmen smiles.

'I'll fetch the van around.' Her husband hurries excitedly from the shop.

After lunch a man in scruffy jeans and an old sweater comes in. 'I'd like the chaise longue. My wife's had her eye on it for months. So, if she comes in, tell her you sold it to a Frenchman or someone leaving Westbay.' He laughs. 'I want it to be a surprise on Christmas morning.'

Carmen wraps a few more gifts and rearranges the shop ready for Monday - Christmas Eve and her last working day before the holidays. She had assumed that she'd be in Florida but now she looks around the shop and whispers, 'There'll be plenty of time to buy more stock. You look quite empty now. I'll soon have you looking lovely again.'

She locks up and then heads upstairs, makes coffee and goes over her accounts. Then late afternoon she takes the unwanted Christmas gifts for José's family and arranges to return them to the online shop.

'All these silly jobs. Always tidying up,' she mutters.

She has a few more errands to run and a few Christmas presents to buy and then she's back at home. She's deliberately blocking out her emotions and focusing on different tasks. She's exhausted.

She runs a hot bath and lays in the water, inhaling deeply the aromatic scent of sage and rosemary. She pushes her shoulder under the water so she can't see her missing breast, wondering what her life might have been like had she never fallen in love with Jack Bailey.

She pulls on a towelling robe and downstairs in the lounge she checks her phone but there are no calls and no messages. Then very carefully it's time to get ready. This is her big moment.

It's show time.

* * *

There are black bamboo torches lighting the paths from the pavement to the teepees. Alongside the pathway runs an illuminated stream that has small wooden bridges to each block of homes. The yellow lighting on the development is subdued and tropical and there's a festive air of anticipation.

Carmen is mesmerized by the beauty, tranquillity and tropical vibe that would normally be out of place at Christmas but which seems perfectly natural here.

The larger flower displays that Eva brought earlier are filled with bamboo and sunflowers and red and white poinsettias and the holly bushes are filled with gold and silver glitter.

'This is posh!' The taxi driver laughs. 'Never seen nothing like this before.'

Carmen gives him a healthy tip then she climbs out of the car, imagining that she's alighting from a beautiful golden carriage. She's wearing a long, beige, woollen dress that shows every curve of her body. Over her shoulder is a matching coat. Her smile is radiant. She looks as if she's stepped into a Hollywood movie.

It's Christmas and suddenly her heart is uplifted and filled with joy. There's a steel band playing Christmas tunes and a machine sending wispy snow into the cold air and over the hot coals of the barbecues. Waiters and chefs are dressed in virgin white aprons and the smell of roasting juices and herbs fills her senses.

The teepee is busy.

Salespeople sit at small tables talking earnestly to couples, some with children, or older people and some have even brought their dogs. There are pop ups on every corner with exquisite photographs showing the colourful and vibrant designs of her show homes.

Martin greets her with a smile and a kiss on each cheek. He's dressed in a black Tuxedo and white bowtie and he takes her arm. 'You look incredible,' he whispers, escorting her through the crowds and toward a set of familiar faces: Harry, Sheila, Eva and Sanjay, Amber, Frances, Jane and Tommy.

'Are we overdressed?' She laughs.

'No more than anyone else.' He squeezes her arm.

Her friends reach out to her.

'You look amazing.' Amber kisses her cheeks.

'This place is fantastic.' Sanjay smiles.

'You've done an incredible job.' Sheila hugs her.

'I think I might buy one.' Tommy laughs.

'I could live here.' Frances grins.

Carmen smiles at them all and after Martin has gone, she says, 'Thank you my lovely friends for all your support and for coming tonight but you really don't have to buy any of the properties. It's just great to see you. The flowers are magnificent, Eva.'

'We're a good team.' Eva laughs.

Champagne flows and they toast each other and themselves.

'Happy Christmas.'

'Congratulations,' says Amber then taking her to one side she asks, 'How are you doing?'

Carmen shakes her head. 'It's been rough.'

'Ben is mortified. He only wanted to help and it seems like everything has backfired.'

Carmen sips her champagne. 'Welcome to my world.'

'None of them are here?' asks Amber.

'I haven't heard from any of them since they left this morning.

Eva pushes between them and pulls Frances with her. 'Tonight is about strong women. Look at what you've done, Carmen. You're an incredible role model and a fantastic mother—'

'Well, I—'

Eva rests her hand on Carmen's arm. 'I have twins a year older than Luis. I know what they can be like. Once my children accused me of having an affair with Amber. Can you imagine? They got it so wrong.'

'No one understands proper friendships,' adds Amber.

'Or marriages,' agrees Frances. 'We're very proud of you, Carmen.'

She looks gratefully at her friends. 'You all made it possible.'

'That's not true,' says Frances. 'I've watched you. You've changed so much since you arrived. After what Tracey did in the vicarage you've blossomed. I love your hair and your new look. I said to you then, out of everything bad comes something good. And now look around you. This is an incredible achievement.'

Carmen raises her glass. 'Here's to my lovely generous friends who are always so supportive.'

'You've been supportive too, Carmen.' Frances's eyes glisten in the firelight. 'You've helped Paul and Sandra with their marriage. They were heading for a divorce and now they're over there and he's looking at new property for Sandra's father to be near them. They want a new beginning in the new year. And, Martin has said that this development wouldn't be the same without you and how right he is....'

Much later Carmen wanders from group to group. She's introduced by Martin to various people and she smiles hiding behind an invisible curtain of shyness. It's as if someone else has designed these homes. As if someone else has guided her and put these designs together. She can't believe her success.

She moves away to a quieter space. Away from the people and the show homes to a dark, quiet corner where she observes, watchful and silent. Her energy is seeping away and her eyelids grow heavy. She's very tired and she knows that none of this really means anything to her. It's her family who are important but they're not here. She hasn't heard from any of them. They're too busy at the house in London that they call home. But for Carmen it's someone else's home. It's not hers. This is where she can be herself where she can grow and develop and where she can live amongst friends.

Martin finds her. 'You can't hide,' he teases, taking her elbow. He insists on introducing her to a stream of people and later Sheila is beside her exclaiming how proud she is of her two sons.

The stress of the past few days is having an effect and, combined with the alcohol, Carmen drifts in and out of the conversations. One young woman with brown hair is keen to know where she sourced the wallpaper and Carmen taps her nose.

'That's my secret.'

'Is that your signature?' she asks.

Carmen puts her arm around the young girl. 'I have more than one signature.'

'You do?'

'This is just the beginning.' Carmen smiles, invigorated by the champagne and praise, and taps her foot to the rhythm of the steel band playing, *Let It Snow.*

'Did you arrange all this too?' asks the girl with undiluted praise.

'No,' Carmen lies.

Martin had taken her suggestions for the opening literally but what's the point of saying you planned all this if your family aren't here to witness your success? 'You know, you should be blonder.'

'Like Barbie?' the girl replies without smiling.

'Absolutely. It would take years off you.'

A waiter passes by with a silver tray and he offers Carmen a fresh glass. When she turns around Barbie has gone so she moves behind the steel band to hide, her shoulder resting against the pillar of the teepee. She's had far too much champagne, but not nearly enough to dull her sadness.

'That's a sight, isn't it?' The stranger's voice interrupts her reverie and automatically she stands straighter concentrating on his words. 'I love a good brass band, don't you?' he asks, as the music changes.

'Yes.' She hopes he will go away.

'The carol they're playing is lovely,' he insists. 'I like *O Holy Night*, do you?'

'Yes.'

'It's all been designed and orchestrated very well, don't you think?'

'Yes.'

'I love Christmas, do you?'

Carmen turns her head to regard the stranger at her elbow. He has long grey hair in a ponytail and three-day old stubble covering his hollow cheeks. He's wearing a black Chanel suit and white shirt with a narrow red leather tie.

'Normally,' she replies.

'Would you buy a home here?' he asks. 'On this development?'

'Probably.'

Carmen thinks of all the houses, and the places and the countries where she's brought property and her heart sinks. They've lost them all. Covid stopped people from travelling and they hadn't been business savvy enough to know that they should pay off their mortgages. They'd lived on borrowed money. They owed a fortune on their house in London with its ten bedrooms, pool and football pitch - it was no wonder the banks were foreclosing on them on Monday.

'I wouldn't buy one.' The stranger beside her laughs. Clearly the worse for wear with the free alcohol. He leans closer. 'They're not for me. Would you believe there are pictures of life-seized animals in the house? Imagine eating your breakfast and you've a bloody pelican beside you. It's enough to put the fear of God into you.'

'They're not pelicans.'

'Alright parrots.'

'Macaws.' A dormant anger rises in Carmen. She's spent the past month working hard, furnishing everything to perfection, and some low-life with no appreciation of art is ridiculing her work.

He giggles and taps his beer glass against her champagne flute. 'Nice meeting you.' Then he wanders away, barely managing to keep his balance along the softly lit path illuminated by fiery beacons.

Carmen raises her glass to his retreating figure. 'Piss off.'

* * *

The evening is a great success and although Carmen has enjoyed herself, she's bitterly disappointed her family aren't here to share her success. This is the one thing that she's worked so hard for yet none of them could support her. None of them realise how hard she's pushed herself to get here.

'Are you okay?' Amber regards her seriously.

Carmen shakes her head. It's partly exhaustion and partly the alcohol. She doesn't want to speak but then she asks.

'What's the point of anything, Amber? When your family aren't here to see your success or to witness what you've had to overcome to get here?'

Amber links her arm through her friends, she walks her down the path, still illuminated by burning flames, toward the teepee. 'Sometimes there are things that you just have to do for yourself.'

'Does it matter?' asks Carmen. 'Is that selfish?'

'It matters to you.' Amber guides her to a car. Ben sits at the steering wheel and she opens the back door.

'It's all about you, Carmen. You've given so much and finally it's all about you.'

Carmen ducks her head as she climbs into the back seat. Enveloped in the quietness of his car, she leans her head back and closes her eyes. Amber climbs in the front and the engine purrs into life.

'What's it all about?' she whispers into the darkness of Ben's car. 'Who cares?'

But no one is close enough to hear.

Chapter 23

Sunday morning dawns and Carmen sleeps like she hasn't slept for years. She wakes with a thick head and a vague recollection of the events from the night before. She remembers the overall ambience and how pretty the development and show houses had looked. But she doesn't remember speaking or saying goodbye to Martin or Sheila. Sadly, she realises, she had been so exhausted that the champagne had gone straight to her head. It was two nights in a row of heightened emotion with alcohol.

She showers slowly. Today she's not in a hurry. There are no show homes, no Florida wedding and there's certainly no family. She can't remember a day when her calendar has been so clear.

It's Sunday, the day before Christmas Eve. Tomorrow they foreclose on the house in London.

She stands with the hot water in the shower beating down on her neck and shoulders realising she has a few important things to do.

Jack calls just as she's getting dressed. 'Hi baby.'

'Hello stranger,' she replies.

'How was the opening last night?'

'Amazing. I'm sorry you missed it.'

'Me too but to be honest Cammy, it's important that I spend time with Elena and Luis now. We're sorting things out and I want them to understand about the book....'

'How are they?'

'Okay.'

'How's it going?'

'Elena's labelled the kitchen boxes and she's deciding what we keep, but I wish you were here to help.'

'I meant how's it going with the kids?'

He blows out his cheeks. 'It's been tough. I've been trying to get them to read the last chapter in the book, but you know how headstrong they are! I can't imagine where they get that from.' He laughs. 'Look, there's a couple of things you need to know.'

Carmen tenses.

'I've been asked on breakfast TV tomorrow.'

'Christmas Eve?'

'Yes, but this is my opportunity to clear the air and to put my story forward. Is that alright?'

'If it's what you want to do.'

'And I want us all to spend Christmas together so I've booked rooms for three nights in The Savoy for us all. We can have a family Christmas in London. Go ice skating in the park, see the lights in Regent Street, go out for dinner. We can make it very special. What do you think?'

'A hotel is not home.'

'But it's a five-star hotel,' he cries.

'This is my home, but it can also be *our* home.'

'We don't have a home any more.' Jack is tetchy. 'I thought you'd be excited. I've managed to get the kids onboard again and hopefully we can all put the past behind us and spend

Christmas together. At least we don't have to go to Florida.' He laughs.

Carmen doesn't respond.

'What's wrong?' he asks.

'I don't know what to say to you any more, Jack. This is clearly something that *you* want to do again. Whether it's the TV show or spending the Christmas holiday in an expensive hotel, but you've given no thought to the future. What happens in January? Luis will go back to university. Elena will be flying. Where will you be? What are you going to do with your life?'

'Well,' he stutters, 'we can talk about that. Can't we?'

'When?'

'Well, I don't know - I'm tired. I've flown across the world and worked hard these past few months and I'm knackered. It's been emotionally exhausting. It's nice to come home but we're packing up the house, Cammy. It's sad and it's hard work. And, on top of all that, you're not here to help.'

'I have a business to run.'

'Great!' His sarcasm burns her ears. 'Well, just in case you're mildly interested in your family and what we're doing, the storage men come early tomorrow. I'm doing the breakfast TV show and then we're going Christmas shopping in Bond Street. If you want to join us for Christmas Eve dinner - then you'll know where to find us.'

'Fine.'

'What do you mean, fine? Are you coming?'

'No, Jack. I want to be at home for Christmas.'

* * *

Carmen's first stop is to Yusef and Ozan's salon.

'Hello, you gorgeous lady. Look at you. Always so stylish and chic.' Yusef claps his hands and dances around her in delight. 'How lovely to see you smiling.'

'You bring out the best in me.' She laughs. 'I wasn't sure you'd be working today.'

'Honey-Lady, we work *every* day. These luscious guys here have got to look hot for their gals over the holidays.' He pats a client on the shoulder and teases. 'And man, don't some of them need a *lot* of work!'

The stranger in the seat grins back at her in the mirror.

She pushes an envelope into his hands and he looks surprised. 'This is for you as a small thank you.'

'What is this, lovely lady?'

'It's a weekend away. The Ritz in London and tickets to a show of your choice.'

Yusef frowns and his smile freezes. 'Why?'

'Because I'd like you and Shelley to go away for two nights and have an unforgettable weekend in the new year.'

Yusef grins. 'Shelley knows that every night with me is unforgettable, baby.'

Carmen explodes laughing. 'Well, have a rest and see a show.' She pats him on the shoulder, but he pulls her into a big hug.

'Thank you,' he whispers. 'It's not necessary, but I appreciate it, and Shelley will love it too.'

Carmen hugs him back. 'I can't tell you what you've done for me without bursting into tears. So, go and have a great time together.'

He kisses her on the cheek and then pretends to appear shocked and horrified. 'Wait! Can I kiss you or is there some evil social media king on the prowl?'

Carmen laughs aloud.

Yusef continues in a stage whisper, 'I believe the evil Viking, Baron-Von-Eric is six feet deep in the river.'

'What?' Carmen covers her mouth with her hand.

Yusef laughs. 'Only joking, Señora. But you can live in peace. He has been given the boot from Westbay - never to be seen again.'

* * *

Carmen's second gift is for Ben and Amber, but she needs to buy the vouchers. She opens the door to the Beauty Salon and Tracey is sitting behind the reception desk. She looks alarmed to see Carmen and she stands up, defensively backing away from her.

'Morning.' Carmen smiles.

'I haven't done anything,' Tracey stutters. 'I haven't taken any pictures.'

'I know.'

Tracey frowns. 'You do? Then what do you want?'

'Two vouchers for a Balinese back massage.'

'They're expensive.'

'I've also heard that you're the best person around here to do them.'

'Really?' Tracey's voice softens and her hostility weakens. 'Do you mean it or is this a trick?'

'I mean it. The vouchers are a Christmas present for Ben and Amber. They do so much for everyone else.'

Tracey tentatively approaches the desk to access her computer to print off the vouchers.

'This is a nice salon, Tracey.'

'Is it?' Tracey's hands are shaking.

'I know what Eric did and also I know it wasn't your fault.'

'Really? How do you know?'

'We can all be victims of persuasive men and sometimes we don't all make the right decisions but that doesn't have to make us bad people, does it?'

Tracey shakes her head. She prints off the vouchers and hands them to Carmen. 'I really like Luis. He was kind to me and I thought we were friends.'

'You were very kind to do his nails and to make him feel welcome here.'

'The other stuff wasn't my fault. It was Eric's idea to—'

Carmen holds up her hand. 'I understand, but that's all in the past now. I've heard this salon is up for sale?' Carmen regards her carefully. 'Do you really want to leave Harbour Street?'

She passes her debit card over the machine that Tracey is holding out.

'I don't know what to do. I'd never had any glamorous friends before. People like Luis and you who are naturally beautiful and elegant. I mean, you're A-Listers. And to think I met Jack Bailey, too. My Dad couldn't believe it. He's a massive football fan and then I messed it all up. I'm not with Eric any more.'

'You deserve better.'

'Ever since I ripped the wig from your head no one speaks to me. It was awful. I'm so sorry.'

'That's okay. To be honest you've done me a favour.'

Tracey looks unsure and Carmen continues.

'I think Westbay is a very forgiving place and I think we need a decent beauty salon in Harbour Street.'

'You do?' Tracey's bottom lip trembles. 'I put it up for sale because I didn't know what to do. I'm so ashamed.'

'In one more week it's the new year. I think you can start afresh here in Harbour Street.'

'Really?'

'Yes. Happy Christmas, Tracey.'

'I'm sorry about what I did. But to be honest your hair is much better shorter. You look even more stunning.'

'Thank you.'

'Perhaps you should tell Luis. They might get theirs cut too.'

Carmen smiles. 'I'll leave that up to you. Should he ever visit here again.'

* * *

Carmen's final stop is to Ian at the greengrocers.

'That tree?' Ian says pointing at the Nordic Spruce. 'Will it fit in your flat?

'I can always cut it in half.' Carmen jokes and Ian looks aghast until Carmen bursts out laughing. He helps her carry it down Harbour Street and up the stairs.

'It will fit perfectly in that corner,' she says.

After he's gone Carmen finds solitude in the carol service from the cathedral in London on television. The music fills the room and brings peace and tranquillity to her heart. It's Sunday evening and Christmas Eve tomorrow - a big day in Spain - and she phones her parents. She imagines them in their white-washed farmhouse with an electric radiator pushing out heat into a damp room. But who was she to judge? It's only now that Carmen realises that it's their home. It's where they're comfortable. They refused all her offers to move into another property. It is what they want. It suddenly dawns on her that she's always been living in someone else's home; her parents, Jack's, the palace prison....

Carmen talks to them in her mother tongue. Her soft Andalusian accent fills the room and their voices are warm with love. It's a rewarding conversation and she fends off conversations about her family. Yes. Luis is happy at university. Elena is much happier now that she's not getting married. Jack. Yes. He's happy to be at home in the UK for Christmas. She talks with optimism and hope and it lifts her spirits. Their voices are excited and they're laughing. They will spend Christmas with her cousin in the valley next door. Carmen promises she will see them in the spring. Her promise is reinforced with sincerity, both as an adult, and a parent. She knows they will be counting the days to her visit.

With a glass of Cava in her hand, Carmen spends the rest of the evening thinking about her family as she makes Christmas decorations from paper: bows, bells, angels and snowmen that she colours with different pencils. She adds silver and gold glitter and then hangs them on the tree with coloured wool. It's different from any previous Christmas tree decorations and she's pleased with the result. It's only after all her jobs are complete and she's finished the bottle of Cava that she turns off the room lights and stares at the golden twinkling lights on the tree.

'Gracias, por hacerme sonreír. Thank you for making me smile.'

* * *

It's Christmas Eve morning. It's always been one of Carmen's favourite days of the year when she would make a special meal for the family. Sometimes a paella or sea bass baked in salt or a whole salmon roasted in the oven. It's a day associated with lovely memories of the children opening one present in front of the fire before Christmas Day.

Before Jack bought the palatial prison, they'd lived in a modest house. It had been cosy and comfortable and they'd all been happy. The children were babies and they'd been a part of the local community. No one had taken any notice of who they were. Later they'd invested in property and they'd travelled in the school holidays. Carmen had always made a point of taking them to their grandparents in Spain. They needed to know where they were from and she had encouraged them to speak Spanish.

After scoring the winning goal in the FA cup, Jack Bailey became a household name. He was playing with the likes of Beckham and Lineker and that's when he'd surprised her with their new home. It had a swimming pool, cinema room, football pitch and even a bodega. The walls separated them from her friends and neighbours. Even the school runs were different. She told herself it was because the kids were growing older, but in truth, people saw them as elite. The A-Listers. A WAG. They went to all the star-studded events, premiers, charity balls, concerts and they mingled with the rich and famous.

They'd been married for four years when Jack tore his ligament. He was twenty-eight. There were two years of operations, agonising physiotherapy and then returning to the field before he finally admitted it was all over.

They never talked about money or finance or mortgages.

Jack looked after everything. Carmen organised the decorating and furnishings. She hadn't realised how much she enjoyed all that work until it stopped.

She coped with his depression, his anxiety and his drinking. For a while she could manage his gambling, but she couldn't cope with the palatial prison. She had always felt she was an imposter and when she told Jack he'd laughed.

'But you're a famous model. You've walked half-naked down a catwalk with everyone staring at you.'

He'd never understood.

When she was a model, she'd worked hard. But it was acting. It was all about pretending to be someone you weren't. Someone who looked confident, elegant and beautiful. When she was pregnant with Elena, she was relieved she'd never have to pretend like that again. She didn't want to cope with the vultures and predators who hovered around her hoping she would be vulnerable and give in to their needs.

She shudders and, as a distraction, switches on the TV while she makes coffee in the kitchen. Then suddenly she hears Jack's voice. She settles onto the sofa to watch him. He looks handsome in a red jacket and jeans. His hair is longer and his eyes are twinkling. He loves the fame and the limelight. It's like a drug and she realises he'll never be able to give it all up.

On his left, Luis wears a purple jumpsuit, hooped gold earrings and enough eye make up for a musical theatre. On Jack's right, Elena looks more nervous. She's wearing blue jeans, a Christmas jumper and her fake professional smile that doesn't reach her eyes.

Carmen takes in her family. They're all seated on national television and she shakes her head. Tears well-up in her eyes.

'It's family,' Jack says confidently. He leans back, crosses his legs, his arms splayed out behind his two children. 'You tell me one family that hasn't had a disagreement.'

The two popular interviewers agree. They encourage him to talk about his book.

Jack's energy is captivating. His voice warm and secure. 'The thing is, truth matters. You can't pretend. Not with the whole world watching and I felt that many people who'd read my book just selected some parts to sensationalise it. These are the bits my kids read. But...' He leans forward. His blue eyes are intense and his energy is magnetic. 'You need to read it, until the end. Until the very last chapter, because that's where the truth lies. I talk about the challenges we faced but I also talk about respect, love and kindness.'

'So, family is important to you?' asks the female interviewer.

'Of course. It always has been and always will be. These guys are the focal point of my life.'

'And Luis, did you think your dad didn't understand you?'

Luis preens and smiles. He flicks long wavy hair over his shoulder and his familiar voice floats into the room.

'I get it. It's people of his generation. It's a pronoun hiccup but the most important thing is that Dad cares. He's cared enough to write this book.'

Carmen sips her coffee and shakes her head.

'Por dios, Jack. Why did they have to go on TV with you?'

'And Elena,' asks the male interviewer. 'Where will you be spending Christmas?'

Her voice is timid. 'Here in London.'

The interviewer smiles. 'And I suppose your lovely wife Carmen, who as we all know is recovering from breast cancer, will join you. Will she Jack?'

Jack smiles confidently and looks directly at the camera as if looking into her eyes. 'We've never spent a Christmas apart.'

Carmen reaches for the control. She turns off the TV and hurls it on the sofa. 'What have you done, Jack? Why have you forced the kids to go on television?'

* * *

Carmen opens the shop at nine thirty. Her head is full of the family after watching them on television. She's furious with them all. The shop is busy and she sells ornaments, a lamp and a small reading table. She wraps the gifts carefully making small talk, wishing her customers a Merry Christmas. It's mid-morning when Amber pops over with a latte.

'Happy Christmas, Carmen. I can't stop, it's manic in the café, but see you later for a drink?'

Martin arrives just before lunch. 'How are you after Saturday night?' he asks.

'Did I embarrass you?' She smiles weakly.

Martin laughs. 'There were people worse than you. Why do you ask?'

Carmen shrugs. 'I was very tired. I spoke to lots of people but it was never my intention to let you down.'

'You didn't let me down. You're going through a stressful time at the moment.' Martin regards her carefully. 'Any news from the family?'

'They were all on Breakfast TV this morning.' She turns away.

'I saw it. Was it alright?'

'I hated it. They probably loved it.'

'Elena is very interesting. Very much like you.'

'Elena is nothing like me! She's rude and abrasive when she's upset.'

Martin laughs.

Carmen pouts. 'I won't be angry with you.'

'Regardless of family emotions I just called in to wish you a Happy Christmas and to say that your invoice has been paid. The monies are in your account.'

'That's prompt. You had thirty days.' Carmen senses the pressure releasing in her heart and the tension evaporates. She has no money worries now. Although she'd lived well in the past few months and invested in materials and stock for the shop, this money would now clear her debts. She could survive well into the new year without worrying

'I believe in paying my bills on time. And Mum said, if you're on your own, you'd be welcome to join us for lunch on Christmas Day.'

Carmen shakes her head. 'That's kind but I really won't be on great form. I struggled through Saturday night and ...'

'Struggled?' Martin laughs loudly.

'Okay, so I drank too much and now it's probably all over social media.' She bites her lip. 'Is it?'

'Well, as far as I know there's nothing on the internet and the two important people who had long conversations with you on Saturday night were very impressed.'

Carmen shakes her head in bewilderment. 'I don't remember any long conversations.'

Martin perches on the edge of the desk. 'There was a girl with mousey hair and you said she should dye it blonde like Barbie.'

Carmen covers her hand to her mouth. 'I did?'

Martin nods seriously. 'She's from *Interiors Magazine*

and she wants to write an article on you. She loves the tropical wallpaper and the themes you have going on. She was so impressed with the show homes that she's considering moving here from London with her boyfriend. They can both work remotely and travel up to town when they need to. It's only an hour away.'

Carmen shakes her head remembering only snatches of the conversation. 'I was tired,' she says in defense. 'But if she's happy then that's good.'

Martin laughs. 'How are you going to defend your conversation with my father?'

Carmen laughs nervously. 'I didn't meet your father. I didn't even know he was coming.'

'I went to get him the day after our dinner in the pub when I met Elena.'

'I wondered where you'd gone.' Carmen smiles smugly. 'But you can't accuse me of anything...'

'I can.'

'No.' Carmen waggles her index finger her anger rising. 'No. No. No. I didn't speak to anyone else.'

'You spoke to him.'

'No.'

'Yes.'

Carmen stares at him. 'Well, maybe in the show homes. There were a few people, and they asked me a couple of questions, but it was early on.'

'He was probably as drunk as you.'

'I wasn't...'

'He has white hair tied back in a ponytail and he probably cornered you in the dark.'

Carmen has a recollection of a lively conversation with a

man by that description. 'It couldn't be him.'

'Why?' Martin asks.

'Was he wearing an expensive suit and red leather tie?'

Martin laughs. 'That's him.'

'Impossible! How is he building a big complex in Surrey?'

'He's sober when it matters. He's very maverick and that's what makes him so brilliant.'

Carmen is trying frantically to recall their conversation, but she's muddled. Her head is tired and she's extremely exhausted. She just wants to go upstairs and lie down.

'So, he's asked me to tell you that having seen your designs he wants to contract you immediately.'

'He does?'

Martin grins. 'Before anyone else snaps you up. Congratulations, Carmen. You've just landed a million-pound contract.'

'What?'

'He has a government contract to build over ten thousand homes. My project, by comparison, was literally the tip of the iceberg.'

'But I don't understand. Why are you so happy?'

'Because we'll be like family. I may even work with him for a while in Surrey, but also...' He pauses and Carmen waits expectantly but she's too tired to think ahead. 'Perhaps Elena might be around a little bit more?' he adds.

Carmen stares at him. So much is happening and she has hardly slept.

'I doubt very much Elena will be coming back here,' she says.

Martin stands up. 'Never say never.'

'You're not James bloody Bond.' She laughs.

'No, but I am an optimist. I think she likes me.'

'That's not hard.'

He grins. 'Well, I'd better go. It's another busy day and sales are going well. And I do believe you are all paid up to date. As I said before, it's gone into your account today. That's for the payment of your invoice for *my* show homes plus Dad's generous retainer.'

'Retainer?'

Martin smiles. 'I told him that was essential.' Carmen is speechless. 'So, you'll be able to stay here in Westbay and we can look forward to working together again in the new year.'

After he's gone Carmen checks her online bank account. Her invoice is paid in full but when she sees the amount that has been deposited as a retainer she has to sit down.

There's also an email from Martin's father confirming her status in his new build. This is beyond her wildest dreams. Thinking of dreams. She checks her watch.

There are still a couple of hours before the end of business, but she turns the closed sign on her shop, locks up and pockets the key.

It's Christmas Eve and there was just one more very important thing she wanted to do. It was an enormous risk but perhaps dreams do come true at Christmas.

She dials the number stored in her iPhone.

Chapter 24

Carmen walks into the church as most people are walking out. The nativity play is over and families with young children are pushing their way excitedly outside. There's a lovely warm atmosphere and Carmen's boots are quiet on the cement floor as she wanders down toward the altar.

It had been her intention to seek out Frances but now she realises that she's missed the quiet solitude of a church. There are red and cream poinsettias around the feet of Jesus on the cross and as the church empties out, footsteps dwindle, voices fade.

Carmen gazes at the stained glass windows and she spends a while looking at the biblical scenes before lighting three candles.

One for Jack, Elena and Luis, one for her family in Spain, and the last candle for her friends and new life in Harbour Street.

She sits in a pew near the front and thinks of her family. Their house has been repossessed and they would now be in The Savoy. Jack will be using money from his dancing show in Australia or perhaps money from the book tour. Either way, the hotel is expensive.

Jack had blamed Covid for their financial problems, but the truth was they had lived on borrowed money. He'd believed there was an inexhaustible supply from his new-found celebrity status that would pay their mortgages and bills forever.

How he'd got on television at such short notice was a mystery and although she didn't like Simon, his agent has proved to be wily and perceptive.

'Carmen?' Frances appears beside her. 'May I join you?'

She slides along the pew and smiles. 'I'm sorry I missed the nativity.'

Frances' eyes are serious. 'How are you? I saw the family on TV this morning.'

Carmen grins. 'The vicar has time for morning television on Christmas Eve?'

Frances laughs. 'Shush, don't tell anyone what I really do.'

'You'll be telling me next that you get drunk on brandy pudding.'

'I'm more partial to a bottle of Sancerre. Graham's got me hooked on it.'

Carmen regards her friend. She's humbled to be sitting quietly beside this busy woman who makes time for everyone regardless of the time of year.

'How's Marjorie?' Carmen asks.

'We're going to take her over to my mum's for lunch tomorrow. She seems to have perked up in the past few days. She loves Christmas and I think the carols on the television have been a solace to her. And, of course, she's happy.'

'I'm pleased she's rallying Frances, and that you and Graham will be able to spend Christmas with her.'

'Me too. Thank you.'

Carmen crosses her legs. 'Christmas Eve – it's your busy time of the year. Do you have any plans?'

'We're going to my sister's for dinner and then the whole family will come here to midnight mass. What about you? You're welcome to join us. Don't be on your own.'

'I'm having some friends coming over for drinks in an hour. I'd love it if you could join us too.'

'Rain check until the new year?'

'Definitely.'

They walk down the aisle companionably and at the door they pause to look at each other. Frances holds her arms out. 'I'm so happy that you're staying here in Westbay. It's been hard for you, but you couldn't have picked a better place to live.'

Carmen smiles. 'I'm blessed.'

'God always works in mysterious ways.'

'This is my home now, Frances.'

'Happy Christmas, Carmen. May God be with you.'

'Feliz navidad, Frances. Vaya con Dios.'

* * *

She arrived home later than she expected and her guests arrived minutes later, carrying bottles of wine and champagne and delicious food.

Carmen rummages for the Christmas tablecloths and napkins she'd ordered online a few days ago. 'Thank goodness for the Internet.' She laughs.

'Where are the glasses?' Ben calls, from the lounge.

'I'm starving,' says Eva. 'I've never known Christmas Eve to be so busy.'

'I've brought a bottle of whiskey. It's freezing outside,' Sanjay says. 'Will that go with smoked salmon and all this delightful fish?' He grins.

'Everything goes with everything in this house.' Carmen laughs carrying large platters of green salads and pasta salads into the lounge where she places them on the table. 'There's enough to feed an army.'

Eva carries a large tray of crayfish, crab and lobsters. 'I'm so pleased you closed the café and the Bistro over Christmas, Amber. Now we'll get to eat all this delightful food.'

Ben pours the fizz. 'If we didn't close up then none of the staff would get any holidays. Everyone needs a break.'

When they've all had a drink, Carmen gives her gift of the Balinese massages to Amber and Ben. 'Hopefully this might relax you both.'

'You must be exhausted going backwards and forwards to London, Ben,' Eva says. 'And this year you have no foster children with you for Christmas?'

Amber takes the champagne flute that Ben offers her. 'We just can't do it. It's all too much. We really need to have a holiday and Ben is going to focus more on his charity in the new year.'

'What do you want to do with your charity?' asks Sanjay.

They sit around the large coffee table in the centre of the room and Carmen hands out plates and red napkins. She puts the Christmas tree lights and Christmas music on and she lights candles.

She gives her gift of the blue and silver Chinese vase to Eva and Sanjay.

'It's the one I saw in your shop that I loved,' Eva cries. 'I thought you'd sold it!' She hugs Carmen tightly.

Carmen smiles. 'I saved it for you. I wanted to give you something you like.' She sits beside Sanjay on the sofa and looks around at her small group of friends. 'I'm so lucky to have met you all.'

Ben talks about his plans for his charity and how important family is at Christmas. 'It doesn't have to be a biological family,' he says. 'It's just about being with friends who care.'

Carmen's thoughts turn to Jack, Elena and Luis. She wonders if they're already in their hotel rooms in The Savoy or perhaps they've gone ice skating?

Were they thinking of her?

Normally on Christmas Eve she would be in the kitchen with her family all around her. They'd have music on and they would be laughing and singing Christmas songs with the aroma of cooking around them. Last year she hadn't been well but she'd roasted a whole sea bass in the oven. Jack was always good at entertaining. He was the fun dad making everyone laugh, organising games while Carmen was the mum in the kitchen making sure the meals were organised like clockwork. She made hosting look effortless.

This is the first year that she's had nothing to do.

When Carmen told her friends she wanted to celebrate Christmas in her new home, Amber had insisted on bringing all the food. There was enough to feed at least a dozen people.

Amber, like Carmen, is a feeder.

Carmen sips her champagne happy to listen to her friends' voices. There have been a lot of changes this year: her cancer diagnosis, losing the house, Elena's wedding announcement and Luis going off to university. She could never have imagined her new life in Westbay.

Jack's celebrity status has increased for better or for worse but one thing she knows for sure. She has been true to herself. But tonight is not a time for nostalgia; it's a time for new beginnings. Carmen lifts her glass.

'Happy Christmas. To new beginnings and wonderful friends.'

They all raise their glasses and echo her sentiments. Then, to their surprise, there's singing in the street.

'Carol singers,' cries Amber.

Eva grins happily. 'At last!'

'Let's sing with them?' Ben leaps to his feet.

'Come on.' Sanjay laughs.

'Is this normal?' asks Carmen.

'Every year!' Eva leaps up excitedly. 'We must go down and sing with them. Come on. Lead the way, Carmen.'

They are all swept up in the excitement. Carmen leads her friends down the stairs and on the bottom step, she stops and turns to her friends lined up behind her.

She whispers, 'They're not very good.'

'Silent night, holy night, all is calm...'

'Open the door.' Ben laughs.

'Hurry up!' cries Amber.

Carmen flings open the door and standing in front of her, singing at the top of their voices are Jack, Elena and Luis.

* * *

It's mayhem. Luis and Elena fling themselves at her and she's pushed against the wall with the strength of their love.

'Surprise!'

'Did you guess it was us?'

'Happy Christmas, Mama!'

They have their arms around her. They are all laughing and talking at the same time. But Carmen is shocked. She can't take it all in.

'Why aren't you at The Savoy?' she stutters.

'You hardly think we'd spend Christmas without you?' cries Elena.

'It wouldn't be Christmas without the family together,' adds Luis.

'Come on up,' cries Amber, leading the way upstairs.

Elena follows Amber and Eva. 'Come on, let's celebrate.' She links her arm through Sanjay's and pulls him with her.

Luis is already hugging Ben, and they stagger up behind. It's chaos as they get settled; coats, boots, cases and Carmen stands in disbelief.

Jack carries bags upstairs and Ben and Amber and Sanjay and Eva help as coats are removed, drinks poured and fragmented conversations are interrupted.

Carmen's whirling mind is trying to make sense of it all.

Amber holds up a bottle of fizz. 'I thought you were never going to get here—'

'The train was late.' Luis complains.

'It was hard keeping the secret,' says Sanjay.

'You all knew?' asks Carmen.

'That's why there's so much food.' Eva grins. 'We could barely stop laughing when we saw your face and all the food.'

Ben laughs. 'It's been hard to keep quiet.'

Elena links her arm though her mother's. 'We wanted to surprise you, Mama. You've always done so much for us. You've always been so understanding and kind and I'm so sorry for being so horrible. I'll make it up to you, I promise.'

'You don't need to do that, Elena. We're family.' She hugs her daughter fiercely. 'This is so wonderful. I can't believe you're all here.' Carmen disappears into the kitchen for more plates and Luis follows her.

He puts his arms around her and kisses her cheek. 'Feliz navidad, Mama. I'm sorry that I behaved so badly. I didn't understand what you went through until I read the last chapter in Papi's book. Neither of us did.' Carmen puts her arms around his waist. 'You're incredible, Mama. I'm very proud of you. Te quiero.'

'I love you too, my darling.' Carmen wipes her damp eyes on Luis' shoulder.

'Mind the red jacket, Mama. I don't want the velvet to get too wet. It's my favourite.' He laughs.

Carmen pulls away laughing. She pushes more plates and napkins into his hands. 'Here, take these in the other room while I get my emotions under control.' She pushes his shoulders away from her and turns to look for kitchen roll to wipe her nose.

Then Jack's arms are around her waist. 'Hello, Cammy. Happy Christmas.'

'Hello Jack.' She turns grinning and he kisses her on her smiling lips.

'You've got a wet nose.' He laughs.

'Your eyes are twinkling again.'

'That's because we're all together.'

She rests her head on his shoulder. He smells of spicy cologne and cold air. It's so comforting to have him, Elena and Luis together again. 'I think my heart might burst,' she mumbles against his chest.

'Surprised?'

'Yes. Very.'

'Happy?'

'Never been happier. What happened to The Savoy and the

ice skating?'

Jack looks at her. His arms still around her waist. 'Er, the hotel wasn't such a good idea. The kids vetoed it anyway. So, we just went shopping and you know Luis. They take longer than anyone to make up their mind about anything and then, because of them, we missed the train and had to wait an hour.' He raises his eyes to the ceiling.

Carmen smiles. Jack has remembered the correct pronouns.

'You're here now.' Carmen leans against her husband enjoying the strength of his muscular body against hers. She can't stop smiling. She wants to place her nose in his neck and inhale his body scent forever.

'I love your hair short like this. It makes you look younger and much more... mischievous.'

Carmen hugs him tighter. 'I probably should have done it months ago.'

They walk arm in arm into the lounge where Luis is in deep conversation with Sanjay about the merits of Indian food and a typical Christmas meal. Elena is taking a keen interest in business and asking Eva about her flower shop.

In the corner, standing beside the Christmas tree, Ben and Amber are engrossed in looking at Ben's phone together.

'I hope you'll stay after Christmas and get to know everyone?' Carmen squeezes her husband's arm.

'Well, on the back of the show yesterday I've been asked to host a quiz programme in the new year.'

Carmen disentangles herself. 'Let's not discuss all this now.' She moves away from him.

'But, Cammy, I have other plans—'

'Not now, Jack.' Wearing her best and brightest smile she squeezes onto the sofa between her children. There is nothing that could ruin this joyous moment. The family homecoming. This is more than she could ever have hoped for. She didn't want to know about Jack's plans for the future.

Elena squeezes her mother's hand. 'Te quiero, Mama. Feliz navidad.'

Ben raises his glass.

'Er, excuse me. I have a small announcement to make.' The room falls silent. 'I've just received official news that my charity has a sponsor. This is more than I could have dreamed of...'

There are cheers and applause.

Amber smiles happily and wipes her gleaming eyes.

Ben continues, 'With this sponsorship the children found on the streets will be better looked after. They will have a roof over their heads and a safe place to live. They will have guidance about living healthily, living smarter and help with interviews and finding work - to become independent. There will also be the possibility of apprenticeships for them. They will have a future.' Ben raises his glass. 'A bright and happy future that they deserve.'

Elena whoops and Sanjay claps the loudest.

Amber slips her arm around Ben's waist. Filled with emotion Ben clears his throat. 'There will also be opportunity for them all. All of the kids in the charity - boys and girls - will be involved with different sports. They will have new opportunities. Especially in football.' He nods at Jack. 'Meet our new charity sponsor, Jack Bailey.'

* * *

It's a memorable evening of celebration and happiness. One

that they will all remember. After the guests have gone, Luis goes upstairs to bed and Elena insists on sleeping in the lounge. 'I'm going to lie awake,' she teases. 'I want to see if Santa finds us here.'

In the quiet of their bedroom, Carmen realises it's the first time Jack has shared a room with her in months. The last time he was here they'd argued and he'd slept in the spare room.

They're whispering about their evening, as they undress, talking about their friends in Harbour Street and their children.

'I'm so pleased you spoke to Luis and Elena,' she says. 'They're happy about the book now?'

'They understand us both much better. They understand what we've been through and it's an important lesson in marriage. You need to give each other room to breathe.'

'What wise children we have,' she teases.

'I've learnt so much from Luis. I've felt so much remorse, Cammy. You know that time when I'd gambled so much money and we were so hard up that we dressed him in Elena's old clothes. I thought it was all my fault that Luis loved women's clothes.'

Carmen giggles and climbs under the duvet. 'Silly! I think Luis only wore an old jumper or two of Elena's. They were unisex anyway and too new to throw out. I don't think for one minute that you...'

'Luis put me straight,' Jack laughs quietly as he pulls off his shirt. 'so to speak - and Elena's been amazing. She realises that we wanted her to be independent so that she wouldn't be taken advantage of. All your experiences in the modelling world have helped you shape our daughter to become a strong woman. We both want her to have her own career and not to always be recognised as the daughter of a famous model or footballer.'

'She's found her path now.'

'As a cabin crew attendant?'

Carmen pulls the duvet under her nose. 'I'm not sure. She was chatting away to Eva about her shop, but I don't know.'

'At least she didn't marry that controlling pilot plonker.'

Carmen giggles. 'I can't believe you're a patron of Ben's charity. That's amazing. It's a wonderful thing to do.'

Jack climbs into bed and pulls her into his arms. 'I want to do something with a purpose, Cammy. And it was only when talking to Ben while he was driving me up to London that I realised I could use my contacts and my skills to help him.'

'Skills?' Carmen laughs.

Jack grins. 'I've been to his place a few times in Kings Cross. We've looked at it and I'm going to open a football academy. I think I'll be able to get finance from some of the old pros and managers. Ben and I have great plans for the future.'

Carmen snuggles against Jack's chest and she realises how much she's missed her husband. His heart is beating faster. His chest rising quickly as he speaks excitedly about the future and plans for the charity. She listens with a growing sense of calm.

'I want to make a difference, Cammy,' he whispers.

For the first time, Jack is talking about using his contacts and his experience to help.

'It's only an hour from London and I won't have to be up there every day. I'll be able to work from home,' he pauses, 'Cammy, are you awake?'

'Yes, Jack. It's lovely listening to you. You sound so happy and excited.'

'I have a purpose. Football is something that I've always been passionate about and an academy is perfect.'

In the dark, Carmen smiles and wiggles closer to him. Jack snuggles so their faces are inches apart. 'I'm also passionate about you,' he whispers.

'Really?' Carmen pushes her hips against his.

'There's no one in the world. Only you, Cammy. You're all I've ever wanted. I love you.' He kisses her and when they pull apart, she whispers.

'Do you think we can we still make love quietly like we used to when the children were small?'

'I think we should give it a try,' Jack replies. 'I think we need the practice.'

Chapter 25

Christmas morning is bright and sunny. Amber and Ben have left croissants and pastries for breakfast. Carmen prepares coffee while they wait for Jack who is upstairs and the last one to use the shower.

Luis is wearing a red and black sparkling dress with scarlet Christmas leggings. Their makeup is subdued with pink and purple hues around their eyes. Their hair is tied back in a loose ponytail.

Luis shows Carmen their phone. 'It's a message from Tracey. She says that you've persuaded her to stay here in Harbour Street, is that right?'

'I don't think she was to blame for everything. Her boyfriend, Eric, was a bad influence.'

'They're not together now,' Luis says.

'She needs a good friend. Someone who will be kind to her.'

Luis smiles. 'She's a decent person.'

'The opportunity is there for you both to be friends – if that's what you want.'

Elena looks radiant in a silver jumper and long black skirt.

'Have you heard from José?' Carmen asks.

'He doesn't want any contact with me.'

'Does that upset you?' Carmen asks.

'Surprisingly, not at all. Who would have thought that I could get over him so easily?'

'You do look happier.'

Elena smiles. 'It makes me realise what a narrow escape I had. He's a control freak. I also think that talking to Papi helped me. Working as cabin crew is fun but I don't know if it's what I want any more. I don't have to escape my family...'

'There's nothing to be ashamed of.' Luis lifts their chin and flicks his ponytail over their shoulder.

'You're young enough to change your career, Elena.' Carmen finishes laying the breakfast table by placing red candles in the centre of the small table.

'I was thinking you might need help in the shop, Mama?'

Carmen puts her arm around her daughter and grins. 'Only if it's what you want to do. This is *my* dream but you're welcome to help me while you work out what it is that *you* want to do...'

'I did say that you and Papi have put me off marriage for life but that's not true, Mama. I'm sorry. You've both shown me what a true marriage is and how you need to communicate and work through problems.'

'You also need to find the right partner,' adds Luis with a smirk.

Carmen is still hugging her daughter when Jack comes downstairs. His blue eyes are twinkling and he strides into the kitchen and kisses Carmen on the lips.

'Papi, stop! That's gross!' Luis pokes out their tongue dramatically.

'Get a room!' agrees Elena.

'We have a table at The Ship for lunch,' Carmen explains. 'Paul has opened the pub for all the people who are on their own on Christmas Day.'

'You were going there on your own?' Luis asks. 'That's sad.'

Carmen shrugs. 'I was going with Amber and Ben. But now you're all here it will be much more fun.'

Over breakfast they chat easily falling back into their natural banter of teasing and pretend rivalry, laughing and enjoying each other's company.

'Happy Christmas, Mama.' Elena passes her present across the table to her mother. As is the family Christmas tradition they share a present at breakfast.

Carmen smells the box and smiles. 'My favourite sage candle?' She opens the box, pulls out the green candle and lights it.

'It's for new beginnings.' Elena smiles.

Luis' gift is a grey and red trilby. 'It will suit you, Mama. And it will keep your head warm. Do you think I should get my hair cut too?'

'No!' say Jack and Elena together and they all laugh.

Jack's gift is a gold keyring. 'This is for your front door. Where's the key to the flat and we can put it on the ring?'

'Let's do it later, Jack. Now, I just want to enjoy this special moment.' She pours more coffee. 'How about a lovely walk before lunch?'

* * *

The air is crisp and dry, the wind cool on their cheeks. They huddle up and link arms as they walk down Harbour Street pausing to window shop and greet friends.

First, it's Femi and Lawrence with their three children and Femi's grandmother. They are on their way back from the church service. Then in the harbour they see Jane and Tommy with their dog Coral, and Yusef and Shelley who are having a walk before lunch too.

They walk along the promenade chatting happily, watching the gulls, listening to the roar of the sea. As they walk back toward the town, Carmen leads them along the boardwalk, past the yacht club, and through the alleyway. She stands outside Marjorie's Merchant's house.

'What do you think?' she asks.

'It's lovely,' says Elena.

'It's got character,' agrees Luis.

'It's beautiful. It's also got a SOLD sign up in the garden,' says Jack.

'It belonged to Marjorie - Frances's mother-in-law. She had to go into a home.'

'It's sad to leave such a lovely home,' says Jack.

'Papi I think Mama's fallen in love with it,' says Elena. 'Will you buy this house for Mama?'

Jack laughs. 'I bought the last one. I think she's perfectly capable of choosing her own home now.' Jack rubs his head. 'It's a pity it won't be this one. It's already sold.'

They stand silently staring at the house.

'It *is* sold,' Carmen says. 'I put a deposit on it yesterday and made them take it off the market. Happy Christmas everyone. This is our new home.'

'Really?' Elena's face lights up.

'How many bedrooms?' asks Luis.

'Four and two bathrooms.'

'It's smaller than I'm used to.' He places his hand on the gate.

'Don't be such a prima-donna.' Elena nudges Luis. 'You'll be back at uni in a few weeks.'

Carmen looks at Jack. 'What do you think?'

Jack slips his hand through her arm and grins. 'I can't wait to see inside.'

'I've arranged for us to see it after the holidays. David Chesent, the estate agent, is meeting us. We can look around it together.'

'This is so exciting,' says Elena. 'Do Amber and Ben know?'

'I've told no one.' Carmen smiles. 'This is our Christmas present. It's our family Christmas present.'

'You'll have great fun doing it up and making it home, Mama. I know it will be perfect.' Luis says. Then he links his arm through Elena's and they walk on ahead toward The Ship.

Behind them, Jack and Carmen walk more slowly arm-in-arm.

'You don't mind I bought it?' she asks.

'You're happy and the kids are happy.' Jack grins. 'I'm happy.'

'All our things are in storage so once the house is refurbished, we can move in. There's no chain.' She smiles.

'Our very own home by the sea,' he replies. 'Your dream. Our reality.'

'Elena said she may want to work with me so she could live with us here or she can be independent and have the flat above the shop. Just until she gets sorted out. What do you think?'

'That's a good idea.'

'Will you commute from here, Jack?'

'We're never spending so long apart again. I've missed you too much and life is too short. I want us to be together.' He squeezes her arm.

'I've made quite a bit of money and I've also been paid a deposit to work on a new development in Surrey.'

Jack grins. 'I've also worked out our accounts and while we've lost the Prison Palace, we're not poor. We can easily afford this.'

'And have money left over for Ben's charity?'

He grins. 'And have money left over... I can even invite you all to lunch in The Ship.'

* * *

The pub is warm and Christmas lunch smells delicious. They take off their coats and introductions are made.

'It's a pleasure to meet you, Jack,' Paul says, shaking his hand. 'Your wife saved my marriage.'

Jack grins. 'She saved mine too.'

Sandra takes Carmen to one side. 'I'd like you to meet my dad. He's moving into one of the new homes so he'll be nearer to us. And, thanks to you, no one this Christmas is left on their own—'

'It was all Paul's idea.' Carmen protests, smiling at the twins running around at the far end of the pub. 'He wants to make you happy.'

'You helped him see sense, Carmen. Thank you. We have our family back again.'

Corks pop, drinks are poured and Martin appears in the doorway. After the introductions he says, 'I'm on my way to Mum's for lunch. I only called in because I thought you might be on your own.' He looks around the pub and his eyes rest on Elena.

'Have a glass of fizz,' says Jack, offering him a glass.

'I thought I would be alone.' Carmen smiles. 'This is a lovely surprise having my family here.'

'Thanks, Jack.' Martin takes the glass. 'It's great to meet you.'

Carmen notices that he keeps glancing in Elena's direction but then Martin turns his attention back to her. 'I have some more good news. *Interiors and Furnishings* emailed me and they want to feature our homes in their magazine. They want an interview with you.'

'That's great! Well done, Cammy.' Jack raises his glass. 'Cheers everyone. Happy Christmas.'

When normal conversation resumes, Elena and Martin are chatting together in the corner of the pub by the door. Elena is smiling as she pushes a tendril of loose hair behind her ear and leans her head to one side, while Martin speaks quietly and stares deeply into her eyes. They both laugh and Elena rests her hand with familiarity on Martin's jacket.

Jack leans closer and whispers in Carmen's ear. 'Do you think Martin was hoping that Elena would be here?'

Elena laughs louder and Martin steps closer to her.

'Isn't that romantic?' Carmen smiles.

'This is a magical Christmas, Cammy. I think this is the perfect place for us.'

'Where's that keyring?' she whispers, nudging him gently.

'I'll need to buy one for all of us now.' He grins and places his arm around her shoulder. 'Who would have thought it? Our new home in Westbay, Cammy. It's not just for Christmas. It's for life.'

Carmen throws her head back and laughs. 'It all happens here in Harbour Street, Jack Bailey. Just you wait and see...'

The End.

Janet Pywell's Books

The Westbay Romance Series:

Someone Else's Dream
Someone Else's Child
Someone Else's Truth
Someone Else's Home

Ronda George Thrillers:

The Concealers
The Influencers
The Manipulators
The Ronda George Thriller Boxset - books 1-3

Mikky dos Santos Thrillers:

Golden Icon – *The Prequel*
Masterpiece
Book of Hours
Stolen Script
Faking Game
Truthful Lies
Broken Windows

Boxsets:

Volume 1 – Masterpiece, Book of Hours & Stolen Script
Volume 2 – Faking Game, Truthful Lies & Broken Windows

Also available in Audible

Other Books by Janet Pywell:

Red Shoes and Other Short Stories
Bedtime Reads
Ellie Bravo
The Novel Mentor

For more information visit:
website: www. janetpywellauthor.com

All books are available online and can be ordered through major book stores.

If you enjoy my books then **please do leave a review** from wherever you purchased the book. Your opinion is important to me. I read them all. It also helps other readers to find my work.

Thank you.

About the Author

With a thirty-year background in travel and tourism, Janet lived and worked in Spain for twenty years and Ireland for ten years where she had her own marketing company. She has travelled extensively.

Janet gained an MA in Creative Writing at the Seamus Heaney Centre at Queen's University while living in Belfast (2013). She has been a tutor at Canterbury Christ Church University (CCCU) on the MA & BA Creative Writing programme and taught English to foreign students (TEFL).

As a mentor to writing students of all ages she enjoys sharing her knowledge and experience. She is highly motivated and driven and she takes pride in helping others achieve their dreams to improve their writing.

With a passion for writing Janet has studied online with the University of Southampton (Shipwrecks and Submerged Worlds), the University of Glasgow (Antiquities Trafficking), the University of Kent (Forensic Psychology), and at the UEA - University of East Anglia - (An Introduction to Screenwriting) to enhance her knowledge and, to add authenticity to her work.

In April 2022, Janet Pywell published her first non-fiction

book: **Ten Simple Steps for Writing Your Book**.

Janet currently lives on the Kent coast.

You can connect with me on:

- https://janetpywellauthor.com
- https://twitter.com/JanPywellAuthorTwitter
- https://www.facebook.com/janet.pywell
- https://www.instagram.com/janetpywellauthor
- https://www.subscribepage.com/janetpywell
- https://www.subscribepage.com/the_novel_mentor

Subscribe to my newsletter:

https://www.subscribepage.com/the-westbay-romance-series

Printed in Great Britain
by Amazon